Michel Vinave
Plays: 2

High Places, The Neighbours,
Portrait of a Woman, The Television Programme

High Places: 'A drama which, from second to second, maintains the spectator in suspense, and which, by the same stroke, achieves the dimension of pure, great metaphysical theatre.' *Le Monde*

The Neighbours: 'A bizarre contemporary vaudeville, biting, disturbing, very subtle and wildly funny.' *Le Figaro*

Portrait of a Woman: 'An intriguing challenging piece.' *Financial Times*

The Television Programme: 'The piece is beautifully plotted and written from the heart.' *Independent on Sunday*

Michel Vinaver was born in 1927. For nearly thirty years he was an executive with Gillette International and this inside experience of the workings of a multinational corporation has provided material for many of his plays. In the 1950s he was labelled a political dramatist, especially after his play *The Koreans* provoked right-wing demonstrations and was subject to government censorship. In the 1960s he suffered from prolonged writer's block, but overcame it with the writing of *Overboard* (1969). Since then he has written eleven more plays and is known as the leading 'dramatist of the everyday'. His work has been produced by every leading director from Vitez to Lassalle; he was the first chairman of the Theatre Commission of the Centre National des Lettres, and is generally acknowledged as France's major living dramatist.

This publication supported
by the French Ministry
of Foreign Affairs.

MICHEL VINAVER

Plays: 2

High Places
translated by Gideon Y. Schein

The Neighbours
translated by Paul Antal

Portrait of a Woman
translated by Donald Watson

The Television Programme
translated by David and Hannah Bradby

edited and introduced by David Bradby

METHUEN DRAMA

METHUEN DRAMA CONTEMPORARY DRAMATISTS

This collection first published in Great Britain 1997
by Methuen Drama

Contents

Chronology   vii

Auto-Interrogation: Vinaver interviewed by Vinaver   xiii

Introduction to the Plays   xxi

HIGH PLACES   1

THE NEIGHBOURS   99

PORTRAIT OF A WOMAN   155

THE TELEVISION PROGRAMME   221

Michel Vinaver: Chronology

1927   Born in Paris of Russian-born parents of Jewish origin, his
        father an antique dealer and expert in Russian art, his
        mother a civil lawyer, later head of the Section on the Status
        of Women at the Secretariat of the United Nations. Early
        schooling in Paris. His first play, *The Revolt of the Vegetables*,
        written at the age of nine: all the vegetables in the kitchen
        garden get together to overthrow the tyrannous regime of
        the gardener, which is only achieved with great sacrifice on
        the part of the artichoke.
1940   On the German occupation of France, the family moves,
        first to the 'Free Zone' in the South. Then, in 1941, they sail
        for the USA. Secondary schooling completed at the Lycée
        Français of New York.
1944–45 One semester only at Wesleyan University, Middletown,
        Connecticut, followed by one year spent in barracks in
        France after volunteering for the Free French Forces.
1947   Completes his BA in English and American literature at
        Wesleyan. Returns to France; goes to England for a spell
        with his uncle (Eugène Vinaver, Professor of French
        Literature at Manchester University), where he translates
        T. S. Eliot's *The Waste Land* into French. Desultory studies in
        the humanities at the Sorbonne.
1948   Completion of his first novel, *Lataume*, published in 1950 by
        Gallimard on the recommendation of Albert Camus. Start
        of a lifelong friendship with Roland Barthes.
1951   Publication of a second novel – it will be his last – *L'Objecteur*,
        reflecting the Cold War which was then raging, and his
        experience of the absurd in the army: awarded Fénéon prize.
        Translates Henry Green's novel *Loving* into French for
        publication by Gallimard; this will be later a source for his
        play *Iphigénie Hôtel*.
1953   Decides against living by his pen and advertises for a job in
        the *International Herald Tribune*, although lacking in education
        or experience in either business or the law, is taken on by
        Gillette, then moving its French headquarters from Paris to
        Annecy. Moves from Paris to live in a house near Lake

Annecy that had been acquired as a summer residence by his maternal grandfather in 1923 shortly after he emigrated from Russia fleeing the Soviet Revolution. Is put in charge of Gillette France's legal and administrative service.

1955   Becomes involved in a new summer theatre festival run by Gabriel Monnet in Annecy. At Monnet's request, he writes his first play (since childhood), *Aujourd'hui*.

1956   Retitled *Aujourd'hui ou Les Coréens*, it is performed by Roger Planchon's young company in Lyon, where political disturbances are caused by right-wing groups outside the theatre.

1957   Monnet plans to produce the play for a theatre festival at Serre-Ponçon, where a vast temporary town has been erected for the workers on the hydro-electric dam under construction, but the Minister for Youth and Sports, who is sponsoring the festival, censors Monnet's choice of play. In its place, Monnet stages Sophocles's *Antigone*, with new choral passages written by Vinaver, performed in the costumes for *Les Coréens*. Vinaver writes his second play, *Les Huissiers* (*The Ushers*) – an attempt to dramatise the texture of French political life at the height of the Algerian war and through the agony of the Fourth Republic, following events week by week as they happen. Planchon has plans to produce the play but these fall through.

1958   Adapts (on commission) Dekker's *The Shoemaker's Holiday* for Jean Vilar's Théâtre National Populaire. Vinaver is attracted by the Elizabethan play's unvarnished presentation of the life of ordinary city dwellers, but the TNP production by Georges Wilson upsets him by giving the play a 'Merrye Englande' treatment.

1959   Writes *Iphigénie Hôtel*, ostensibly about the struggle for power below stairs in a Greek tourist hotel, but also dealing with the theme of power in general, and in particular with the generals' attempted putsch in Algeria and their attempted coup in France which culminated in de Gaulle's coming to power. Gillette sends him to Britain for one month as an apprentice salesman and then to Imede, an international business school in Switzerland, on an intensive nine months' general management training programme.

1960   Appointed managing director of Gillette's sales subsidiary in Belgium (forty employees) and moves to Brussels. This is the time of the marketing revolution in Europe, with the engineering of mass consumer product promotions to stimulate desire rather than merely push the goods out. Distinguishes himself with the triumph of the launch of Toni and Prom home perm kits on his market.

1964   Transferred to Milan as managing director of Gillette Italy (300 employees). Rapid expansion of the core business – blades and razors – along with the launch of a line of toiletries.

1966   Appointed managing director of Gillette France, one of the three manufacturing subsidiaries of the company in Europe (1000 employees), which brings him back to Annecy. In the course of five years, launches the Techmatic ribbon razor, the Teflon-treated Gillette Extra Blue Blade, the stainless steel long-life Super-Gillette blade, the Right Guard deodorant.

1967   Overcomes seven years' writer's block, and begins to work on *Par-dessus bord*, a vast Aristophanes-inspired epic concerning the fortunes of an old-fashioned family-owned French toilet-paper-manufacturing firm caught in the transatlantic competition of the boom years of the sixties, and ultimately taken over by an American multinational corporation.

1969   *Par-dessus bord* (*Overboard*) completed: it runs to 250 pages, and would take about eight hours to perform. It is turned down by Gallimard.

1970   Negotiates the acquisition by Gillette of the French family-owned company S. T. Dupont, makers of luxury lighters and 'Cricket' disposable lighters. Is appointed managing director of this firm and will run it for eight years, diversifying the luxury operation with a line of writing instruments, and extending the distribution of 'Cricket' worldwide.

1971   *Par-dessus bord* accepted for publication by L'Arche. After writing a chronicle of exceptional dimension, feels the need to treat the same subject matter in microcosm: the result is *La Demande d'emploi* (*Situation Vacant*), centring on an out-of-work sales executive, his wife and his daughter.

1972   Becomes involved with the Théâtre Eclaté, a young, politically active group in Annecy.

1973   First productions of *La Demande d'emploi* and *Par-dessus bord*. The latter is directed by Planchon in an abridged version and a glitzy style reminiscent of Hollywood musicals.

1976   Writes two short 'chamber plays', *Dissident, il va sans dire* and

Nina, c'est autre chose. An industrial plant he is managing at Faverges (near Annecy) goes on strike and workers occupy the factory.

1977 *Iphigénie Hôtel* produced (eighteen years after it was written) by Antoine Vitez with his Théâtre des Quartiers d'Ivry at the Pompidou Centre in Paris. Writes *Les Travaux et les jours*, inspired by the previous year's events in the factory and by the effects of the advent of the computer in the office world.

1978 Production of *Dissident* and *Nina* at the studio theatre of the Théâtre de l'Est Parisien, directed by Jacques Lassalle – the start of a long and fruitful association between author and director. (Lassalle was to become head of the Théâtre National de Strasbourg in 1983, where he stayed until being appointed director of the Comédie-Française on the death of Vitez in 1990.)

1979 Writes *A la renverse* (*Falling Over Backwards*), centred on the cosmetics industry, and the manipulation through advertising of mass fears and obsessions; it contains some televised sequences and a preliminary reflection on the function of television in society, later given a more thorough treatment in *L'Emission de télévision* (*The Television Programme*, 1988). At the end of the year, leaves Gillette.

1980 Adapts Erdman's *The Suicide*, working from a literal translation done with his father. Production of *Les Travaux et les jours* by Alain Françon, director of the Théâtre Eclaté of Annecy. Production of *A la renverse* by Lassalle at Théâtre National de Chaillot. Publication of a children's book, *Les Histoires de Rosalie*, based on the stories of his grandmother's childhood in late nineteenth-century Russia.

1981 Writes *L'Ordinaire* (*High Places*), sparked off by the story of a plane crash in the Andes several years before, which some passengers survived by eating the flesh of the dead – a play about the cannibal tendencies of big business.

1982 Commissioned by the Comédie-Française to write an adaptation of Gorki's *Summerfolk* for a production by Jacques Lassalle. Begins teaching at the University of Paris III (Censier). Publication of his collected writings on the theatre. Appointed to chair the newly established drama committee of the Centre National des Lettres.

1983 Vinaver's first (and last) venture into stage directing: in collaboration with Alain Françon, he directs *L'Ordinaire* at Théâtre National de Chaillot. First unabridged production of *Par-dessus bord* by the Théâtre Populaire Romand in Switzerland, directed by Charles Joris.

1984   Writes *Les Voisins* and *Portrait d'une femme*. *Les Voisins* traces the intermingled lives of two families who are neighbours in semi-detached houses. *Portrait* is based on the newspaper reports of the trial of a woman who murdered her ex-lover. His version of *The Suicide* is staged by the Comédie-Française, Jean-Pierre Vincent directing. Begins a series of playwriting workshops at the University.

1986   Production of *Les Voisins* by Françon at Théâtre Ouvert in Paris, and on tour at a number of Centres Dramatiques. Awarded Ibsen prize. *Théâtre Complet* in two volumes pubished by Actes Sud. *Dissident, Goes Without Saying* and *Nina, It's Different*, a translation of the chamber plays by Paul Antal, published in *Dramacontemporary France*, PAJ Publications, New York.

1987   Publication of a report, *Le Compte rendu d'Avignon*, written by Vinaver as chairman of the Drama committee of the Centre National des Lettres, on the current crisis of play publishing and the state of the playwright in the French theatre industry. This report triggers a number of initiatives, particularly in the area of national educational programmes. First production of his work in Britain: *Les Travaux et les jours*, translated by Peter Meyer as *A Smile on the End of the Line*, directed by Sam Walters at the Orange Tree Theatre, Richmond.

1988   Appointed titular professor at the University of Paris VIII (Saint-Denis). Writes *L'Emission de télévision*.

1989   Production of *Situation Vacant* (John Burgess's translation of *La Demande d'emploi*) by Sam Walters at the Orange Tree. A second UK production of *Les Travaux et les jours*, in a new translation by Ron Butlin under the title *Blending in*, staged at the Traverse Theatre for the Edinburgh Festival. Vinaver is commissioned by Vitez to write *Le Dernier Sursaut*, an impromptu for the yearly celebration of Molière's birth at the Comédie-Française. Publication of *Portrait of a Woman* (Donald Watson's translation) in *New French Plays* (Methuen) and, in the US, by the Dramatic Publishing Company.

1990   Translation of Shakespeare's *Julius Caesar*, commissioned and produced by the Comédie de Genève, directed by Claude Stratz. Production of *L'Emission de télévision* at the Odéon, by the Comédie-Française, directed by Jacques

Lassalle. Staged reading of *Portrait of a Woman* by Di Trevis for the RSC at the Covent Garden International Festival.

1991 Translates *Time and the Room* by Botho Strauss: a commission by Patrice Chéreau, who directs it at the Odéon.

1992 Production of *The Television Programme* (D. and H. Bradby's translation) at the Gate Theatre, London, directed by Kim Dambaek.

1993 After extensive restoration works, the Vieux Colombier Theatre reopens in Paris as the second home of the Comédie-Française, to be devoted to the work of living playwrights; one of the two opening productions is a revival of *Les Coréens*. Publication of Vinaver's *Ecritures Dramatiques*, a new approach to the analysis of dramatic text, founded on the research and teaching he had developed in the University. Production of *Situation Vacant* (*La Demande d'emploi*) by the Public Works Company in Sydney, Australia, in a new translation by Paul Dwyer and directed by him.

1995 Production of *Portrait of a Woman* by Sam Walters at the Orange Tree, and simultaneously in New York by Peter Sylvester at the Synchronicity Theatre. Production of *Overboard* (Gideon Lester's translation of *Par-dessus bord*) by the Institute for Advanced Theatre Training at Harvard University, American Repertory Theatre, directed by François Rochaix.

1996 Production of *Portrait of a Woman* by Gerry Mulgrew, Communicado Theatre, at the Traverse Theatre for the Edinburgh Festival.

1997 As part of a French Theatre Season in London, three of Vinaver's plays are performed at the Orange Tree Theatre: *Overboard, The Neighbours*, and *Dissident, Goes Without Saying*.

Auto-Interrogation:
Vinaver interviewed by Vinaver

You began by writing novels. But for a long time now you have written only for the theatre. Why?

I do not write for the theatre, I write against it. I use dramatic form because, for me, to write is to begin with something that is loose or untied and, gradually, to succeed in tying it together. In a novel everything is tied up from the beginning: the novel is a trap, whereas with a collection of dramatic lines you are plunged into discontinuity with everything jumbled up.

When I'm writing I pay no attention to how the play will take shape on stage, to the possibilities and constraints involved. I do not 'act out' my plays in my mind – while I am writing they exist for me only in their textual form. It is up to the director to take on this 'raw material' if he wants to put it on the stage (and if he is able). I feel I have a very limited involvement with the directorial choices.

I enjoy thinking about the plurality of possible sequels, continuations, bifurcations. What is important to me is that, if there is a theatre production of the play, it should take the process one stage further – there are many ways of taking the text one stage further, which do not exclude the option of resisting the text. But among these options I do not include side-stepping the text, nor manipulating it, nor ignoring it, nor simply using it. Its non-soluble character must be respected, whether in convergence or in tension.

Aren't you afraid of being betrayed – dissolved, as you put it?

It's a risk. I see no way of completely eliminating it, given my approach.

You are defining and, it seems to me, seeking to justify a positon of irresponsibility vis-à-vis the director, actors, and audience. Not only do you refuse to commit yourself, but you take no interest in the uses (aesthetic or political) that might be made of your work.

I know, it's a problem. In fact, I would not give a play to a director unless I could sense a certain complicity between us ... My starting point is nevertheless the non-solidarity between the end-result of the production and the creation of the text. I am convinced that the work (luckily!) goes beyond any intention I might have had in writing it, or any ideas that I might have about it afterwards. Once the play is written, I do not feel I am in a better position to judge it than any one else.

With The Koreans *you placed yourself in the Brechtian tradition. Is there not, in your demand for irresponsibility, a complete renunciation and . . . a reactionary attitude?*

I was strongly influenced by Brecht: that means a lot, but not everything. I did not take out a membership in Brecht (as one might do in a party, school, or ideology), so it cannot be a case of renunciation. It is true that for a long time I had a guilt complex concerning the question of commitment. Not now. I believe that voluntarism mutilates art. Reality is constituted by the questioning human being. Especially by artistic activity. Therefore the artist can never start from preconceived positions. He starts with undifferentiated, heterogeneous raw material. Like a sponge, he absorbs it and then restores it by *composing* it. His tastes, beliefs, opinions, and judgements are not interesting in themselves, but are just another part of the jumble that he uses.

Must the work that results from this process be called 'reactionary'? In my case I think not ... Not because my opinions, judgements, and so on, are 'progressive', but because the impulse to create is linked to a very profound refusal, or perhaps just a fundamental incapacity, to be satisfied with the state of affairs as it exists, or even to recognise that such a state does exist. Art is the search for a 'new usage' in the Brechtian sense. And to come back to Brecht, a great dramatist and a great writer, his work was fertilised by his political commitment, but it is absurd to think that he wrote *in order* to illustrate his ideas, *in order* to accomplish a mission.

Then in which tradition do you place yourself? With which authors do you feel an affinity?

There have been many influences or encounters, without any sense of my belonging to a movement or tendency. I have the sense that I am quite alone in my search, but surrounded by others who have searched and are searching, and whose work sometimes has a sympathetic resonance with mine. These people belong to the past as well as to the present. They are above all Chekhov (his plays), T. S. Eliot (his poetry), Rossellini, Dubuffet, Rauschenberg, Beethoven (his late chamber music).

You keep speaking of a search, but nothing you say suggests a clear direction for this search. Or an area. Is there one, or is it just a case of any old thing any old how?

Everyday trivia have never ceased to interest me. The constituent matter of daily life at its most undifferentiated, confused, indistinct, and neutral. Starting from zero.

Arriving where?

I have already told you: fragments of unchecked meaning, or rather expressions of meaning (through the play of montages, links, collisions), in the hope that these mini-shocks will combine with one another to form larger explosive phenomena. History emerges from nothing other than the day-to-day magma. So, if one doesn't want to write something useless, perhaps it's best to occupy oneself with provoking small bursts of consciousness at the level of this magma . . .

The theatre of messages, demonstrative theatre, committed theatre, as we have seen over the past fifteen or twenty years, is extraordinarily easily assimilated by the establishment. Oppositional ideologies are rapidly digested and dissolve back into the magma. The way I work makes me difficult to assimilate. Like the Zen archer, I aim at nothing, I concentrate on shooting well.

You speak of magma. Your plays are far from being 'unstructured'. How do you construct them?

I have always experienced, at least since *The Koreans*, an incapacity to tell one story – that is to say to give prime importance to one sequence of events. During the gestation of a play several themes (in the musical sense of the term) present themselves to me and are woven together. As a play is not a musical score, there comes a moment when a framework is necessary, and this is provided by 'story'.

For *Les Huissiers* (*The Ushers*) I lifted that of *Oedipus at Colonus*. *The Shoemaker's Holiday* is adapted from Dekker's play. For *Iphigénie Hôtel*, the plot is constructed from sections of Henry Green's novel *Loving*, interwoven with the assumption of power by de Gaulle and the initiatory rites of archaic tribes. For *Pardessus bord* (*Overboard*), I borrowed from Dumézil the sequence of events in the war between the Aesir and the Vanir in Norse mythology, and from Aristophanes the obligatory structure of all his comedies – transgression, combat, *agon*, counter-transgression, feast, marriage. In *La Demande d'emploi* (*Situation Vacant*), which is my most 'musical' play, I experimented with complete rejection of story in favour of the interweaving of contrapuntal leitmotifs, the overall movement being that of a spiral moving through a structure of 'theme and variations'.

You like to use mythology, which is present in some form in all of your plays. Isn't this rather self-consciously intellectual of you?

The theme of 'entry and exit', the dialectical movement between these two poles, is, of course, linked to the myths of origins – of the Garden of Eden, in which nothing was separated, everything was participation and fusion. The work of T. S. Eliot influenced me considerably – I encountered it when I was eighteen. What he does (and I try to take further) is to establish connections, at the level of language itself, connections that are both extremely intimate yet highly ironic, between the fullness of a past in which everything held together, and the derision of the present, laid waste through the loss of the sacred.

Why 'highly ironic'?

Because this resplendent past never existed as we imagine – it is a false loss. But we need it. It helps.

So this coming and going between a mythic past and today is the explanation for your adopting the Aristophanic structure in Par-dessus bord*?*

I wanted to enclose myself within a structure of maximum constraint, so that within it I could behave with maximum licence. I was also seeking an ironic relationship with the past. For Aristophanes this structure corresponded to a necessity, anchored in the ritual origins of theatre: for the contemporary dramatist, it could only be a frivolous decision, because quite arbitrary. But taking Aristophanes as my confederate helped me with this project: it was a sort of guarantee, allowing me to write something gigantic, pullulating, unbuttoned, scatological. Aristophanes was my ally against self-censorship.

You say you have no convictions, but you are curious . . .

Yes. I am more astonished than many people by the things that happen and by what is generally considered to be perfectly obvious. For me, nothing is obvious, especially the commonest things, like living together (for a couple) or making a sale (for a salesman). I find these things amazing. As if the world began anew every day. At the same time it is as if everything is being repeated over and over to the point of nausea. Hence irony . . .

You are continually side-stepping the problem of the writer's or the artist's responsibility . . . You cannot escape being part of society, and the artist, even more than anyone else, if he refuses to take sides, is in danger of finding his work being exploited by the forces of oppression.

Of course the artist occupies a public role: whether he likes it or not, his output has its influence on social behaviour. To complicate matters, the creator of shows tends, in the current organisation of society, to be hand-in-glove with the powers that be, in the sense that, to be produced, his work requires subsidy, either direct or indirect. Hence the dilemma of those powers who, at the risk of seeing the source of all creative work dry up (an eventuality that would tarnish their image) have to support activity that is turned against them.

Now in reality these are false dilemmas, which stem from the fact that since the Romantic period artists have liked to see themselves as having a mission. For their part, those in power have taken them more and more seriously, and when they have passed certain 'limits' (the 'limits' varying according to the regime) they have been silenced by censorship, or assassination . . . Things would be quite different if the artist were seen as adopting the role of the jester, both within society and standing outside it. The jester is the person who is not only permitted but requested to entertain, by saying what nobody else dares think or imagine, to name the unnameable, to throw into ferment the prospects for the future, to upset the hierarchies. Once he was paid for it.

He was also beaten sometimes.

Picasso and Chaplin have been roughly treated: they are the great jesters of our century. Brecht, if looked at afresh, is more jester than leader of a school. Other jesters might be listed: Joyce, Hemingway, Breton, Aragon, Borges, Ernst, Duchamp, Michaux, Dubuffet, Stockhausen, Xenakis, Rauschenberg, Oldenburg, Godard as far as *Weekend*, and among the 'politically aberrant', Pound and Céline – the work of those two is no less 'salubrious', 'progressive', than that of the great figures who committed themselves on the side of historical progress. Irony . . . What counted was their creative daring, at the level of the material in which they worked.

How do you define the artist as jester?

He is the person whose action, whether dazzling or calm, shatters the conformities and stereotypes of the system and opens up paths not yet imagined . . .

Which will only lead to the construction of a new system, slightly more oppressive than the last?

That is another question. Yes and no. The music of Mozart engendered a new conformism. Nevertheless, it retains to this

day all its liberating force, and will continue to do so for a long
time to come.

*This Auto-Interrogation was originally devised by the author in 1972. It
sets out principles which govern all his subsequent work. It was published
in Vinaver's* Ecrits sur le théâtre. *This translation by David Bradby
first appeared in* New Theatre Quarterly, *no. 27, August 1991.*

Introduction
to the Plays

The plays Vinaver wrote in the 1980s developed the same themes explored in his earlier work: the immediacy of the everyday experience, the relationship between the world of commerce and people's private lives, the competing claims of friends, family, lovers, colleagues, etc. In the course of the decade a new theme emerged as well: the theme of justice. Both *Portrait of a Woman* and *The Television Programme* are concerned with the processes of justice in contemporary French society. The theme of television, and its role in defining our image of the world, is an additional new element in the last of these plays, questioning the representational methods which shape our imginations and govern our ways of understanding the world we live in.

High Places (L'Ordinaire), 1981

This play uses more traditional suspense than is found in Vinaver's plays of the 1970s, without sacrificing his experimental approach to dramatic structure and patterns of dialogue. The story is based on that of the Uruguayan rugby team, whose plane crashed in the Andes in 1972, and some of whom survived by feeding off the bodies of their dead companions. In *High Places* the survivors are not sportsmen, but top-level executives of a prefabricated housing company based in Seattle; they are on a mission to sell their products in South America.

The situation is among the most concentrated and intense of any of Vinaver's plays and can be understood on a number of different levels. As well as enacting an exciting story of survival after a disaster, the play offers a meditation on social taboos and how they may, in extreme circumstances, be broken. The means by which the taboo on cannibalism is broken, and the gradual stages through which the group develops, forms a fascinating study in social dynamics, as the company president loses his grip and others take over. A third level of meaning is to be found in an examination of the common currency of management techniques. By this use of the contrast between the 'ordinary' ways of doing things and the extraordinary situation the characters are now in, the playwright develops an ironic commentary on the workings of business in the industrialised nations. From this there emerges yet another level of mythological or poetic meaning. For, while the incidents of the play remain realistically rooted in the microcosm of the Andes mountainside, the situation of these cannibal industrialists acquires a macrocosmic resonance, conveying the whole relationship between 'First' and 'Third' worlds, and the mindset of Western industrial leaders.

The play is divided into two unequal halves. The first, quite short, shows the group of five executives, plus a wife, a mistress, a daughter and a secretary, in their jet before the crash. They argue about the tactics to be employed on their business trip, about love affairs and family relationships. A clear hierarchical structure is evident and power games of various kinds are shown to be the centre of these people's lives. After the crash they find themselves marooned in a snow-bound waste where everything is unfamiliar, and yet their personal struggle for survival is permeated by the power structures – industrial, political, sexual – that governed their relationships before. In this way, the dramatic situation is used to clarify their relationship to society at large, at the same time as they are most cut off from it. Moreover, the discrepancies that are revealed between their real situation and the limited understanding they display, are used to generate ironic humour, so that the audience appreciates both the horror of their situation and the absurdity of their behaviour.

As the action progresses, however, the existing pecking-order crumbles, and different priorities take over. With the hope of rescue becoming more remote, the characters develop in different ways: some, like the company president, cling, grotesquely, to their prior preoccupations and behaviour, as if nothing had happened, while others open up, gradually, to previously inconceivable thoughts, feelings and conduct. As the days and weeks go by, all succumb to cold and starvation on the mountainside, with the exception of two, Sue and Ed, whose ultimate survival remains a question mark at the end.

This play takes a highly charged dramatic situation but avoids presenting it in melodramatic style; instead, the author makes systematic use of counterpoint, as developed in his more experimental plays such as *Situation Vacant*, in order to achieve ironic and allusive effects. The experience of seeing this play should leave its audience sickened by the political injustice of the relationships existing between industrialised and non-industrialised countries, those who eat and those who are eaten. But nowhere does the play contain a scene of 'protest': the effect is achieved instead by irony and by implication. To witness these overfed executives lovingly discussing the *haute cuisine* of a few privileged restaurants in a country dominated by mass hunger carries a strong ironic charge; to see them doing so when they are unable to feed themselves because their umbilical cord to North America has been severed makes the revelation of their true situation even more flagrant.

On the mountain icefield where their plane has crashed, they move from a position of detachment from the problems of everyday survival on the continent (before the crash) to a position in which they experience, in their own bodies, the hunger and cold of those from whom they had been hoping to make profits (after the crash). The dramatic action places great emphasis on the details of survival. For example, in Scene Six the four remaining characters spend most of the time with their pants down, coping with the problem of loose bowels, which has followed the chronic constipation of the first weeks. But such gestures are carefully selected and broken up so as to avoid a naturalistic presentation. The structure of the play was described by its author as one of '*le montage et le démontage*' [piecing together and taking to pieces]. He described the play's seven scenes as *morceaux* [pieces], defining the word as follows: '*Morceaux* is the state of a body after an accident; it describes what does not automatically hold together – something that must be built, stuck, put together'. The structure of the play thus mirrors the pattern of events presented in it: the characters of the play will try to reassemble the remains of broken objects, bodies, lives, in a way that makes sense to them. They will succeed to a limited degree, but their attempts will often convey meanings to the audience quite different from the meanings they ascribe to their own words and actions.

On the subject of *montage* and *démontage*, Vinaver wrote:

> The process of *montage* involves revealing, on the surface of the text, all the familiar elements that make up the [capitalist] system, whether orderly or disorderly, in such a way that their potential for terror and pity and strangeness bursts forth. The process of *démontage* involves the work done by the text as it reveals intimate life in its minutest pulsations interacting with the large-scale results of the socio-economic machine. (*Les Cahiers de Prospéro*, no. 8, July 1996, p. 10)

In other words, the structure of the play needed to show how the most intimate details of human behaviour can serve the interests of 'the system' or be conditioned by it. This was important if reality was to be respected, since a simple denunciation of the system achieves nothing more than a sense of self-satisfaction on the part of both playwright and audience. 'What these plays reveal is how the system functions, how it is constantly degenerating and regenerating, throwing its agents overboard, or letting them go into reverse, or devouring them as part of its everday fare.' The result aimed for is a comic vision as viewed from within: 'This comic vision of the way the system functions has the peculiarity of being produced by one of the system's devoted agents; a bit as if Harlequin, without abandoning his character, had taken on, for one of his escapades, the status of author.'

The Neighbours (Les Voisins), 1984

The Neighbours centres on the same kind of closely knit group as the shorter plays of the 1970s; here it is two single fathers, Blason and Laheu, and their children, respectively Alice and Felix. The characters establish their identity by contrast with one another within the microcosm of their semi-detached homes and shared terrace; but events from the outside world, though not shown on stage, are often the trigger that sets off a shift in the dynamics of the foursome. These dynamics range from loyalty, love, trust, to vulnerability, hatred, treachery. At the start of the play both fathers have white-collar office jobs: Blason is an accountant with Macassin Brothers, an insurance company, and Laheu is head of quality control at the Universal Biscuit company. The children are in their early twenties, intend to get married and run a restaurant together. Blason's wife was killed in a car accident when Alice was only four years old; Laheu has been abandoned by his wife some years previously. The four of them have come to rely on one another. On special occasions they eat together and share their most treasured secrets, notably the fact that Blason is putting all his savings into buying gold, which he stores under one of the paving stones of the shared terrace.

The events of the play contain a 'whodunnit' element, something common to all of Vinaver's plays since 1985, which supplies an element of suspense to the plot. But it is not a traditional detective story, since the crime is never solved and the audience's interest is displaced, from wanting a solution to the crime, to seeing how it affects the lives of the four characters. The events are divided into three acts. In the first, the four are sharing a dinner held to commemorate the death of their pet dog Elsa; Felix is having some success as a salesman of dinner services and Blason reveals his latest purchase of gold, which Laheu helps him to hide. Act Two covers a period of twelve months in ten short sequences. It begins on the day after Blason's home has been torn apart by thieves, who have stolen all the gold, and it shows the gradual estrangement of the two fathers as each suspects the other of trying to ruin him. It gradually emerges that the theft was the work of a local gang, in the pay of a certain Daphne, a restaurant owner with whom Felix has been doing business; suspicions and recriminations develop between the fathers, but the children remain united. At the end of the act both Alice and Felix have lost their jobs: they decide to set up a roadside stall selling frankfurters and chips together. Their two fathers have fallen out irrevocably, finally coming to blows. The third act takes place a few weeks later. The fathers have both left their jobs, but have unexpectedly made up their quarrel. They now live in adjoining huts at the flea market, where they work together, renovating and selling second-hand furniture. Their children have set up their stall and have acquired a new puppy. In an old sideboard, they discover a cache of gold coins; they decide to give the coins back to the old woman who had sold them the sideboard. As the play ends, Felix is brought in by Alice, having made a suicide attempt.

In *The Neighbours*, Vinaver treats reality in an almost playful manner: what appears to be a simple story is constantly being questioned, turned back on itself, forced to change direction. The abstract pattern of the double is constantly clamouring for the audience's attention and the narrative structure is repeatedly problematised. The construction of the second act is particularly novel, showing brief, almost random glimpses of the year following the theft. Within each episode, it is perfectly clear why the characters behave the way they do, but the events of the separate episodes often seem to contradict one another. Vinaver is using a Brechtian technique in this act, surprising his audience, asking them to reconsider what had previously seemed obvious. In Scene Four, for example, Blason convinces Laheu that Felix could not possibly be guilty of the theft; in the following scene both he and Laheu argue the opposite.

The characters, too, are more extreme, more fragmentary, and at times more grotesque than those in any of Vinaver's plays since *Overboard*. Behind the figures of Blason and Laheu lurk the ghosts of Flaubert's Bouvard and Pécuchet, and in them one can detect their author's admiration for the *Dictionnaire de idées reçues*, Flaubert's great catalogue of the banalities of French life in the nineteenth century. In many

ways they are very similar, being separated only by qualities
that they seem to cultivate in order to maintain their
individuality. For example, Blason loves statistics, Laheu hates
them; Blason is a hoarder, Laheu never has any money;
Blason enjoys working with figures, Laheu enjoys working with
his hands; Blason admires Monsieur Jonc, Laheu admires
Monsieur Delorge. Through their differences, and the ups and
downs of their relationship, Vinaver generates a great deal of
comedy, which the reviewers at the first production noted with
surprise, not having seen Vinaver as a comic author before. In
the *Figaro Magazine*, for example, Jacques Nerson wrote that
the play could have been inspired by Labiche and called it 'a
bizarre contemporary vaudeville, biting, disturbing, very
subtle and wildly funny' (15 November 1986).

As well as its biting comedy, the play incorporates great
thematic richness. Vinaver's encyclopaedic eye for the details
of lived experience in contemporary France ensures that an
enormous variety of subjects emerge in the course of the
dialogue, from the most banal, such as how to lay a table
correctly, to the most profound, such as relationships between
parents and children. But as in all of Vinaver's work, it is not a
case of the banalities providing the background against which
the profundities can emerge: on the contrary, everything is as
significant as everything else, because each thing occurs as it
does in real life, demanding instant attention, not ready sorted
into value-governed hierarchies. Each theme is mirrored at a
number of different levels. An example is the theme of
competitiveness: this is clearly central to the relationship
between Blason and Laheu, but is mirrored, at the level of big
business, in the struggle between Jonc and Delorge. Again, it
emerges at a trivial level in Act Three, as Alice and Felix
discuss the sales potential of merguez sausages as against
frankfurters. Into the texture of this deceptively light-hearted
play, Vinaver has woven most of the concerns that character-
ise the European literary tradition: love, death, suicide,
careers, success, failure, intrigues, deceptions, and the relationship between social status and private happiness or misery.

Portrait of a Woman (Portrait d'une femme), 1984

This play occupies a special place in Vinaver's oeuvre: it is the closest the author ever came to writing a documentary play, since it is based entirely on newspaper reports of a real case, but it is also his only play not set in the immediate present, i.e. the time in which he was writing. The case is that of Pauline Dubuisson, a twenty-three-year-old medical student, who in 1951, murdered her ex-lover; two years later she was sentenced to hard labour for life at the Paris Court of Assizes. The way the trial was conducted, the proximity to the end of the war, during which Dubuisson had grown up, the events of her life and her attitude during the proceedings all contributed to the sensationalism of the proceedings. As a young man in Paris, Vinaver followed the case, collecting all the reports of the trial that were published in *Le Monde*. Collecting and filing newspaper reports on all sorts of matters has always been one of Vinaver's regular activities; he forgot about the Dubuisson case until thirty years later when he came across the file of cuttings. On re-reading it, he was struck by the way in which the court authorities failed to draw Dubuisson into their linguistic field. She adopted none of the attitudes expected in such circumstances: she was neither contrite nor angry, but simply appeared untouched by the court's proceedings. Vinaver decided to write a play that was not exactly a documentary – it did not attempt to reconstruct the crime, its motives, or to focus on the pressures exerted by the society of the time. Instead he based his play entirely on the newspaper reports, and the strange communication gap between the court and the accused.

Out of this failure to connect, he was able to create powerful dramatic tension that is, first and foremost, linguistic. The idioms used by the different characters all carry their own implicit value judgements, whose effect is to deny the truth of anyone else's perspective in the crime. Broadly, the characters fall into four groups, each with their own particular use of language. First, there are the members of the legal profession. The rhetoric of the court is governed by the need to represent its workings in an objectively impartial light and to insist that it concerns itself only with hard facts. But the processes of the law demand that these facts be placed in a tendentious perspective, since the sole aim of the trial is to arrive at a point where guilt can be assigned. The arguments and counter-arguments fly to and fro above the head of the accused, but they do not touch her reality.

The second group is the parents of the accused (whom Vinaver renames Sophie Auzanneau). Their language alternates between brutal sarcasm (her father) and fussy over-protectiveness (her mother). The father's low expectations and fatalistic attitude are all too clear: whether it is his two sons (Sophie's brothers), both killed during the war, or his garden, destroyed by a storm, he always expects the worst. The mother is the opposite: full of concern for Sophie, but mostly at the level of whether she is eating enough, and how long it will be before she gets married and settles down. The third group is that of Sophie's student friends, with whom she at first appears to have more in common, especially Xavier, the young medical student who is attracted by her mercurial, vulnerable quality. But he proves unable to enter her world and understand her anguish; after his initial fascination with her, he starts to find her instability frightening, and drops her for the more conventional Francine.

The last group is made up of the adults she comes into contact with, notably the two older men who become her lovers. Colonna, her lecturer in medicine, has no real interest in her as a person and fails to understand her needs. Dr Schlessinger, on the other hand, does have some understanding of her profound needs, but is unable to meet them because of his age, status and nationality. Both men, in different ways, manipulate her for their own ends. The only person who does not try to manipulate her is her landlady, Madame Guibot. But for all her sympathy, she understands Sophie no better than her parents or lovers.

Vinaver's original dramatic technique, of presenting the action in a continuous but fragmented present, gives the audience an intense impression of Sophie's predicament, torn between the demands of her different 'selves'. The scenes from her life before the trial are highly condensed, and their order does not respect chronology, so each member of the audience has to piece together the different 'stories' of her life in much the same way that one does in reality, when meeting somebody new. This is consistent with the rather 'cubist' dramatic technique often employed by Vinaver. His frequent insistence that his way of working is similar to that of a painter finds particular resonance in this play, which ends in an art gallery, and which is all to do with how one constructs an image of a person. As epigraph to an earlier play, *Iphigénie Hôtel*, Vinaver had quoted Georges Braque's claim that, in his paintings, what was between the objects was as important as the objects themselves. In similar fashion, Vinaver's characters can only be grasped through the actions that take place between them. *Portrait of a Woman* consists of a wealth of insight into how our characters are composed of a constantly shifting network of interactions: between persons; between groups or families; between the individual and the group.

The flashbacks are interwoven with the court scenes so as to clarify the predicament of first the adolescent girl, then the young woman, who is obliged to conform to role models proposed by men. Her father, her boyfriend, her teacher, her lovers, all in their different ways, cast her in roles which condemn her to passivity. In such situations, all she can do is to struggle unsuccessfully to pull her different selves together into one coherent personality. Sophie is never allowed to take a dominant role. If she had been able to develop and impose her view of herself on others, or if she had been able to integrate the different selves that she manifests in her various relationships, then she might have had the strength to survive. She fails because she can only experience life as a collection of fragmented parts, each of them a failure with no centre to hold it together. Her crime is an act of desperation, a protest against the intolerable strain of trying to please too many people and to achieve a sense of her own integrity. The dramatic method perfectly expresses this, as Sophie is torn between answering the officials of the court, her lovers, her parents, her friends, etc., all coming at her from different angles but in the same space at the same time.

There are similarities between Sophie and Camus' Meursault in *L'Etranger* (*The Outsider*): both are victims of a legal process which functions according to its own logic, taking little account of the needs of the character concerned. But Sophie is never able to achieve the positive affirmation of Meursault who, despite being crushed by the pressures of social conformism, is able, before he dies, to affirm his rightness and declare his revolt. This is denied to Sophie, since Vinaver had decided to remain faithful to his source. It would have been easy to write a final speech in which Sophie vindicated herself, but it would have falsified the truth of her dilemma, so painstakingly recreated for the audience in the course of the play. The independent life-style enjoyed by Meursault in Algeria in the 1940s was not available to a young woman of Sophie's background growing up in France in the same period. Sophie Auzanneau is a martyr deprived of a voice, looking forward to the changed world of forty years later, when it *is* possible for women to find an independent voice, and to express it on stage. There is a tragic afterword to this case: in 1964 the real Pauline Dubuisson was released from prison with a remission of sentence for exemplary behaviour; a year and a half later she committed suicide.

The Television Programme (*L'Emission de télévision*), 1988

Although Vinaver's plays are full of dramatic events, these are seldom placed centre-stage. In *The Television Programme*, the event which precipitates the action (not shown on stage) is a murder. The first ten scenes take place alternately *after* and *before* this murder, giving the audience a kaleidoscopic view of the characters by showing them both in ignorance of the murder (just before it happens) and coping with their awareness of it (just afterwards). Through the story of the murder investigation, Vinaver deals with a wide range of themes: the theme of friendship that can easily turn to rivalry in the work-place; the theme of work, and how people come to be conditioned by their occupations; the theme of justice, the workings of the legal process and the manner in which it arrives at its judgements; the theme of spectacle in society – how we experience the quality of our social life through images, representations, performances, and how real-life experience is transformed so that it may be enjoyed as entertainment broadcast through the media, primarily television. As in *The Neighbours*, this heavy-weight material is dealt with lightly, by means of ironic juxtapositions and comic contrasts. As the play progresses, the murder, which was the mainspring for the action, becomes more and more opaque. By the end, the question of the motive and identity of the criminal have ceased to be the sole focus of attention. Real life pales before the glamour of televised reconstruction.

The play is made up of twenty scenes, in which the threads of four distinct stories are woven together, and their characters brought into conflict. At the centre of the play are two middle-aged couples, Monsieur and Madame Delile and Monsieur and Madame Blache (Monsieur Blache is the murder victim). They have known each other for decades and their relationship has gone through many ups and downs. Both men have recently lost their jobs. Now their world is invaded by Adèle and Béatrice, a couple of television researchers, who are working on a chat show to be devoted to the problems of the long-term unemployed. The third couple is formed by a magistrate and his secretary, and the fourth by Paul Delile the twenty-four-year-old son of the first couple, and Jacky, a young woman journalist.

The play opens in the office of the magistrate – a *juge d'instruction* who, in the French inquisitorial system of justice, conducts all the preliminary examinations in a criminal case and can call in as many witnesses as he likes. He is young and ambitious; he has just taken up his first post in the provincial town which is the setting for the play. His one ally is his secretary, who likes to tell him her lurid dreams. These all relate to the cases under investigation and she believes that, through them, the identities of the guilty parties are apt to be revealed. There is something conjugal about the relationship

between her and the magistrate, and through it we see a
favourite theme of Vinaver's work: the complex power
structures of dependence or interdependence that are engendered between people working for long periods in the same
office.

The second scene takes us back to before the murder and
introduces the Delile couple, the themes of unemployment and
of friendship or rivalry at work, and the story of the two
television researchers. The third scene jumps forward again to
after the murder of Blache, and shows the magistrate
interrogating Delile. For the next ten scenes this alternation
between before and after is maintained, giving the audience a
chance to build up its own picture of what really happened.
Each of the scenes contains an interrogation or an interview,
with the result that our attention is constantly drawn to the
process of how one makes sense of one's life when one has to
account for one's actions to a supposedly objective observer.
What is the difference between an event described to a wife or
lover and the same event described in front of a magistrate? If
called upon to face the television cameras and discuss your
own life, how do you present – or re-present – it? The success
of Vinaver's play at this level depends on his skill in writing
dialogue that captures accurately the kinds of expressions
typical of each new combination of character and situation.

Although constructed from commonplaces, this dialogue
maintains a dual focus which permits an ironic presentation of
the characters' situation. The audience is conscious both of
Blache and Delile's need to be true to their own (painful)
experience, and also of how their accounts of that experience
are manipulated to suit the interpretation of the judicial
inquiry or the television researchers. Delile feels obscurely that
if he consents to take part in the programme his own sense of
his life will be falsified. Blache has no such qualms, but
welcomes the chance to play a part for the cameras. Both
reactions are a source of profound if rather disturbing humour.

After Scene Eleven each of the play's four stories reaches
crisis point and the 'before and after' structure gives way to a
more concentrated time sequence. Because of Blache's sudden

death, the television researchers are left with only one candidate for their documentary, but Delile still hesitates. Meanwhile, the magistrate has become convinced of Delile's guilt, and is about to have him arrested when he is confronted by Béatrice and Adèle, who threaten him with public humiliation on their programme if he does not agree to put off the arrest until after the filming is completed. This is the moment chosen by Paul to claim that *he* is the criminal, perhaps to give a good story to the journalist Jacky, with whom he is infatuated. At the same time, in the Deliles' kitchen, Rose Delile is persuading her husband to take part in the television programme. The final scene is set in two places simultaneously: the magistrate's office and the Deliles' house. The Deliles wait nervously for a knock on the door not knowing whether it will be the film crew or the police, while the magistrate wages a desperate, losing battle for his independence, overpowered by the might of the media.

The conclusions to emerge from the play are: 1, the sense of how difficult it is for personal relationships to be free from outside manipulation in contemporary society, and 2, how well-nigh impossible it is to achieve an impartial investigation, whether by television, the judiciary, or any other means. *The Television Programme* is a profoundly political play. But it does not simply provide a rant against the inhumanity of media-driven late capitalism. More fundamentally, it builds up a demonstration, in complex and realistic (and frequently comic) detail, of those forces in our society which, in the name of an illusory liberty of choice, lead us into competitive or instrumental relationships with one another, even when all we want to achieve is simple conviviality.

David Bradby
Royal Holloway
University of London, 1997

Bibliography

1. Works by Michel Vinaver:

Théâtre complet (2 vols.), Arles: Actes Sud & Lausanne: L'Aire, 1986. [Volume 1 contains: *Les Coréens*; *Les Huissiers*; *Iphigénie Hôtel* (shortened version); *Par-dessus bord* (shortened version); *La Demande d'emploi*. Volume 2 contains: *Dissident, il va sans dire*; *Nina, c'est autre chose*; *Les Travaux et les jours*; *A la renverse*; *L'Ordinaire*; *Les Voisins*; *Portrait d'une femme*.]

L'Emission de télévision, Arles: Actes Sud, 1989.

Le Dernier Sursaut, Arles: Actes Sud, 1990.

Ecrits sur le théâtre, Lausanne: L'Aire, 1982.

Théâtre de chambre [Three plays (*Dissident, il va sans dire*; *Les Travaux et les jours*; *Les Voisins*) edited with an introduction in English by David Bradby], London: Duckworth ('Bristol Classical Press' French series), 1995.

2. Critical works on Vinaver's plays:

David Bradby, *The Theatre of Michel Vinaver*, Ann Arbor: Michigan University Press, 1993.

Kevin Elstob, *The Plays of Michel Vinaver: Political Theatre in France*, New York: Peter Lang, 1992.

Anne Ubersfeld, *Vinaver, dramaturge*, Paris: Librairie Théâtrale, 1989.

High Places

L'Ordinaire

a play in seven scenes

translated by GIDEON Y. SCHEIN

Characters

Bob (Robert Lamb), *50, chairman and CEO of General Houses Inc.*

Bess (Elizabeth Lamb), *47, his wife*

Pat (Patricia Fielding), *35, his secretary*

Joe (Joseph di Santo), *40, vice-president in charge of the Latin American division of General Houses Inc.*

Nan (Nancy di Santo), *18, his daughter*

Jack (John Hirschfeld), *48, senior vice-president in charge of research and production at General Houses Inc.*

Sue (Susan Beaver), *28, his mistress*

Dick (Richard Sutton), *41, senior vice-president in charge of marketing at General Houses Inc.*

Ed (Edward MacCoy), *52, senior vice-president in charge of finance and administration at General Houses Inc.*

Bill (William Gladstone), *46, pilot*

Jim (James King), *25, co-pilot*

Scene One

The interior of an aeroplane cabin. **Bess, Bob, Dick** *and* **Joe**
are at a table playing cards. **Pat** *is typing at another table.* **Ed**
is asleep on a berth. **Jack** *and* **Sue** *are in a corner of the cabin.*
He is seated on another berth and she is lying down, reading, her
head on his knees. **Nan** *is painting her toenails.* **Jim** *is*
intermittently either in the cockpit or in the cabin.

Sue   It's over Jack
   That's it

Jack   But Santiago is such a miserable town

Sue   I wish you wouldn't go over all that again
   You know yourself
   That it's over

Jack   You don't love me any more?

Sue   No
   Nor do you
   We went over all that before we left
   It was fine
   Let's not start all over again

Jack   There isn't a damn thing in Santiago
   I can't just dump you there
   I'll take you back to Seattle from Seattle you can go to
wherever you want and I'll pick up the tab
   In the meantime think it over

Sue   You are not dumping me
   I'm cutting myself loose I wish you would get that into
your head

Jack   There isn't a goddamn thing in Santiago you
should have stayed in Rio
   Oh I forgot you didn't like Rio you're the first person I
know that wasn't knocked out by that town

Sue   I am not a tourist

Jack   You could've stayed in Buenos Aires
   There's a lot going on in Buenos Aires

Sue   I want to be somewhere where you aren't Jack

Pat *rises and kisses* **Ed**, *who has been snoring lightly, on his half-opened mouth.* **Ed** *wakes up, startled, and* **Pat** *bursts out laughing.*

Ed   For Christ's sake Pat
   A man has a right to sleep

Pat   Of course he has of course he has

Ed   Not to be disturbed while one is sleeping is a God-given human right

Pat   I know
   Finance and Sleep
   A bird

Sue   Oh Jack

Pat   Landed on your lips didn't you feel it?
   No answer
   When he's not counting he's asleep
   When he's not asleep he's counting
   Maybe he even counts while he's asleep
   Do you Ed?
   Do I count?

Ed   Not so loud are you out of your mind if Bob heard you think of your job

Pat   At the Excelsior
   Ed when I woke up I was starving
   You all warm curled up next to me asleep
   And that huge tray I'll bet it was solid silver
   The waiter was pretty solid too
   The heavy curtains and the carpet can you remember how thick that carpet was?

Bob   Compared to Europe this feels great
   Goddamn European tour
   Jimmy Boy are you dreaming?

Who's going to refill these glasses?
That boy is a dreamer
What good is this co-pilot?

General laughter.

This European trip wiped me out
You have to put so much in and what do you get
back? Peanuts
Here in Latin America things move
In any case you can make them move
What about the peanuts Jimmy Boy?
Thatta boy Jimmy
Those tight-assed European ministers drive me nuts you
come to talk business and they dangle their laws and
regulations in front of you as if you were trying to stick
your hand up their dress
Whereas here
Right Dick?

Bess   Buenos Aires now there's a city

Nan   Gee I really loved wandering through the favelas of
Rio de Janiero at night

Dick   You're damn right

Bess   A city a real city obviously Rio is a great deal
more spectacular

Joe   But Buenos Aires is a city

Dick   No doubt about it things move around here

Bess   Buenos Aires is a *petit* Paris

Bob   All you have to do is push a little
That was the way it was in Europe twenty years ago
what's happening to Europe right now is a real shame

Bess   A jewel

Pat   If you would care to sign these Mr Lamb

Jim   The latest weather reports indicate strong gusts over the Andes

Pat   When you read the first one over I am not sure you will be happy with it Mr Lamb

Nan   Mr Lamb would you choose my nail-polish colour? How about this one?

Bob   Sweet kid

Nan   This one? Take a good look I wouldn't want you to make a mistake

Bob   No I think I prefer that one

Nan   That's Jane Fonda's

Bess   Next time you can do whatever you like Bob but I'll never set foot in the Excelsior again
   The air conditioning didn't work
   I woke up at two o'clock in the morning bathed in perspiration and naturally I was up for the rest of the night
   A hotel of that calibre

Jim   The weather reports now show violent atmospheric disturbances over the Andes

Bess   What an awful night
   Bob I had a strange premonition
   The plane exploded I took a valium not that it did much good
   I told you to lodge a complaint they will never see me in that hotel again not to mention the hot water faucet that leaked
   I am worried Bob

Bob   Nonsense Bess our little Gulfstream Jet is a thoroughbred
   Why shouldn't I like this letter?
   It seems to me that this letter says exactly what ought to be said

Pat   You don't leave him much hope

Bob   He doesn't have any
The books are closed

Pat   In that case sign it

Bob   What's that general's name in Brasilia?

Dick   Figuereido

Bob   He turned out to be quite realistic and I don't
expect less tomorrow

Dick   From Pinochet

Bob   What time's the meeting tomorrow? Jimmy Boy
aren't you being a little stingy with the ice cubes
Look Nan we're approaching the Andes
I have always felt the approach to these mountains is
more spectacular than the approach to the Alps there's no
transition all of a sudden you're in another universe

Nan   I love watching your face Mr Lamb
But you are even more impressive from the back
Your voice and your back are so impressive

Bob   Pour us a drink Jimmy Boy
I want to toast this gracious creature who is discovering
the terrifying splendour of the Andes for the first time

Jim   Excuse me Mr Lamb but Bill is considering turning
back he would like to talk it over with you

Bess   I am absolutely positive that we are going to crash
in these mountains
You know that sometimes I can tell something is going
to happen

Nan   Dad's concerned that I am not interested in boys
my own age
I like strong men
Dad told me how you stepped on everyone to get to
the top

Joe   Nan will you leave Mr Lamb alone?

I would never have taken her along on this trip if I had
known that she would talk your ear off

Nan   My analyst says that my father is doing everything
he can to repress my spontaneity
   He's right I don't like boys my age they are phoneys
and snobs I don't like luxurious houses
   Like ours and like yours in Crockton Hills
   I like slums that's where people really do live
   Like in Rio
   Without lies without hypocrisy

Joe   Honestly Nan
   It's about time you shut up

Nan   You see

Bob   It seems to me Joe that your daughter has an
intense need to express herself
   She has a strong personality and pointed little breasts
people would love to munch on

Nan   Oh Mr Lamb don't be cruel I know they're tiny

Bill *appears.*

Bill   Mr Lamb

Bob   You see this guy Nan?
   We have flown over 300,000 miles 625 flight hours
together
   On board I'm not the boss he is
   He makes the decisions
   Billy Gladstone is an authentic Vietnam War hero he
got the Distinguished Service Cross from President
Johnson himself right Billy?

Bill   Mr Lamb the control tower in Santiago suggests
that we turn back
   There are hurricane-force winds out of the Pacific
sweeping across the valley colliding with warm air currents
coming from the other direction crossing the Andes could
be very uncomfortable

Bob An ace
Modest and secure
He received a bunch of medals do you think he would
ever talk about them?
Safety is his primary concern
He's in love with her
He's in love with our little Gulfstream
Between flights he never stops servicing and polishing
her
He rubs her down isn't that right Billy?
Tell me Billy can we get through
This is an important meeting Billy
General what's his name again?

Dick Pinochet

Bob Is expecting us
He's going to open the gates of Chile for us
This little conversation tomorrow will lead to the sale of
thirty to forty thousand Housies
Pinochet is ripe and one never knows about these
generals ·
One day they're in power and the next day they're
swinging on the end of a rope
Can we get through?
It's your decision
No matter what I must be in my office in Seattle nine
o'clock Monday morning
If we go back to Buenos Aires
We'll have to forget about Chile

Bill exits.

Ed Forget about Chile?

Dick Ed's awake

Joe He's recuperating

Dick From last night's exertion

Joe At the Excelsior

Ed   Where are we?

Joe   Entering into turbulence

Ed   That black wall?

Joe   The Andes

Dick   Above a hurricane

Joe   Just like at the Excelsior

Dick   In the squall

Joe   Ed's given in

Dick   To Rio's lascivious moisture

Joe   Nowhere else but in Brazil

Dick   Brazilian nights are irresistible

Joe   Pat broke the sound barrier

Dick   She grabbed her chance

Pat   Now look

Joe   Poor Ed

Dick   Annihilated

Joe   Three years of work and she finally got him

Ed   She's been running after me for four

Pat   Four Ed? Try six
   I've wanted you for six years and I have had you but
that sky scares me

Nan   Oh Mr Lamb I'll never forget this trip

Joe   Button up your blouse Nan and you can put on
your shoes and socks there are plenty of magazines on
board for Godsake read a magazine

Nan   I feel great barefoot
   My toenails are drying
   Next time Mr Lamb you can take me along without

my father

Bess   An air-pocket

Nan   In Santiago are there beaches too?

Sue   Oh Jack
   I don't want to hear any more about it

Nan   You promise?

Jack   Can you simply decide to forget everything

Sue   Who said anything about forgetting?

Jack   It's the same thing

Sue   Not at all

Bob   Pat
   'And the dinner you had in your garden was delightful'
   'And the candlelight barbecue you had in your garden
was delightful'
   You typed that sentence twice
   Once with a barbecue and once without
   For heaven's sake Pat what's wrong with you?

Dick   The lascivious

Joe   Moisture

Dick   Of Brazilian nights

Bess   Another air pocket Bob

Bob   For Argentina
   Reread it first

Bess   If there is still time

Pat   I'll type it over first

Bob   No reread it first
   I'm thinking of Steve for Argentina
   We need someone solid
   I did think Sidney was solid
   No read it out loud Pat

What do you think of Steve?

Pat   Sorry Mr Lamb
I'm a little nauseated

Joe   Poor wounded heart

Dick   Pierced

Joe   By an arrow

Pat   It's because of all the shaking
(*Reading*.) 'Dear Sidney
As always it was good to see you and Dorothy again.
And the candlelight barbecue you had in your garden was
delightful.

I will summarize my general impressions of my visit to
Buenos Aires. Your presentation of the plans for 1982 was
sloppy. Your 1981 results came in well under budget
primarily because you allowed yourself to relax following
your excellent performance of the past three years. To
make matters worse you juggled the inventory figures in
order to cover up the situation. Even more disturbing,
however, is that you were satisfied arranging a meeting
between me and a subordinate member of the President
of the Republic's staff whereas your instructions to set up
a meeting with the head of state were quite specific. No
need to elaborate further. You will return to Seattle on
November 4th so that we can discuss the measures needed
to straighten out the situation in Argentina and to discuss
your personal future.

Once again thank you for the lovely barbecue. Love to
Dorothy from Bess and myself.

Sincerely.'

Jack   What about Pete?

Joe   Pete?

Jack   Pete could run Argentina

Bob   I need him in Japan
I'm transferring Jeff from Japan to France that won't do

that boy any harm
 Let him get a taste of Europe let him see what it's like
to have to run when you're up to your knees in muck

Joe I'd leave Jeff another year or two in Japan
 He's just beginning to grasp what's going on in Japan

Dick To run Argentina what we have to have
 Mind you Steve has a head on his shoulders
 But under certain circumstances Steve could and you
admit the circumstances in Argentina

Joe They are extremely special it's not that Steve isn't
totally reliable but take Larry Larry isn't Tom
 Tom wouldn't bend but there's something about Tom

Jim *appears.*

Jim Could I have your attention please fasten your
seatbelts and bring your seats to an upright position

Bob For landing?

Jim Not yet and please extinguish your cigarettes we are
flying into an area of extreme turbulence

Bob But where are we?

Jim Over the Planchon Pass two-thirds of the Andes are
behind us Bill has had to change course and altitude

Bob If we have to turn back

Jim We passed the most difficult point we'll make a
turn to the right and descend to a lower altitude where
there is less wind
 We should encounter only another quarter of an hour
of disturbance

Nan A break in the clouds
 I can see the mountains

Bess One can almost touch them

Nan Great

My camera

Bob   Drinks Jimmy Boy

Jim   Bill would like me back right away will you excuse me

Jim *exits.*

Dick   We need a guy that's solid a real hard ass and Steve I wonder if Steve

Joe   Steve in Brazil there's no way to tell

Dick   He did get terrific results but

Joe   Brazil is not Argentina I'm not suggesting that Steve would bend

Jack   Steve gave way in Brazil at exactly the right time Larry is somehow stiffer he might crack

Joe   Not Larry no he won't crack he takes it right to them and asks no questions

Dick   Larry's got a lot of balls all right

Jack   But not much of a brain

Joe   Somehow I wouldn't mind seeing Argentina run by a guy who doesn't ask himself too many questions and Tom

Jack   Steve has proven that he's flexible he's flexible and tough
    Whereas Tom

Joe   Is tough maybe a little too rigid considering the circumstances in Argentina

Bob   I trusted that boy Sidney
    To see him break down like that
    What I like about Tom is his directness he'll reduce a problem to two or three essential issues
    And then he'll dive in

Jack   Sometimes he'll miss

Bob   But I'm afraid that in Argentina he'll collapse just like Sidney did

Dick   Argentina has that softening effect on managers but Tom

Nan   We're in the clouds again

Sue   No that's snow snow
  Bess doesn't feel well at all
  Look
  That peak that ridge it looks like an ocean
  That peak above us

Bob   Larry?
  Maybe basically Larry is
  Larry did inherit a rotten situation in Chile and he sure as hell turned it around

Dick   Yeah but women are Larry's problem women and alcohol so between him and Tom

Jack   Tom is reliable although I can't say that he's sharp

Joe   Tom's reliable maybe not sharp but fierce nothing'll stop him in El Salvador Tom has held out against all odds the trouble with Steve Steve is not hard Steve is an idealist he could be gotten to whereas Tom Tom

Jack   Larry's got more punch

Dick   But when it comes to women he's got a problem and he can't hold his liquor in Argentina I don't know whether Tom

Joe   If we want a guy in Argentina that's reliable he's got to be tough and Steve

Jack   Exactly Steve flexible as he is

Dick   Steve

Jack   Is hard to the core

Dick   I'm not sure

Joe   All things being equal better than Tom

Jack   I have the feeling

Joe   What?

Jack   Look at that snow field

Dick   That's a cloud

Jack   No it's snow

Joe   It's so close

Jack   You could almost say

Nan   That isn't true

Sue   We're flying a little low

Dick   We're skimming the snow

Pat   Are you sure?

Bob   What's going on?

Joe   The plane's pulling up

Dick   It's about time

Jack   But look

Nan   What?

Sue   The mountain just ahead

Joe   He's climbing

Bess   God be with us

Jack   No

Joe   What do do you mean no?

Jack   He can't

Sue   Oh my God we're going to hit it

Noise. Blackness.

A giant screen. We see the words appearing on a teleprompter:

AP OCTOBER 21. THE CHILEAN AUTHORITIES HAVE
ANNOUNCED THAT ALL ATTEMPTS TO LOCATE THE
GULFSTREAM TWIN-JET PLANE BELONGING TO THE
AMERICAN FIRM GENERAL HOUSES INC. THAT HAS BEEN
MISSING FOR EIGHT DAYS SOMEWHERE OVER THE ANDES
HAVE FAILED. FOLLOWING A WEEK OF INTENSIVE SEARCHES
BY ALL AVAILABLE MILITARY AND CIVILIAN PERSONNEL, ALL
FURTHER ATTEMPTS TO FIND THE PLANE HAVE BEEN
HALTED. IT IS BELIEVED THAT ALL PASSENGERS AND CREW
HAVE DIED EITHER AS A RESULT OF THE ACCIDENT OR
DURING THE EIGHT SUBSEQUENT DAYS, DUE TO THE
ALTITUDE, THE LACK OF FOOD AND THE SEVERE WEATHER
CONDITIONS THAT PREVAIL DURING THIS TIME OF THE
YEAR.

THE PLANE, WHICH LEFT BUENOS AIRES FOR SANTIAGO ON
13 OCTOBER AT 10.00 A.M., HAD A CREW OF TWO:
WILLIAM GLADSTONE AND JAMES KING. THE PASSENGERS
INCLUDED: MR ROBERT LAMB, THE PRESIDENT OF
GENERAL HOUSES INC., ACCOMPANIED BY HIS WIFE
ELIZABETH AND HIS SECRETARY, MRS PATRICIA FIELDING.
ALSO ON BOARD WERE THE FOUR RANKING VICE-
PRESIDENTS OF THE FIRM: MESSRS RICHARD SUTTON, JOHN
HIRSCHFELD, EDWARD MACCOY, AND JOSEPH DI SANTO, THE
LATTER ACCOMPANIED BY HIS DAUGHTER NANCY. MISS
SUSAN BEAVER WAS ALSO ON BOARD. THE PRIVATE JET
HAD LEFT SEATTLE, CORPORATE HEADQUARTERS OF
GENERAL HOUSES INC. ON 4 OCTOBER ON A BUSINESS TRIP
TO LATIN AMERICA. THE SENIOR MANAGEMENT OF THIS
LARGE MULTINATIONAL ENTERPRISE SPECIALIZING IN
INEXPENSIVE PRE-FABRICATED HOUSING, MADE STOPS IN
BRAZIL AND ARGENTINA AND WAS TO HAVE RETURNED TO
SEATTLE FOLLOWING A BRIEF STOPOVER IN CHILE. ALL
THE PASSENGERS WERE AMERICAN. RESPONDING TO US
GOVERNMENT CRITICISM OVER THE HALTING OF THE
SEARCH, THE SPOKESMAN FOR THE PRESIDENT OF CHILE
STATED THAT ALL POSSIBLE MEANS WERE UNDERTAKEN,
LIVES WERE RISKED AND THAT THE SEARCH HAD

CONTINUED FAR LONGER THAN IS REQUIRED BY
INTERNATIONAL LAW AND CUSTOMS APPLYING TO AN
AVIATION ACCIDENT.

*The screen disappears. Light comes up on the fuselage of the plane
which is dug into a snowy slope. Five survivors are discovered inside
the cabin blown open at both ends by the accident. A wall of
suitcases serves as a shield against the wind.* **Pat** *and* **Dick***, both
wounded, are curled up tightly against one another, sucking
alternately on a snowball.* **Bess** *is trying to get snow into a 'black
and white' bottle and is shaking it.* **Sue** *lying flat is rhythmically
massaging her side.* **Bob** *is doing an inventory. They are all
listening to a portable radio that is transmitting the final phrases of
the AP bulletin. They are all wrapped up in several layers of
clothing, blankets and all available materials. In the vast snowy
distance one will soon make out three human forms moving slowly
towards the plane.* **Jack***,* **Ed** *and* **Nan***, their silhouettes appearing
voluminous and deformed by their eccentric makeshift outfits. They are
wearing 'snow shoes' made out of aeroplane seat cushions, which
make them walk bow-legged.*

Bob   One hundred and twenty-five black olives three
chocolate bars a bag of potato chips twenty-eight pieces of
sugar
      Twenty-eight plus twelve equals forty pieces of sugar

Dick *rises and one can see that he has a metal object protruding
from his stomach.*

Dick   Before the wound closes up completely
      Before it's too late
      Please Bess

Bob   Four boxes of crackers in each box sixty-four
crackers eleven cartons of cigarettes six cans of tuna

Dick   For the love of God Bess
      Your were a nurse

Bess   That was thirty years go
      Better leave it alone

Bob   One tube of anchovy paste six slices of Dutch
cheese two bottles of ketchup three bottles of grapefruit
juice a little less than half a salami

Bess   Till we get back to Seattle there a surgeon can
remove it
  If I pulled it out you could haemorrhage

Dick   Would an infection be any better?
  It's rusting inside
  Bess I feel the rust
  It's getting harder and harder to hold myself up when I
turn over in my sleep

Bess   In order to rust it needs air
  Don't be a child

Bob   A quarter of a pound of shelled almonds a pound
and a half of peanuts eight slices of rye bread

Bess   Butter?

Bob   No butter

Dick   But Bob
  Are you sure we'll get an import ban?

Bob   He is a man of vision
  No more slums
  A Housie in place of each and every hovel
  We will surround every town over ten thousand
inhabitants with a ring of Housies

Pat   My legs were my best asset
  I have many friends in Seattle
  They all told me my legs were really something

Bob   In return for which Pinochet is giving us a five-year
income tax exemption and with that import ban he is
protecting us against all potential competition
  You saw Larry's report

Dick   You're certain about the monopoly?

Bob   That was the essential condition Larry was
unequivocal about it
   In three months we break ground production should
begin in eighteen months and in five years there won't be
a slum left in Chile
   Five bottles of tomato juice the dregs of a bottle of
vodka a bag of potato chips

Bess   You counted it already

Bob   This is a different one that makes two bags of
potato chips

Bess   But this second bag's already been opened

Bob   One third of a bottle of gin

Pat   Dick rub my feet

Bess   And that's all?

Pat   I'll rub yours
   If I have the strength I promise
   Rub
   Are you rubbing?
   I don't feel anything

Bess   I said so over and over again
   But no one would listen

Dick   It looks a lot better Pat it's less purple
   Certainly has a lovely curve

Pat   You're very funny Dick I'm cold fortunately I have
your voice to warm me
   I hope they don't have to amputate
   I'd rather they cut off my head
   I don't find my head nearly as attractive as my legs
   My legs are my best asset
   By far

Dick   Your pretty little feet are perfect

Pat   When I say legs I mean the whole thing from hip

to toe
  My friends tell me that my legs are flawless
  You simply have to believe what everyone says
  Pat your legs are the finest part of your anatomy by far
  Besides Dick it's no secret
  For David my ex it all started with my legs
  At the university pool he kept looking at them
  A long hard look
  From a distance
  Then he came over and lay down next to me I didn't
even know who he was he stared at me
  But I knew it wasn't my face that attracted him
  He asked me what I was interested in he told me he
was interested in geology I told him that I couldn't make
up my mind between art and US history
  Are you rubbing Dick?

Dick   I'm rubbing

Pat   Don't give up if you rub long enough the
circulation will start again I know you're going to save me
Dick
  When David left me after being married three years
  He regretted losing my legs
  He told me he missed them
  He missed my legs

Dick   I understand

Pat   Do you understand Dick? The rest
  The rest isn't that important

Sue   Give me a sip Mrs Lamb

Bess   It isn't time yet to distribute water

Sue   One sip of water
  I'm so thirsty

Bess   So is everyone else snow's not a very good thirst-
quencher
  It takes an incredible amount of time to get it into the

bottle and I'm the only one working you could help you know I'm the only one doing anything around here

Sue   I melted snow for hours this morning
Now I am tired
My whole body hurts
It's as if everything was all torn up inside me
I'm thirsty

Bess   Everyone's thirsty
You'll have to wait

Sue   One sip now

Bess   Who forced you to go on this trip?
What right do you have to be on this trip?
I have never understood what business you have being on this plane
If there is one thing that Mr Lamb cannot stand it's a *fait accompli*
To my knowledge he never authorized Jack to bring a girlfriend on this trip
As far as I know this is not a pleasure trip this is a business trip
Everyone is here for a reason

Sue   This is a business trip for me too Mrs Lamb
My business is to leave Jack
This way I can get as far away as possible
Free of charge for which I am very grateful to General Houses Inc.
Rest assured I won't be making the return trip with you
I'm staying in Santiago
Even though there doesn't seem to be much happening in the city of Santiago

Bob   Santiago is a lousy city there is nothing to see there in Rio the slums have a certain character but
Pinochet wants to raze two-thirds of suburban Santiago he has included the project in his five-year plan Pinochet is far-sighted he's a man of vision

For GH this is unquestionably the largest contract we
have ever negotiated in Latin America
Housies' crowning glory

Dick   Which we shall negotiate provided

Bob   It's as good as done

Dick   Provided we get to Santiago
But they have stopped searching Bob
Pinochet has written us off

Bob   That communiqué did irritate me
But Reagan won't let us down
Evidently Pinochet is using all possible means to bring
pressure to bear on the negotiations with the US over
arms sales
He's using us that's fair enough
But Pinochet doesn't know Reagan
And anyway we're not going to wait for Pinochet to
come and get us
If he doesn't find us we'll find him
We'll know more soon

Jack *and* **Nan** *enter, followed by* **Ed***, all three are totally
exhausted.*

Jack   You tell them Ed

Ed   You tell them Jack

Jack   Nan

Nan   What should I say?

Jack   Tell them first about your father

Nan   We found Dad
Hard as a rock

Jack   Tell them about the valley

Nan   There is no valley

Pat   Ed did you think about me

Ed   How have you been Pat?

Pat   I was worried about you
I am relieved

Sue   Jack are you all right?

Jack   Nan tell them

Ed   About the crevasse and Jack

Nan   All of a sudden Jack Jack disappeared

Jack   A huge hole

Nan   He just vanished

Ed   It's beyond me how Nan knew exactly where he had gone through

Nan   It only took a few seconds to uncover his head

Ed   But it took the rest of the day to dig him out

Jack   At least we know now that there's no point in trying to get through that way
There is no valley behind that wall just another wall even higher

Bob   But look at the map
That valley does exist

Jack   It exists somewhere
Where we made our mistake is locating our position on this map
We are somewhere but where?

Ed   A rock ledge stopped his fall
Joe's broken body was hanging there

Jack   He sure got the best deal of us all
For him it only took several minutes

Ed   During which he must have had a chance to tell himself a lot of things
From the minute the tail broke away from the fuselage

and he was ejected
  Until he hit that ledge
  He had time to think

Bob   Something doesn't fit
  Your theory simply doesn't make sense because we are
here
  These two mountains are this one and that one
  Where do you think we are if not right here?
  For God's sake

Bess   Oh Bob

Bob   Everything substantiates that

Jack   Except that there is no valley

Dick   Pinochet halted the search they announced it on
the radio

Bess   God will not abandon us
  It wouldn't do any harm if we would all pray together
  If our prayer reached him
  It wouldn't hurt if I weren't the only one praying

Nan   Mrs Lamb can we have something to eat

Bess   Ask Mr Lamb

Bob   This business about Joe upsets me
  I was counting on Joe
  In my five-year plan Joe was a key element
  He was to assume broader and broader responsibility
and now you are an orphan

Nan   Mr Lamb I'm hungry

Bess   Mr Lamb has assumed the responsibility of
rationing personally

Nan   You were getting Dad ready to be your successor
weren't you Mr Lamb?
  He told Jenny and me

Dick   What

Who said that?

Nan   He told us

Bob   It behooves the man at the top to groom the men who one day will take his place and lead the business on to even greater heights

Your father was one of the two or three individuals who were qualified to become the next CEO of this company now we're back to square one

A boss has no greater responsibility than to plan for his own departure no one lasts forever

Just this once one piece of chocolate for each member of the expeditionary force

I did an inventory we have one hundred and twenty-five black olives three and a half bars of chocolate two bags of potato chips forty pieces of sugar four boxes of crackers six cans of tuna one tube of anchovy paste five bottles of tomato juice

Ed   That will last three maybe four days

Jack   Did you go look over there
In the nose of the plane
How's Jimmy?

Dick   I just brought him some water it's hard to believe

Ed   Maximum four days Bob

Dick   That he's still alive
Billy got a better break

Sue   It's been eight days and Jimmy hasn't moved an inch

He has no idea where he is

He doesn't even know that the nose broke off

He talks about his house on Hamilton Bay he thinks he's in his own house he talks to his dog Blackie

He has no idea that the instrument panel is implanted in his pelvis and his insides are hanging out

Still at times he asks for his gun I looked but I couldn't

find his gun
   I love you Jack
   Given the circumstances I think I can say that
   I can also say I don't feel hungry any more
   I'm ready for it to be all over
   I only wish I could put Jimmy out of his misery

Pat One ought to
   It's not an easy thing to say
   Billy is dead he's now useless Jimmy's going to die and
Joe is down there in the snow and if we don't eat we're
all going to die
   I don't know if that's such a good idea

Bess What?

Pat To let ourselves all die

Bob Who's said anything about dying?
   We have an expeditionary force whose mission is to
find a way out of the Andes
   Failure on a first attempt was to be expected
   The northwest route is blocked? Fine tomorrow they'll
go and climb the southwest pass
   There has to be a way out

Ed This expeditionary force needs two or three days of
rest Bob
   And when it goes out again it will need supplies

Pat The dead we must be allowed to eat them

Bob Her legs are doing that to her
   Rub her legs Ed God forgive her the poor little thing is
raving
   Dick has been rubbing her legs all day

Dick From day one I said it over and over again
   Jack didn't want to listen he made us lose precious time
   This is the way out
   The mountain in front of us has to be this one and if it
is then Bob is right the way out is that way

If I could walk I would leave right now and prove it

Jack   That's the way out huh?

Dick   Obviously

Jack   The oracle has spoken

Dick   Another two or three days?
They have to leave tomorrow morning Bob hopefully
it's not too late already

Jack   Bob you know what I have always thought of your
little protégé here
Today Dick Sutton will hear it from me personally
I can stand stupidity when it isn't combined with
arrogance and I can stand simple arrogance without
stupidity
Joe's death suits you fine doesn't it Dick?
The door's open the top is a hand's reach away

Dick   That's too much
Bob you are the only one on the twenty-ninth floor
who hasn't heard what everyone is saying from the
lowliest typist to the divisional directors
Everyone agrees that Jack is responsible for the major
mistakes that have shaken Wall Street's confidence and set
our stock tumbling down

Jack   The mistake was to hire him
I suppose that was probably because he was the son of
the president of Harvard

Nan   Oh Jack don't say anything bad about Harvard
Dad and I spent my sixteenth birthday sailing the
ocean just like we do every Sunday
He said to me Nan Harvard is the top university in the
US and I Joe di Santo a Harvard graduate would like my
daughter to go there if you get into Harvard I will ask
Mr Lamb

Bess *has taken* **Dick** *to the side, opened his clothes. She places
one hand on the metal object protruding from his stomach, looks at it*

a moment and pulls. **Dick** *bends over.* **Bess** *holds the object in her hand and lets it fall from her fingers. She wipes the wound clean, she wraps a bandage around* **Dick**'s *waist as he straightens up, throws out his chest, smiles.*

Nan   But there was no need to ask you Mr Lamb you beat us to it you asked him one day what would Nan like if she gets into Harvard? Ever since she was a little girl Nan has dreamt of taking a trip in the company plane and you said let her buy a pretty new bikini I will watch her swim at the Copacabana Mr Lamb I am sure if Dad knew that there were only a few olives and a few crackers left
    He would agree with Pat

Scene Two

Three days later. A bright sunlit day. The aeroplane seats have been laid out on the snow. The survivors, in shirt-sleeves, are lying in them as in lounge chairs on a terrace. Their faces are emaciated and wrinkled. Movement has become slow and heavy. At times even speech has become difficult. **Dick** *and* **Nan** *are melting snow into bottles.* **Ed** *and* **Jack** *are busy sewing seat covers together to make knapsacks.* **Sue** *is cutting out circles from the tinted plastic sun visors in the cockpit in order to make sunglasses.* **Bob** *is repeatedly counting and sorting the remainder of the food.* **Bess** *is dozing.* **Pat** *is the only one who is inside the cabin, the interior of which cannot be seen.*

Nan   My darling sister Jenny has already been to Europe twice Jesus am I jealous and each time she goes she sends dozens of postcards
    Venice and Amsterdam
    Those are her favourite cities
    Mr Lamb I'd love to see Europe
    Will you take me along next time?
    Which are your favourite cities?

Sue *gets up and disappears into the cabin.*

Bob   Continents age like people Europe has grown old it's shrivelled up

I used to love Europe

I opened up the gates to Europe when no one at GH believed in its potential

During the sixties

A tidal wave that made history

Right Jack?

Thanks to Europe between 1962 and 1968 GH increased its gross sales 600 per cent

Jack   I didn't believe him any more than the others did

Top management at the time was convinced that Bob would fall on his ass

That marked the beginning of his rise to the top

They had to make a little room for him and once there he eliminated all of them

All except me

General laughter.

Bob   Because my good man it didn't take you long to jump onto a winner's bandwagon

Jack   And because I'm such a lovable guy right?

Laughter.

Bob   Let's just say there were some damn good ideas floating around in that ugly head of yours

There's no room for sentiment in business Nan or let's just say business first sentiment later

Jack   Look who's talking Nan Bob is the most sentimental man on earth

Europe was primarily a love affair

And the people that surround Bob are picked above all on the basis of personal inclination

Bob   Jack's right he is absolutely right

Instinct is what breeds success in business

Those who don't have it can operate the machines

Sue *re-enters.*

Bob I have a feeling for this continent now
It's a strange thing Nan every time I set foot in Latin
America something inside me goes off

Sue I think we should carry Pat out here so she can
take advantage of the sun

Silence. **Ed** *and* **Jack** *get up and enter the cabin.*

Sue It was your turn to clean the cabin Mrs Lamb
wasn't it?

Bess I did

Sue No you didn't
The stench is intolerable there is a pool of urine at
least one person urinated while they were sleeping

Bob There
I've made two piles
Both are equal
But I have an announcement to make of interest to
everyone
I have to wait because it involves Jack and Ed too

Ed *and* **Jack** *reappear carrying* **Pat**. *They set her down on three
seats arranged side by side.*

Bob Two pieces of chocolate and four crackers have
disappeared
I counted over and over again and four crackers and
two pieces of chocolate are missing
As a result I have decided to institute a surveillance
system
You will all watch each other and report to me any
incidence of pilfering that may occur
I have taken note of all comings and goings that seem
to me to be suspicious
These two piles are equal and this is all we have left
The first few days we ate and drank freely
Because we expected to be rescued at any moment

Now the valley leading to the coastal plain begins right
behind that ridge

The expeditionary force will leave tomorrow the three
of you will take one of the two piles

The other is for the five of us who will remain behind

Sue   We won't get very far on that Mr Lamb

Ed (*to* **Jack**)   Four or five olives and some crackers per
person

He's got to be kidding

Jack   His strength

Is that he sees only what he wants to see

He refuses to see that there no longer is an
expeditionary force

We've been eating practically nothing for the last three
days

Who's got the strength to walk even a couple of
hundred yards

Nan get up

Nan *tries to get up.*

Jack   She can't

Just carrying Pat was enough I'm wiped out

Sue   Mr Lamb we wouldn't get far on what you've got
in both piles

Bess   Bob I am stunned I am not used to disagreeing
with you but it's unfair I object

The food must be divided into eight equal parts

Aren't the members of the expeditionary force in better
shape than the rest of us? Weren't they chosen because
they have been hurt the least?

Those who stay behind like Dick don't they need even
more to regain their strength?

Dick   I'm for even distribution are you going to deprive
Pat of what she needs to get on her feet again?

Sue   Mr Lamb there's not enough here either for them

or for us
We have got to add some meat if we want to survive

Sue *opens a bag and adds several pieces of meat to each stock.*

I cut these up last night
I am not a butcher so this is the best I could do
The expeditionary force shouldn't leave for several days
that will allow enough time to build up their strength
Don't you agree? Jack?

Jack I am
I must admit that I'm
I don't know I'm surprised
I can't say that I disagree

Ed In theory I don't either
But to actually do it is another matter

Sue What else can we do?

Ed I mean to actually eat

Sue I know
The first couple of mouthfuls are going to be very
difficult
After that I don't know

Nan Mr Lamb I could never do it
Yet do you remember when Pat first brought it up a
few days ago

Sue The meat is dried
I spread it out on top of the cabin this morning

Nan When Pat said it
I heard Daddy's voice say
Do it

Dick I'd like to know Miss Beaver who gave you the
authority

Bess No one did
Bob aren't you going to say anything?

That girl shouldn't even be here
That girl didn't belong on the plane
She's poisoning the atmosphere
Bob I feel sick say something
God is watching he's waiting for you to take a stand
You who cannot stand being faced with a *fait accompli*

Bob   Yes

Bess   There are certain things which are sacred

Pat   Life

Ed   Pat woke up

Pat   I wasn't sleeping
While you were speaking to me I heard bells ringing
I heard the bells that are right outside my window in
Seattle Saint Vincent's church a red-brick church all
covered with ivy
It's surrounded by a garden honeysuckle grows in it
In the summer the scent floats up all the way into my
room

Jack *moves away. So do* **Bess** *and* **Dick** *in another direction.*
Nan *disappears into the cabin.*

Pat   If I could only sleep

Sue   You did doze off Pat

Ed   You look a little more rested

Pat   I've got to be in top shape for Monday night
Monday night is our annual meeting
I am only the vice-president but the president doesn't
understand anything at all about legal issues she has
entrusted me with the task of drafting the new
amendments to our by-laws
There will be strong opposition

Jack *sings a traditional American folksong.*

He removes a sheet of aluminium from inside a broken seat and bends it into the shape of a curved bowl and constructs a spiggot at the bottom of the bowl. He fills the bowl up with snow and sticks it into a bottle which he has shoved into the snow allowing the snow inside the bowl to melt in the sun.

Bess   Dick I'm scared
He is losing control
Only you can
It's happened several times during his career he'd fade out and each time he'd bounce back stronger than ever
I have faith
He said to me often Dick and Joe are my two rising stars
Now you're the only one left
Grab hold of the reins Dick
I'm scared
It's dangerous
A man like Jack simply waits for his moment
He has always spun his web around my husband
A girl he simply picked up in a drugstore in Seattle
And he's a sceptic
I had decided not to
And then
These business trips really wear me out particularly since you can never be sure of the hotels but I adore the bazaar
In all these countries you can go broke buying all the cheap arts and crafts that are spread out on the ground and I love to bargain

Pat   I really must be in top shape for this meeting there's bound to be a confrontation do you know what my opponents
We don't have anything against unwed mothers they say but their mentality is simply not the same
Let unwed mothers go and form their own organization

Sue   But what is your organization?

Pat   I am vice-president of the Young Divorcées of

Seattle

The age limit is currently thirty-five after thirty-five those who want to can ask to be transferred to the Divorced Women of Seattle but it's just not the same

One of the amendments I'm proposing will extend the age limit from thirty-five to forty

In today's world a woman between those ages is still young

We are not against men

But we must defend ourselves

Sue   Against what?

Pat   You simply wouldn't believe it

I mean the number of young divorced women who wouldn't mix under any circumstances with unwed mothers

They claim that the mentality just isn't the same

We in the executive committee believe we have the majority but the point is we want to avoid a split

You see my opponents will focus their attack on the amendment that will change the name of the club from Young Divorcées of Seattle to Young Separated Women of Seattle

Sue   You certainly are active Pat

Pat   I am also the treasurer for the friends of the Museum of Fine Arts

Paintings

I'd spend my life looking at paintings

What about you Sue?

Sue   I try to stay unattached

I like being able to leave without creating a fuss

I have fun

Pat   Your son

Sue   Doesn't need me

Pat   Jack

Sue   That was just a passing affair

Ed   I don't believe you
Sue I'd like you to join the next expedition
It's important to be light when the snow softens in the heat of the sun

Jack *approaches, carrying his melting device.*

Sue   It's time to eat
Don't you think?

Bob *has joined* **Bess** *and* **Dick**. **Nan** *reappears.*

Jack   I bring you progress a Promethean device
It produces water instead of fire

Bob   It's a beautiful day Bess
And the scenery is overwhelming
Remind me when we get back to give Donald Sutton a call I want him to keep an eye on our little urchin Nan
After all he is the president of Harvard I'll ask him to make things easier for her this younger generation doesn't like to show its feelings and so eventually something breaks down
Joe was crazy about his daughter look at Nan no way of knowing what she feels
As to Argentina all things considered

Jack   Total automation see?

Sue   Jack are you coming? we're going to eat

Jack   A practical device to harness solar energy
A 100 per cent reduction in manual labour

Sue   What about you, Nan?
It's easier if we all do it together

Bob   As to Argentina
The kid's adorable I think she is finally going to cry
Come here Nan rest your head on Mr Lamb's knees

Nan *doesn't move.*

Sue   Ed take some

Nan   I cleaned the cabin and it's true it stunk the odour
of piss was horrible I went to give Jimmy something to
drink
  Jimmy was dead
  His throat was cut

Bob   As to Argentina
  I'm leaving Jeff in Japan for another year or two

Jack   Did you do that Sue?

Sue   Someone had to are you coming?

Bob   Admittedly it takes a while to grasp the Japanese
mind and Jeff so there we are I'll leave France as it is
and put Pete in Argentina

Bess (*screaming*)   She killed Jimmy

Dick   That is the best solution
  Pete is the man we want in Argentina
  And that of course would allow us to leave Larry in
Santiago

Bob   And Steve in Brazil
  Let's not rock the boat any more than necessary Dick
no waves

Dick   But who will replace Joe?

Sue   Are you coming Mr Lamb? Dick and you if you
please Mrs Lamb

Bob   Now what happened to Sidney is not entirely his
fault

Sue   What about you Nan?
  Come on Nan come on Nancy come on

Pat   My daughter's name is also Nancy and my son who
is one year older is named Walt I'm not worried about
them they're in an excellent boarding school my nextdoor
neighbour is an insurance agent I left him the keys and

he'll take care of my plants and my dog I took out
insurance it's a good policy I'm sure that policy covers
everything that one could need

My neighbour told me that Prudential is probably the
most solid company in the US they are building the tallest
skyscrapers everywhere

Life disability and bodily injury but I must read the fine
print it's so small

I have a friend in Boston who told me that the tallest
skyscraper in the city belongs to Prudential and do you
know that in Chicago the tower that they built has been
for quite a while now the tallest building in the United
States but now in New York

Sue, **Ed** and **Jack** *begin to eat.* **Bob**, **Bess** and **Dick** *watch
them.*

Bob   Bad surprises like that Sidney's falling apart
I am not making excuses for Sidney
I have no use for excuses

Pat   Sue they say that in New York
There are now two buildings in New York that are
even taller

Bob   A Sidney in Argentina today and tomorrow there
will be another one somewhere else
Better get that into your head Dick
Bad surprises like Sidney are over

Dick   His success

Bob   He wasn't properly supervised
Sidney was under your authority

Dick   He was Bob

Bob   Our managers are not controlled
But that's going to change
He fell apart men will always fall apart
But when a man shows signs

Forewarned is forearmed
Good management begins with prevention

Dick   I know that Bob

Bob   You do?
So what did you do about it?
A boy like Sidney with such potential
If he had felt himself controlled
That's exactly what happened
It's what Professor Peterson in the most recent issue of the *Harvard Business Review* called the Anglers' Syndrome every manager at every level is a potential angler the primary responsibility of a manager's superior at any level is to watch for the early symptoms

Dick   How many times have I heard you say Bob
Once we've selected a manager we must trust him he will only grow if
He is nurtured by the confidence of his superior

Bob   Confidence yes
Confidence and
Control I have always said one won't do without the other
You can trust when you know that the controls work
The tighter the screws the greater the confidence
I've said that over and over again but only those who want to listen hear

Bess   God will punish those who offend him
God is merciful
God will punish those who allow this to happen

Bob   Peterson got it right
Every manager tends eventually to relax
That's Peterson's second law every system under pressure tends to release that pressure
There are two compensatory mechanisms control and stimulation

If these mechanisms don't work together

Bess Didn't I say that?
Didn't I always tell you that you were kidding yourself about Sidney?
. Sidney isn't worth a thing he's a flatterer
He's a philanderer with no heart which upsets me because of Dorothy
Dorothy is so sweet and she'll have to be so brave
She is so infatuated with her Sidney who when it comes down to it thinks only of his own pleasure in fact he actually brings women home openly and in front of the children
Bob do you see them? Do you know what they are doing?
God will not forgive us he will not forgive you for letting them do it
Poor Dorothy has already had two nervous breakdowns
And look at Nan

Nan *is vomiting.*

Nan Don't pay any attention to me Mrs Lamb
I'm just emptying myself out
I've decided to try it myself
As soon as I feel better
Dad would have insisted
And in the end I would have obeyed

She looks at **Pat** *who holds a piece of meat in her hands.*

Pat is too tired to eat
We have to eat before we drop
Dad always succeeded in getting me to do what he wanted my will vanished when he spoke my analyst was surprised that my psychological identity resisted
Dad's love for me was all-consuming I was a piece of food that he crushed and ground up between his teeth
I was chewed up and chomped on from my head to my toes

I felt very strange watching from the window of the
plane as he fluttered and swirled further and further away
and then landed in the snow

He got up and walked staggered fell and then there was
nothing

Nan died that moment and I became Nancy di Santo a
woman a woman who will never be swallowed up by
anyone again so long as she lives but if I die here Mr
Lamb

Bess   They aren't saying a word over there

Do you see them?

Or maybe it's me

They are choking on shame

They are stuffing themselves with

I don't know whether they cut up Billy or Jimmy it
must be Billy a part of Billy I don't dare think what part
they chose and you you talk about Peterson's Law

When they are finished with the first two they will go
look for Joe

Joe was their colleague on the same level as they were

Bob   Her father

Bess this generation surprises me did Nan cry even
once?

Joe had a way of taking things in his stride

There will be so much to do when we get back you
will remind me to call Donald

Although no one is irreplaceable I can't quite imagine
GH without Joe

And without Joe the Benjamin Franklin Country Club
just won't be the same

He was one of the five or six best golfers

And an ace on the skating rink

It really was something sitting on the terrace before
dinner on Saturday night

Watching Joe and Jenny

Watching them skate

Scene Three

Five days later. Dawn. Awakening. **Bob** *and* **Bess** *are lying down tightly huddled together in the more comfortably furnished part of the cabin.* **Dick, Sue, Ed** *and* **Nan** *in the same position in another part of the cabin. After a moment* **Jack** *enters from outside covered with snow.*

Sue   Could you shit?

Jack   Yesterday there were large flakes
Today dense small ones
They're falling heavily
It's been coming down for three straight days

Sue   Did you shit Jack?

Jack   I didn't try

Dick   Two Douglas C-47s
Reagan

Bob   I knew it

Jack   I carried Pat outside

Dick   Thank God we have a strong president

Bob   They won't just give up on us
They definitely won't stop until they find us

Jack   I don't believe it Bob
Our only chance is to get this transmitter working again
In order to get it to work we have to retrieve the batteries from the tail of the plane
We have to find the fucking tail of this plane
Before it's completely covered with snow

Sue   Pat will be covered fast
Pretty soon we won't know where to dig to find her

Ed   We need something
To mark the spot where she is

Nan   In the meantime we have a little more room

    She took up space for two
    I will not spend another night like last night

Sue Because her knees wouldn't respond any more
    She couldn't bend her legs

Dick Two Douglas C-47s will take off this morning with a specific command from President Reagan to comb the Andes

Ed Do you have any suggestions?

Jack I don't believe it for a minute

Ed (*his eyes searching out every corner of the cabin*) Something like a stake

Dick You can hear it for yourself on the eight o'clock bulletin

Ed Something long and rigid

Nan In any case I will not sleep here any longer I am going to sleep next to Mr Lamb
    Mrs Lamb you can take Pat's place

Dick They will undoubtedly rebroadcast the information it was about four when Nan got up to pee and of course she stepped right on my wound

Nan Me?

Dick Of course

Nan I didn't move

Dick I couldn't fall asleep again turned on the radio and caught the middle of the six o'clock bulletin
    They also announced that there were guerrillas looking for us

Ed That's not so good

Nan Did she really have
    Mr Lamb were her legs really as beautiful as she said they were?

Bob   There are no more guerrillas in Chile
Pinochet wiped out all the rebels

Nan   Under the table I mean underneath the table

Jack   Almost all

Nan   When you dictated your letters you must have
looked at them it's just natural how could you not have?

Jack   There are still a few left

Jack *is playing with the transmitter, which had been dismantled
and taken from the cockpit. Dozens of different-coloured wires are
visible.*

It's entirely possible that even in these somewhat
inhospitable mountains a small group of them could
survive
The invincible hard core

Nan   They say that all bosses have a thing for their
secretaries' legs

Jack   BAT is to connect the battery
ANT is to connect the antenna

Nan   Today is Wednesday

Jack   We need two volunteers
Before the tail of the plane

Ed   Thursday
Our sixteenth day out here

Nan   Pat's all covered with snow
Her legs don't hurt any more I'd like to go look at
them may I?
I hope you didn't leave her there all dressed?

Jack   Why?

Nan   Don't you think her clothes would be useful?

Ed *has made a long stake by tying together several curtain rods end
to end.*

Sue   Congratulations Pat said you couldn't do anything except count

Nan   And sleep

Ed   I'm going

Nan   I'll go with you

She tries to get up but can't. **Ed** *leaves.*

Sue   You have to eat Nan

Bess   Nan eat please

Bess *hands her a piece of meat.*

>   The Holy Communion
>   When Jesus died he gave us
>   His body to save us

Sue   It's the last dried piece we've got

Bess   Jesus
>   Above
>   Desires it

Sue   I saved it specially for you

Bess   Thanks to Jesus it's nothing else but meat

Sue   Don't think about it

Bess   Jesus is in heaven with God and his angels
>   Eat

Dick *is holding the radio in one hand and with the other is trying to adjust the antenna made out of electric wires and metal rods.*

A Voice   ... of the US Air Force that has placed two Douglas C-47s and their crew at the disposal of the Chilean authorities. The search could begin again tomorrow weather conditions permitting. A spokesman for President Reagan stated that he was pleased with the cooperation of the Chilean government in getting the operation off the ground again, while indicating to the

families that there was little hope of finding anyone alive.
General Villegas Commander of the Chilean security
forces reported the monitoring of a communiqué broadcast
by a clandestine transmitter belonging to terrorist
elements. According to the communiqué a brigade of the
so-called Allende Popular Liberation Army was searching
for any trace of the survivors of the private jet belonging
to the multi-national corporation. They intend to
capture any survivors in order to demonstrate to the
whole world their determination to carry on their
proletarian struggle. These declarations are not taken
seriously considering their obvious publicity value.
Nonetheless the spokesman added that a military ground
detachment would be sent to locate the wreck. In Moscow
Mr Leonid Brezhnev, first secretary of the Soviet
Communist Party, met for two hours with Mr Kania and
the Polish delegation at the Kremlin. According to a joint
communiqué released simultaneously in Moscow and
Warsaw all problems between the two countries have been
discussed in a spirit of warm and fraternal cordiality. The
communiqué underlined that both countries were in total
agreement on the means needed to

Ed *returns, covered with snow, he distributes the clothing he has
brought in from outside.*

Bess God in heaven

Sue Eat Nan

Bob And you still don't believe it?

Jack No I don't
Our only chance
Is for me to get some juice into this damn box

Dick He just heard it and he says he doesn't believe it
I made the whole thing up right?
Invented the two Douglas C-47s?

Jack Oh I'm sure that two Douglas C-47s will roam
around up there and I'm convinced that we will see them

flying back and forth over our heads
  But I don't think they'll see us from up there

Dick   Bob make him shut up
  He's got no right

Jack   Unless of course Dick Sutton's fertile imagination
can give birth to a brilliant idea that will make us visible
from up there

Bess   That's good Nan
  Now a bite for your sister Jenny

Jack   For example some way to transform the
unfortunately very pale colour of this cabin into some
vivid colour

Bess   One for mother

Jack   I eagerly await Dick's suggestion because dumb as
I am I think we've tried everything
  However all of a sudden the amazing Dick Sutton is
going to come up with an idea a simple idea like all great
ideas

Dick   (*grabs the transmitter out of* **Jack***'s hands, throws it
violently on the ground and kicks it*)   All that just because he's
scared
  This transmitter is a piece of shit
  How many days has he been playing with it?
  And how many days have we already lost?
  All that just to delay our departure because he's afraid
Scared shitless
  He's afraid to go out even though we know damn well
that behind that pass

Jack   I've no right to destroy hope?
  So you destroy the equipment?
  Dick you don't have a prayer this piece of hardware is
unbreakable
  The plane may blow up but the transmitter will survive
  You'll have to come up with another idea

To leave now with the snow coming down isn't it either
But assuming the snow will stop how about coming up
with some bright idea on how to draw a huge coloured H
on this landscape
H for Houses
One that the C-47 pilots can see

Ed   Or the guerrillas

Sue   Nan what are you making?

Nan   A stake
If they find us
What will they do?

Ed   Who knows?

Bess   They'll do the worst things imaginable

Sue *attaches two rackets to her shoes.*

Ed   Pat has almost completely disappeared

Sue   Who volunteers to go with me?

Nan   This should be planted
Where Dad is
So we can find him later too

Bess   They rip out the men's tongues
Rape the women and tear them apart

Sue   Mr Lamb why don't you help me look for the
plane's tail section?

Bob   Me?

Sue   Why not?
Why should it always be the same people?
I'll take your stake Nan
It'll do you good you know
The danger is in going numb
Also we have to try to take a shit
Come on

Bob   Yes however that won't do I can't leave here in case something happens
I belong here Sue

Nan   Take the guerrillas for example
What would you do if they came?

Bob   That's a good question Nan if they come

Nan   What do they want from us?
What have we done to them?

Bob   They'll have to deal with me
If they lay a hand on us they must be told what it will cost them

Nan   They say they're fighting for the people
The poor
Mr Lamb aren't you also working for the poor?
Isn't General Houses

Bob   That's right Nan
We work so that poor people can have decent housing a little comfort that seems simple enough but
The problem will be to find a common language

Nan   I took two and a half years of Spanish

Bess   But will they want to listen?
Nan can translate Bob

Bob   I'm used to making myself understood

Sue   Who's going with me?

Bess   They are fanatics

Ed   I wonder though they are probably disciplined people
They execute their orders they receive them from Brezhnev

Sue   Mrs Lamb what do you say?

Bess   About what?

Ed   Via Fidel Castro

Sue   How about a little walk with me?

Bess   Me?

Sue   Yes you

Bess   For God's sake Bob explain to this girl that I am
incapable of walking
I've always hated the thought of walking tell her Bob
I've never even made it once around my garden and here
where no one seems to do anything there is so much I
have to do

Sue   You mean cutting up the meat
Right? And cleaning?

Bob   In all aspects of daily life Nan as in business

Nan   And in love?

Bob   I suppose in love too
The hardest thing is to find a common language
My conversation with what was that general's name?

Dick   Figuereido

Bob   Clearly demonstrates if that conversation had not
been carefully planned

Dick   And long in advance

Bob   If Steve hadn't done his homework
Before planting the seeds if one hasn't ploughed the
ground
That's why picking the right man is the most important
thing if one picks the wrong man
And Steve Steve was definitely

Dick   A concept like ours needs to penetrate
If Steve hadn't worked in Brazil patiently to infiltrate

Bob   You see a concept doesn't penetrate all of a sudden
it has to wend its way in

Dick   In successive stages

Jack   Steve is tenacious if you try to slam the door in his face he'll have his foot in the door
That's exactly why neither Tom nor Larry Larry even less than Tom

Dick   But Pete

Ed   Steve I can easily see Steve in Argentina

Dick   Or Pete

Bob   It only took Figuereido half an hour to grasp the entire problem
He was easy picking
We spoke the same language

Dick   God it was amazing
That moment when Figuereido began to lick the entire length of his cigar
Steve knew he prepared you for it
And you scored
After that he didn't ask you any more questions except how we dealt with the waterproofing
The game was over

Bob   When he got up
How he embraced me

Scene Four

Four days later. Bright sunlight. All are busy making a giant H in the snow out of all available means on board: seats, suitcases, pieces of fabric, clothes, varied debris and bones. Everyone participates except **Bob**, *who isn't in sight, and* **Jack**, *who is connecting the wires from the batteries to the transmitter.*

Bess   That's it I cut it up in pieces and roll it in breadcrumbs
The secret is not to leave it in the oven more than a

few minutes
  Just enough time for the crust to form crisp and lightly golden
  Put it in a casserole with a knob of butter a pinch of paprika and some capers

Ed Sylvia's speciality was tournedos Rossini she spent a summer in Paris as an au pair girl

Bess A teaspoon of brown sugar and a tablespoon of fresh cream

Ed Every time she made it our guests complimented her the last time she made it she already knew that she was dying the Bradshaws and the Glasses were having supper at our house

Sue I make it with a skewer we eat it while munching on celery sticks which Danny picks that same day from our garden

Bess Danny?

Sue My son

Dick Have you ever tried to slice some radishes into cream cheese lightly spiced with herbs and pepper?

Nan On Sundays the kitchen is mine I love being creative sometimes it's a dismal failure but sometimes like the Sunday before we left I cooked a duck stuffed with apricots it wasn't as successful as my crab stuffed with spinach I stuff just about everything I cook but what's Mr Lamb doing?

Sue In the fall he and I go out and pick mushrooms

Ed It's pretty pale on that side
  That part of the H fades into the snow

Bess We don't have much left in fact there's nothing

Ed We should collect the bones
  Close up a bone appears to be white

But when Sue and I climbed up that crest
We couldn't make out either the plane the seats or the
people from up there the only thing that stood out against
the snow was the bones

Sue   That's right
Mrs Lamb why don't you make a pyramid out of all
the little bones and the bone fragments left over vertebrae
clavicles even the most insignificant bones the hands and
feet
The pyramid will cast a shadow
We need as much contrast as possible

Nan   Where is Mr Lamb?

Bess   I told you for the fiftieth time he went to try to
loosen up his bowels

Sue   The forest comes right up to our door he knows
every corner of it we collect chestnuts too

Nan   Mr Lamb is a shirker

Bess   Nan

Nan   He is and as far as his bowels are concerned
except for Sue we're all in the same boat
He's hiding

Bess   This entire situation depresses him so much

Sue   If he wants to relieve himself he'll have to extract it
I didn't tell you Ed
I used your pipe
I shoved the tip of the pipe all the way up my ass
It was worse than a forceps delivery
I couldn't even scratch the first piece out with my nails

The sound of a plane gradually growing louder. **Jack** *hesitates for a
moment and then joins them in a frantic dance around the H. They
wave different-coloured fabrics in the air.* **Bob** *enters and joins the
dance. The sound fades, grows louder again and then fades out.*

Bob   He saw us

Jack   He would have signalled us

Dick   How could he?

Bob   He couldn't do anything more than fly right over us

Dick   Right now he's transmitting our exact position on his radio right now

Bob   To send a helicopter

Dick   He couldn't afford to lose any altitude

Jack   He would have passed over us two or three times he would have made a circle

Bob   He saw us he saw us

Bess   Oh Bob are you sure?
   Bob the first thing I'll do

Nan   Oh a shower

Bob   At Nickie's

Nan   A hot shower then bed

Bob   The kidneys in Madeira sauce at Nickie's

Bess   A long bath the sound of hot water flowing

Sue   To take off all my clothes
   To slip naked in between the sheets

Nan   Before washing?

Dick   Before eating?
   We'll dine at Nickie's first

Nan   First I'll wash

Ed   I'll shave

Bob   The veal kidneys at Nickie's are better than at Prospero's
   They're the best in Latin America
   On the whole Nickie's can't hold a candle to Prospero's

in Buenos Aires which is undoubtedly the finest restaurant in Latin America
Prospero's is unquestionably the best restaurant on the continent
But the kidneys at Nickie's are better than at Prospero's
And you have to admit that Nickie's is the finest restaurant in Santiago

Dick   One could say the only restaurant

Jack   No

Dick   What do you mean no?

Jack   No
Sans Souci is a superb restaurant

Bob   It is superb but Sans Souci isn't in Santiago you've got it mixed up
Sans Souci is in Lima ,

Dick   No it's in Quito

Jack   Really?
Ed talked about tournedos Rossini
The tournedos at the Sans Souci

Ed   Is staggering five years ago Sylvia and I took our final trip together she had already been told she didn't have much time I took her to the Sans Souci it is not in Quito I am absolutely positive it's in Lima I have never been to Quito naturally Sylvia ordered a Rossini

Jack   Listen
It has a way of gently melting in your mouth

Ed   You can cut it with a fork I said to her

Dick   But don't you have to make reservations several days in advance
At Nickie's?

Bob   No problem
Considering how long I've known Nickie

You know he's a Russian
I'll give Nick a call personally and tell him Nikita better
get the large round table in the corner of the terrace

Bess   With candles

Nan   Silver candlesticks and a white tablecloth

Bess   Embroidered

Bob   Lobster
We'll begin with an assortment of shellfish
The clams and the oysters are brought in the same
morning from Valparaiso

Dick   Followed by the kidneys in Madeira
And for dessert

Bess   We'll have them bring the wagon

Bob   They have a baba at Nickie's
They have a bitter-sweet chocolate cake covered with
wild strawberry sauce

Bess   I can't help it
I always wind up taking the profiteroles

Nan   Oh God and then
A huge
A huge big bed I'll wrap myself up in the sheets
A down comforter oh

Jack   Nan are you all right?

Nan   It's too much
I don't think I'll go to Nickie's
Just a deep bed to sink into
A pillow
Sue and you?

Sue   I don't know
It's getting dark and cold

General hesitation. **Sue**, *the first to do so, removes a piece of
clothing from the H and wraps herself up in it. Soon, after all, the*

others do the same and the H disintegrates. **Jack** *returns to his transmitter,* **Bess** *settles down next to him.* **Ed** *goes to cut meat and is joined by* **Nan**. **Bob** *goes inside the cabin.* **Dick** *and* **Sue** *sew.*

Nan   I can tell Ed
   By the way you're looking at me
   You think I did it

Ed   In inventory accounting you have to consider the entries the withdrawals and the stock
   The stock on day D equals the stock on day D minus one plus the entries minus withdrawals
   The numbers have to balance
   If they don't you have a leak
   I began at GH as an assistant stockboy five years later I was the manager of the raw material stockroom
   It's a job I know something about
   Today's the third day in a row I've wound up with a negative balance between the stock on day D minus the stock on day D minus one on the one hand and consumption on the other

Nan   And you suspect me Ed?
   I know who it is I saw him
   You remind me of a professor I had last year his name was Bach he was a quiet man like you Ed he'd never raise his voice what makes me think of him is that sometimes the colour of his eyes would change and you could tell that something was wrong

Bess   He doesn't seem to have it all together any more
   It's as if his life were a record
   And someone had scratched it
   Jack he's always listened to you
   Bob is slipping away from me Jack
   And you're the only one who can try

Jack   This is fascinating because you've always hated me
   Yet you're making the effort to come and talk to me
   You're adapting to the circumstances Bess

Whereas Bob Bob's problem is he's gotten used to having things go his way

Bess   He is so stubborn about certain things
For example the small wound at the base of his back that he got during the accident I wanted to take care of it now it's infected

Dick   I have been watching you Sue

Jack   Given our circumstances
Things don't necessarily go our way
Events remain rigid and stubborn yet he he is determined to control them the way he used to
Just like in Seattle
Basically Bob is disoriented
So he steals

Bess   What are you saying?

Dick   Bob yes Bob has decided that I should lead the next expedition Sue
So if you would agree

Jack   Yes he

Sue   Me?

Nan   There's no doubt about it

Ed   Everyone is under suspicion
I as much as anyone else

Dick   But without Jack
We don't get along we never did

Sue   Do you and I?

Dick   You would still accept my authority as the leader of the expedition wouldn't you?
If Jack and I left together we'd be at each other's throats but not you and I
What's more I have discovered

Nan   With my own eyes

Sue   What?

Dick   That I like you

Sue   I'm flattered

Nan   He broke into the larder when he knew the rest of us were asleep and I had gone out to pee and was squatting

Jack   The strangest thing is Bess that he takes more than he can use

Sue   Perhaps you should know

Jack   He must have a personal larder somewhere a secret hiding-place

Sue   Your boss instructed Bess to keep a special eye on me
   That's natural
   I don't belong Jack dragged me into your world

Dick   It's quite natural that Bob

Sue   Should suspect me as far as the stealing is concerned
   Maybe you ought to know

Bess   He was born in Philadelphia and his family was poor
   They didn't eat every day
   Let's keep it between you and me Jack please

Jack   The main thing is it must stop

Ed   Nan we must not

Nan   What?

Ed   Talk about it

Nan   Now you look just like Professor Bach
   Seriously Ed you'd let it go on?

Jack   Bess you know that there is very little left to eat

Bess   There will be more soon enough
For Godsake we don't have to bring it up

Dick   I can't believe it

Sue   If we let it go on there won't be anybody left to
believe period

Dick   You could be wrong

Sue   Yeah Nan probably made a mistake
She made the mistake of seeing him

Dick   She could have been dreaming

Sue   In that case Jack dreamt it too
Because he also saw him

Bob *appears.*

Bob   Everybody's very quiet
I have finalized the planning for the next expedition
I am increasingly concerned about the level of our
supplies
What were you talking about?

Jack   About things that aren't very important any more
since the C-47s saw us what's important is that they did
see us
The helicopters will arrive any minute
Let's not talk about any more expeditions

Sue *takes* **Nan** *a few steps away. They light a fire using the
wood from Coca-cola cases and cook bits of meat in a casserole.*

Bob   The most important thing is to do what needs to
be done
Let's talk about the twenty-ninth floor there are offices
on that floor
Management offices your offices my office offices that
are there in order to get things done and there are the
hallways
They are spacious and have thick wall-to-wall carpeting
there are sofas where one can sit comfortably chat or one

can simply relax one can't even hear footsteps
I have noticed recently that the population on the
twenty-ninth floor is spending more time in hallways than
in their offices
The halls are alive with soft chatter
Uninterrupted rumour
Sarcasm and machinations
Naturally while that is going on nothing of what should
be accomplished
Is getting done

Nan   This too?

Sue   Yes

Bob   It's no great mystery
The secret meetings in the halls

Nan   And this?

Sue   Yes

Bob   Gossip has replaced action
But all that's going to change
Immediately
Some people have nothing to lose by waiting

Jack   There's nothing to lose and not much point in
waiting

Bob   Really?
Things are going to change and that goes for those who
are listening to me now too even if there have to be some
casualties
I'll bring Pete back to the States and make him my
right-hand man in Seattle he'll take Joe's place
Pete is a solid guy
I'll put Larry in Argentina

Dick   Larry?

Bob   Larry has shown what he's made of
If we could have met with that General what is his

name?

Dick   Pinochet

Bob   The contract is practically in our pocket
And Larry ought to get all the credit

Dick   Larry appears to have done his job but Bob
We have to protect ourselves against bad surprises let's wait
Until we have seen Pinochet

Bob   I will see Pinochet but you would be a lot better off
If you stayed out of it in fact I would strongly advise you to shut up
This affair is no longer any of your business

Dick   But Bob

Bob   You can start thinking about
France

Dick   What?

Bob   Two or three years out in the field where you can reacquaint yourself with the hard realities of life will do you the most good
Up to your knees in the muck
You'll report to the Paris office on December 1st
Christmas in Paris Dick

Ed   I can understand your rationale Bob but at the same time
Since Joe's gone do you think this is the right time to clear out our ranks even further? I suggest we take time to think first

Bob   Take time?

Ed   Restructuring is fine but let's not rush into it

Bob   Rush into it?
That's what you do best taking time not rushing into

things
    The result is that nothing gets done controls are
ineffectual and so we are confronted with one bad surprise
after another right
    Sidney juggles the inventory in Argentina? Sure what
do you expect Sidney juggles the inventory we catch him
at it when it's too late and everyone stands around
looking stunned
    There aren't going to be any more bad surprises like in
Argentina do you understand Ed
    There won't be any because I've decided to transfer
you
    Some place where you will have time plenty
    Plenty of time

Jack Fortunately the ladies are over there taking care of
our immediate needs – dinner
    The smell is mouth-watering
    Surely this will be our last meal here because the
helicopter
    Although it might be a little late this evening for a
helicopter it won't come any more this evening will it Bob
    But tomorrow morning right Bob?
    After dinner we'll have to think about
    Packing right?

Bob And prepare ourselves for a stopover in
Washington if I know Reagan
    He will want to greet us personally at the White House
but we won't stay long I can see what's going on in your
mind
    But that won't go on much longer
    Your way of denigrating everything is over
    There won't be any room for that on the twenty-ninth
floor from now on

Bob, *suddenly stricken, sinks slowly to his knees.* **Bess** *holds him.*

Bob From now on there will only be room for men
with conviction who know how to communicate their

conviction from above down the ranks
I want I want I want the twenty-ninth floor

Bob *collapses.* **Bess**, **Dick**, **Ed** *and* **Jack** *surround him and try to revive him with mouth-to-mouth and other forms of resuscitation.*

Bess   Oh Bob

Sue   Taste it Nan

Nan   It's spicy
You could almost call it
You could almost say it's salty

Sue   It is
I cut the large and small intestines into little balls

Nan   Without emptying them?

Sue   That's the secret

Nan   I forgot what salt tasted like
It's fabulous

Sue   If we let it simmer for another minute it will be even better

Ed   The heart's beating

Nan   You're sure that we can eat that?

Sue   I put in a brain too

Nan   You are sure

Jack   The nostrils are moving

Nan   That this won't make us sick?

Sue   Look a testicle

Nan   Really

Bess   God be praised

Dick   The wind is picking up
Let's move him into the cabin

Sue   We can call them now

Nan   It will be hard

Sue   No it won't

Nan   To tell my mother

Sue   Nan Mr Lamb is dying

Nan   This piece?

Sue   Taste it

Nan   It's soft it melts in your mouth my teeth love it

Sue   It's the liver

Ed   His pulse is beating

Nan   Hmm and I love the thick grease all around it

Bess   Bob

Dick   His lips

Jack   Are moving

Sue   A kidney

Bob (*leaning on his elbow*)   And you tell Nickie
For a long time the CIA claimed they believed
Larry warned me I tried to intervene on Leslie's behalf
in Washington Leslie
Poor Nickie he saw it coming
He fought it as best he could me a KGB agent?
They picked him up and questioned him
And then everything was arranged
Thanks to Leslie I have to say that Leslie

Bob *collapses again and they try to revive him again but this time*
Bob *is dead. Everyone gathers around the fire.* **Sue** *serves the stew.*
A meal.

Jack   If you stay in Santiago
You could get Prospero to hire you

Nan   Nickie

Jack   I mean Nickie
Unless of course you come to realize
One can't live in Santiago
Then you'll go back across the Andes and take a job as
a chef at Prospero's

Sue   Nan has become adventurous
My kitchen assistant wanted to taste every piece
She wanted to know the name of every dish

Bess   Don't tell me

Ed   Nan? She's regained her strength

Nan   And my weight
I want to be part of the next expedition

Sue   We've burned the last pieces of wood
Our next meals will be cold

Scene Five

Six days later. Inside the cabin. Night. A full moon.

Bess   What's that noise?

Nan   The wind

Bess   Are you sure? It sounds like footsteps
Whispers

Ed   Ten million

Dick   Dollars?

Ed   Maybe fifteen they could ask for fifteen million

Jack   It's just the wind
A gust of wind

Dick   They'll try us before a people's tribunal
They'll condemn us for crimes against the people

Sue   At least they know
   How to find the valley

Ed   These people don't keep their word
   Once the ransom is paid

Nan   The women too?

Bess   I can hear it again
   There must be at least a dozen of them

Ed   A whole squad

Dick   We don't have a single weapon

Bess   They'll strip us and search us

Nan   The women too?

Jack   It's just the wind

Ed   And we'll die frozen where we stand
   Pinochet won't agree

Sue   To pay the ransom
   Jack sing us your song

Jack *sings.*

Dick   Fifteen million

Nan   They'll strip the women
   Unbuckle their belts

Bess   And rape and quarter us

Jack   Not at this altitude
   They'll wait until we reach the valley

Ed   Do you hear them?

Jack   Just try to get an erection at 13,000 feet

Dick   I hear steps

Bess   Voices murmuring

Ed   They are surrounding the cabin

Jack   We're lucky we crashed this high up
No erections up here
No corruption
The flesh remains intact in perpetuity

Sue   They'll tear off the men's pricks

Jack   And our ears

Nan   They can do to me whatever they want
I just wish they'd get here
What are they waiting for?

Jack   I'll tell them that we are ready to receive them

Sue   Not all alone you won't

Jack *exits. A moment later* **Sue** *joins him. They look around, bent over to resist the force of the wind.*

Bess   No germs either
If Bob were still here he could tell you
I used to get a cold in Seattle from every little draft
I used to consume
A box of Kleenex a week

Ed   Did you notice that man Figuereido didn't have a
single file folder or document on his desk a box of cigars
a box of Kleenex and a little flag that's how one governs
Brazil
He couldn't stop blowing his nose

Sue   Jack it's so cold
Yet it's like the first time we met
I wanted to tell you that
Jack I'm afraid

Jack   No sign of any guerrilla
You see

Sue   That's not what I'm afraid of

Jack   The wind has never blown like this before
I want you as much as I did the first time I saw you

Santiago is such a thankless place

Sue   I love the wind
   I'm afraid
   It's like a little girl's fear
   Just like when Dad used to step down on the
accelerator
   Hold me in your arms

Jack   I can hardly breathe

They kiss.

Sue   Let's go back

Ed   'Assuming you build your factory in Manaus'

Jack *and* **Sue** *re-enter the cabin.*

Jack   The infidels have fled in disgrace

Sue   They got away

Ed   As soon as I heard him say those words
   I knew we had won
   It was merely a question of deciding where to locate
the factory
   You should have seen Bob
   He remained totally impassive as if unconcerned
   He was terrific

Bess   That little girl is freezing
   Come here Sue let me warm you up
   How could you even stick your nose out in this weather

Sue *nestles in between* **Bess**'s *legs.* **Bess** *massages her lightly
and blows softly in her face.*

Ed   You should've seen the general trying to convince us
   In Manaus you would benefit from the cheapest manual
labour in the hemisphere
   No strikes in Manaus Mr Lamb because no politics the
unions are under our control strikes are against the law
and besides the workers don't want any

In Manaus labour is docile Mr Lamb docile and cheap
all salaries are frozen
The land's free the government will pay to bring water
and electricity to your factory and you'll pay no taxes for
the first five years

Dick   And Bob just kept on staring at him
Wait till the news of Bob's death hits Wall Street
There'll be quite a commotion

Ed   Wall Street will react favourably
The stock will go up
There will be a wave of speculative buying

Dick   The speed with which
Bob's image deteriorated on Wall Street

Jack   The fair-haired boy for such a long time

Dick   Everyone's favourite

Jack   And then disgrace

Ed   Brutal
GH sent to purgatory

Bess   It was unfair the way those financial analysts lost
confidence in him they're murderers
Bob suffered a great deal he wouldn't talk about it but
he began having trouble sleeping
   I took him to see Dr McBride in Los Angeles who is
the best known specialist on stress Bob couldn't even finish
his bowl of cornflakes and his fried eggs in the morning
   I have a feeling the wind stopped

Sue   That feels great Mrs Lamb

Bess   He was counting heavily on this Latin American
trip to reverse the trend
   But God wanted him to die before he could regain his
position in the financial community

Dick   There's not a cloud in the sky and the wind has
stopped

My wound is completely healed
Today's the day

Bess   That was his deepest regret
That and never having had a daughter I only gave him
two sons

Ed   This trip could've easily done it if Sidney hadn't
I don't understand how Sidney could have
If we could have seen and talked to Videla in person

Jack   Viola
General Videla was thrown out now it's General Viola

Bess   Some sons
They gave him no satisfaction
No ambition
That's why he latched on to you Nan
He felt very close to you
He would have looked after you
He would've replaced your father

Dick   Sue today's the day
Shall we go?
This outing will be it

*Dawn. Sunlight. Morning routine. The cabin is cleared. Everything
that is used as bedding is laid out outside. They hand out meat and
water.*

Nan   Why not me?
Why is it always her and never me?

Bess   Jonathan lacks perseverence and that's what
disturbed Bob most
The boy can't follow through on one single idea

Dick   You see that ridge?
Behind that ridge there's another one still slightly
covered by fog

Bess   I told Bob that it can't possibly be laziness he just
doesn't have anything that he feels like doing but one of

these days he'll find something that will excite him

Dick   Somewhere around the middle of that ridge is a
slight indentation
Behind that is the beginning of the valley
The valley seems to point east
That's what misled you Jack
I've had some experience with this kind of topography
You see everything like a mechanical engineer nature
follows another logic that valley hooks around it curves
I've gone on so many ski trips with my parents since I
was a kid in the Austrian Alps I am not sure whether my
knowledge is inherited or acquired
But I've never gotten lost in the mountains I have an
instinct for how the geological formations relate to one
another
When a valley runs into an obstacle it forms around it
I can see that valley as if I were there
I can see the sea
Sue is in better physical condition than you are Nan

Nan   I've regained my strength

Dick   Sue's got more resistance
I'll take Sue and you Ed the three of us will go

Ed   I'm a fact addict I'm afraid
Your valley is a dream and I don't think much of
dreams

Dick   You have no mountain experience

Ed   I'm a numbers man

Dick   So let yourself be guided

Nan   I'm going with you Dick and that's all there is to it

Jack   You saved my life Nan I want to reciprocate
Don't go if you do it's a one-way ticket

Nan   All Dick has to do is think about something and
you'll say exactly the opposite

You tried to get this transmitter to work right? And?

You gave up didn't you? Didn't you say it was our last hope? And now you are trying to frighten us again I have had enough of you and your cynicism all you do is hurt I would rather believe

It's very simple I can't take any more I will not stay here for one more day

Dick *and* **Nan** *prepare to leave. The others help.*

Ed   Where did these pieces come from?

Jack   They were buried in the snow by the nose of the plane I marked the spot

Ed   Bob's larder?
Eighteen pieces

Jack   It all adds up
And even two olives
Everything neatly organized

Bess   You will be careful won't you Dick?
I wish you would take down Jonathan's number when you tell him what happened don't be overly brutal about it

There's no point in giving you Gordon's he's a nomad he must be somewhere in Ethiopia right now

Gordon is an artist he decided to become an artist because he hated money

It's still too early to tell whether he has any talent
Naturally Bob wanted to know so I said
Why don't we invite Randy Sheffield for dinner one night?

He's the chief curator for the Seattle Fine Arts Museum isn't he? Randy is a very nice man

I told Bob we could show Randy some of Gordon's canvases without telling Gordon naturally

Randy wouldn't refuse to give you his opinion after all you are a member of the museum Board and one of its principal donors but Bob said no probably because he was afraid of what Randy would tell him

Ed   The rest of the vodka bottle too?

Jack   Does the inventory report balance?

Bess   So without telling Bob I went to Pat
As treasurer of the Friends of the Seattle Fine Arts
Museum she had a great deal of contact with Randy
I am not even sure she didn't have a crush on him
Randy has remained a bachelor in fact some people say
that

Ed   I propose that we allocate what's left of the vodka to
the expeditionary force

Bess   That's very often the case among the best artists
Sometimes I wondered about Gordon
It would be natural for a boy to bring a girl home
from time to time
Oh Ed about you and Pat
I am convinced that Bob knew nothing escapes him
and you know Bob and his principles
I couldn't understand Ed

Ed   To be honest Bess
I couldn't understand either

Dick   The lascivious

Jack   Moisture

Dick   Of Brazilian nights?

Bess   It was an awful night and I told Bob
Bob you should lodge a complaint but you know Bob

Nan   Ed I'm happy you slept with Pat that night

Bess   When it came to certain things I knew Bob well
It wasn't worth pushing he was very loyal to his hotels
Bob would have gone back to the Excelsior
I know that it's on an expense account but have you
any idea how much a night at the Excelsior costs?

All embrace **Dick** *and* **Nan** *who then depart.*

Ed　We had just gotten married Sylvia was at the wheel of the old Buick she said to me

Bess　Oh Ed you were so patient with Sylvia and so brave
It appals me to think that one has to pay such prices
With so much misery all around us

Ed　Half an hour before she died she leaned her head against my shoulder and repeated the same sentence
Ed never forget that I'm just a girl passing through your life
You remember her ringing laughter

Bess　How many times

Ed　An instant before she died she let me hear her laugh

Bess　Bob and I both said to each other that Ed ought to remarry
Ed is not a boy who can live alone

Ed　Yet as you see

Bess　One evening we introduced you to Marjorie
You remember how Bob scolded you

Ed　Even after Sylvia's death
I wasn't free of her

Bess　Even so you needn't have been so rude
Poor little Marjorie
You never even looked at her

Scene Six

Nine days later. Three figures squatting in the snow, their pants down to their ankles.

Ed　But he did know how to surround himself with people who weren't all sycophants

Like you Jack
And if I can be so bold
Like me

Sue   You think you got rid of it all
And suddenly it explodes all over again
Look

Ed   What is it?

Jack   A condor
First sign of life
Since we've been here

Sue   No I've seen a fly

Jack   We should write that in the log
On the thirty-fifth day

Ed   Neither you nor I Jack
We are both good seconds
He was a mover

Sue   Look a second one and a third
Their wingspan is enormous

Jack   That's the largest surviving bird since the disappearance of the pterodactyls

Sue   I don't like their beaks

Jack   They're like vultures
They're no danger to us

Bess *appears. She drops her pants, rolls up the blankets she has been using as a coat and crouches down.*

Sue   At the beginning we only ate the noble parts

Jack   Until you made your famous stew

Sue   There are still leftovers strewn all over the place
You got the runs too Mrs Lamb?

Bess   Let's drop the formalities Sue
You can call me Bess

Sue   We'd better gather them up and keep them away from those birds

Jack   We can store them in Bob's makeshift larder
  The hole is very deep

Ed   Bob's death has left a large void the more I think about it
  The more obvious it is that neither you nor I can fill it

Sue   So Bess you too?

Ed   I don't see anyone filling it not even Dick

Jack   Least of all Dick

Bess   Dick might Dick maybe oh Sue
  My insides

Ed   It goes from one extreme to another

Bess   The constipation was better God knows
  Right now Dick and Nan could be walking out onto the plain

Jack   Or the condors could be working on what's left of them
  In the valley

Sue   Just when you think it's all over

Bess   God protect them

Ed   I lean towards the second hypothesis

Jack   At any rate Bess Dick didn't measure up either
  Neither Dick nor Joe nor any of the puny princes
  That was Bob's weakness he let himself be seduced by those interchangeable Harvard boys
  But Bob was another matter he was a shining star the kind that comes along rarely in the business world
  He was a giant and he would have bounced back

Sue   It's like an earthquake
  It comes in intermittent tremors

Just when you think it's over it strikes again

Jack   And Wall Street would have gone on its knees again
Thanks to the Latin American coup
His European venture twenty-five years ago was a stroke of genius
But this one is even more remarkable
It's the work of an extraordinary mind
Because it is politically so well controlled
Bob had a flair or an instinct you just don't get at Harvard
GH's crowning glory was the idea of replacing the cardboard and tin shacks with fully equipped homes costing one-fifth the price of those built with traditional building materials
These homes will give man back his dignity
In the current economic climate that's exactly what these generals need
What do you know about earthquakes?

Sue   I learned all I need to know in Chiapas Mexico
The prison I was in was ten miles from the epicentre

Jack   What prison? You lived in Mexico?
I didn't know that

Sue   There are a lot of things you don't know about me

Jack   When the condors come
Spring can't be far behind
And neither can a whole new set of problems

Ed *wipes himself, stands up, fastens his pants.* **Sue, Jack** *and* **Bess** *do the same. They all proceed to gather up the remaining pieces of meat that are scattered around.*

Ed   Like what?

Jack   The threat of an avalanche and the conservation of food
I am also concerned about the stability of our shelter if

the snow melts all around it
  One day it will simply roll over and then

Ed   Three good reasons not to wait around

Jack   I think we're really going to have to think about
getting out of here

Sue   All four of us?

Jack   I'm not sure that Bess would

Bess   I'm not moving
  I'm fine right where I am
  You three go

Sue   We can't leave you

Bess   You'll come back and get me with a helicopter
  I'm not afraid to stay here alone for a little while
  Can that be?

Sue   Yes

Bess   Look a butterfly
  Here we go again

She drops her pants and squats.

Ed   Skinny little thing

Sue   There isn't much warning
  He looks very surprised

Ed   He has a right to be
  He won't find much around here

Bess   This time I've got my pants full

Jack   Ed that's an interesting sign
  The flowers couldn't be too far away

Sue   The intestines
  Are thawing out

Ed   A sign of spring

Bess   Maybe he's like us far away from his home base

Ed   Blown all the way up here from the coastal plain by a strong gust of warm air

Jack   A butterfly only lives for one day

Sue   On the other side of that mountain

Ed   The plain

Sue   What a word
It makes you dream
I will wait for you with Bess
You two go

Ed (*picks up a piece of bridgework*)   A golden bridge
Gold in snow makes quite an effect
Sue has to go no matter what she's the steadiest of us all
Especially if we have to climb to the top of that mountain
The wall to the top seems completely smooth
From here anyway it looks totally vertical

Jack   We don't have any alternative

Ed   I'm not too fond of sudden drops

Bess   Oh Jack Bob always thought highly of you even if you did have your slight misunderstandings
And he trusted you Ed on any question of management he relied totally on you
All three of you have to go

Bess *stands up, wipes herself and closes her pants.*

I sewed two knapsacks and have enough thread left for a third one.

Jack   Why didn't you tell me?

Sue   You never asked any questions
As far as you were concerned
I never existed until we met

Ed   I'll stay with you Bess
No one can survive here alone
One has to talk

Sue   Thank God I met you
Right?

Ed   If only to talk

Jack   You stayed there

Sue   Three years those three years there
Changed everything

Ed   Dizziness
Whenever I lean over a staircase

Bess   Never mind Ed you'll climb up with your eyes closed

Sue   In that village I actually considered myself a brave girl
   The first time they served large worms with a crunchy skin sizzling in a rather dubious layer of fat
   I took one small bite of worms and one big bite of fried bananas to get it down
   There were four of us young American romantics on an unauthorized dig
   They caught me and took me to a prison in Tuxtla Guttierez that's where I met this boy he came from Madagascar he had killed someone
   Together we created Danny

Bess   You were a butterfly

Sue   Worms become butterflies

Jack   But not all worms

Ed   There aren't any worms here the bodies don't fill up with worms

Bess   We escaped so much ugliness so much misery
   I find it miraculous

I feel like a cloud dividing itself into smaller clouds and all those clouds

I will never be bored here

It's as if I knew everything

Everything starts over and over again

Each one of you must take at least three pairs of pants and leave a good layer of air between each pair

It's a good thing we've got a lot of pants

These are the pants Bob wore for his visit with General Figuereido and that he would have worn to see General Pinochet

The suit is custom-tailored we had it made during our last trip to New York

I said to him Bob the fabric in London is better and much cheaper

But he never stays in London long enough

And anyway on a late afternoon in London Bob would rather go window-shopping on Bond Street

Sometimes we would go into an antique shop

The *Time-Life* guidebook says that Chile is a mini-England

With a very sophisticated and kind people

Jack   Sleeping out up there without a shelter

Bess   And wonderful bazaars the peasants come in their wagons with all sorts of folk things

Baskets embroidered blouses and authentic pottery that is still cheap

Jack   We have to be prepared to spend several nights exposed to the wind

There's a danger of freezing to death at night

You can go to sleep and never wake up

This sleeping bag is only good for two

Ed   If we squeeze together it will be fine for three

It will be in our best interest to be close together

What's also important is our feet

Bess   Our house is so full of these things from every

country
 And now that Bob is gone

Sue   Bess I'm staying with you
 I'll tell you the peasant stories from Chiapas I had a
cassette with me
 I taped the legends straight from an old Mayan chief

Bess   And who knows?
 I'll call Randy Sheffield and have him look at the
collection

Sue   He was bursting with laughter
 As he explained to me how the world began out of a
mouse's asshole
 I found out later that he was pulling my leg

Bess   I'll propose a donation
 In June they just opened an ethnology department
thanks to Pat's small gifts drive
 She worked tirelessly to get the people to part with
their
 Naturally the Fine Arts Museum of Seattle specializes in
the Northwest American Indian
 But they could open a room with Bob's name the
Robert Lamb room

Night begins to fall. One after the other, they re-enter the cabin.

 I am not afraid of remaining alone Sue
 I have so much to think about
 And then there is so much to do here the days will
pass quickly I don't know how to explain it but I don't
feel like I'm waiting any more I feel as if this is my life
and I have arrived
 This cabin feels like a home and I feel at ease here
 Ed and Jack you will join forces and together take over
General Houses right?

Ed   Neither Jack nor I

Bess   But surely the two of you together

Ed   Neither one of us has it Bess
We just don't have Bob's driving force

Bess   All right then just go out and buy the people who
do there are head-hunters out there for that
But it's up to the two of you to preserve the continuity
of spirit that Bob gave the company
I know that Bob would have wanted it that way
And please call Chris my gardener tell him not to wait
for me before he starts pruning
Sue I have the oldest roses in Seattle you will come to
see them won't you
My grandfather planted them when he was only sixteen
you can't imagine what a scandal there was in my family
when Franklin Roosevelt brought him to Washington as
Secretary of Agriculture
My family had voted Republican for centuries
Everything seems natural to me today

Sue   The condors have gone

Ed   They found better things to do elsewhere

Bess   Poor Nan

Jack   That's right
Dick and Nan are a royal banquet
GH will get along without me Bess
I will not go back to the firm
We have to decide who's leaving with me tomorrow
morning
Ed? Sue?

Sue   Ed

Ed   Sue

Bess   Ed and Sue
You'll both go

Ed   You're not going back to General Houses? You've
got to be kidding Jack? To protect our feet we need to
rub in a thick layer of grease between our shoes and our

socks
I tried it grease drained from under the skin acts as a good insulator

Jack   Socks made out of the skin itself are even better
You just take the skin from an entire forearm with its subcutaneous grease
The problem is that we need forearms that are still intact
How many do we have left?
And passports we can't forget our passports
GH and I are going our separate ways
That happened all of a sudden last night

Collection of all necessary material for the expedition. They pack knapsacks.

GH and I are parting company Sue
I want to live differently

Sue   And do what?
The company is in your blood

Jack   My stick with the little wrist-strap

Sue   And your sunglasses
I don't believe you

Jack   I don't need GH to live
GH is over

Sue   What will you do?
How high do you think that mountain is?

Jack   I don't know

Bess   God Jack I don't believe you either
And don't forget to tell Nickie

Sue   When you get to the other side of the mountain
When you eat at Nickie's

Ed   That one is 14,000 feet assuming it is this one
Just try to tell from an aeronautical map

If it is

Sue   The moon is growing

Ed   Yes it will be a beautiful day

Jack   It would be best to leave early
Before the snow starts to melt
There's a long crossing to make
Just to reach the foot

Ed   Of Mount Iquiquerica if it's the one

Jack   For my bar mitzvah
I got a stamp from Mauritius
It was worth three thousand dollars
It's worth $150,000 today
We could go away on that money

Sue   Go where?

Jack   What's that?

Sue   An old scar

Jack   What will you do tomorrow morning? Are all three
of us going?

Sue   I don't know yet
Jack I'm beginning to believe you

Bess   I wish you wouldn't worry about me

Sue   Okay let's go to sleep

Ed   You'll think it over during the night Sue?

*They stretch out and snuggle up close together, all bundled up. They
fall asleep. Darkness. A distant and muffled sound grows louder. An
avalanche. A very long silence.*

Sue   Jack

Ed   Sue

Sue   Yes

Ed Bess

Sue   Ed

Ed Yes
  Jack

Sue Bess
  Jack

Ed Bess

Scene Seven

*Seven days later. The cabin is almost entirely filled with snow. Off
to the side a narrow space has been dug out to act as a shelter.
There is also a passageway between the shelter and the outside.
There are the remains of the wall of suitcases. The fuselage is buried
under a thick layer of snow.* **Sue** *is asleep.* **Ed** *is sitting and
writing.* **Sue** *wakes up.*

Sue   I'm cold
  How can you write
  Aren't your fingers cold?
  Warm me up

Ed *and* **Sue** *try to warm each other up by massaging and rubbing
each other.*

Sue   What are you writing?

Ed A history
  Of what has happened
  So that people will know

Sue   What people?

Ed The whole world
  We'll both sign it

Sue   And roll it up
  Put it in a bottle

Ed Someone some day
Will find it here
And will also find this letter to my brother

Sue They'll forward it
Milwaukee is that where he lives?

Ed He's my older brother he drives a taxi in Milwaukee
We never wrote each other
You
Don't you want to write to Danny?
Every Christmas I sent him a cheque and his wife
Millie answered
She always wrote the same thing 'Dear Ed thank you
for your cheque it couldn't have come at a better time
Millie'

Sue I slept like a log last night

Ed You sure did
I watched you while I wrote

Sue You worked all night?   ˙
I feel great this morning
It's the first night since the avalanche that I didn't wake
up several times jolted by that sound in my ears

Ed And without screaming

Sue I screamed?

Ed You did

Sue So you wrote everything down that happened to us?
I would never have known how to do that
Read it

Ed In order that the truth be known I Edward MacĆoy,
senior vice-president of administration and finances at
General Houses Inc., and I Susan Beaver, hereby relate
everything that occurred following the accident on
October 13th.
The pilot William Gladstone died instantly on impact.

Joe di Santo, vice-president of GH died that same day
having been ejected from the plane after said plane had
hit the mountain and broken into several sections, with all
occupants on board.

The co-pilot James King, critically wounded during the
crash, died on the eleventh day; he could not be freed
from the cockpit. Patricia Fielding, the chairman's
secretary, had her legs crushed in the crash. Gangrene set
in and she died on the fifteenth day.

Robert Lamb, chairman and CEO of General Houses
Inc., died on the twentieth day as a result of a back
injury incurred during the crash, and apparently from
cardiac arrest.

Nancy di Santo, Joe di Santo's daughter, and Richard
Sutton, senior vice-president of GH, died some time after
the twenty-sixth day while on an expedition to find help.

Elizabeth Lamb, the president's wife and Jack
Hirschfeld senior vice-president of GH, died the night
before the thirty-sixth day during an avalanche.

The above has been written the morning of the forty-
second day by the two surviving passengers who are about
to leave this site in order to find inhabited territory.

Sue   Ed

Ed   What?

Sue   I can't sign that

Ed   Why not?

Sue   I can't and don't ask me to
I can't explain why

Ed   If you don't sign it
They won't believe it

Sue   What difference does it make?
Let's hurry up and leave
Do you ever go out?

Ed   What?

Sue   I mean in Seattle

Ed   Rarely

Sue   But generally
What do you do at home after coming home from work?

Ed   I read the *Wall Street Journal* and all the other financial papers
Forbes Fortune Business Week Barrons Management Today
It takes a lot of time to keep up to date
The in-depth studies in the *Harvard Business Review* cannot be simply skimmed
I cut out and file the articles that are of the most interest to me

Sue   And then you go to bed?
Ed all of a sudden I have become intensely curious about you
I warn you there isn't a thing I won't ask
How much do you earn?

Ed   I

Sue   How much?

Ed   One hundred and ten thousand

Sue   How much did Mr Lamb make?

Ed   Three hundred and eighty thousand

Sue   By becoming president your salary will more than triple
Ed I wonder

Ed   What?

Sue   I wonder whether I should marry you
As president of General Houses you need a wife
Someone at your side to reassure you and relax you
There are constant shake-ups and the battles are tough
Bess was marvellous and I am sure she gave wonderful

receptions
    Beautiful tablecloths exquisite china and silverware
    All done with tact and simplicity

Ed   You amaze me Sue

Sue   But you aren't saying no?
    If I marry you Ed
    Imagine on Sundays we'll go to mass you are Catholic
aren't you?
    You'll hold Danny's hand and tell him not to
masturbate during the service
    Danny could play tennis at the Benjamin Franklin
Country Club
    If I marry you the only danger is that I'll run off with
the cash
    Overwhelmed by the dollars
    I can scarcely resist a hundred-dollar bill my heart
starts to palpitate
    And Danny doesn't like seeing me with a man as
serious as you are
    What a shame
    Because I like you Ed
    I find you very funny

Ed   That's the first time any woman has said that to me
    I am not very relaxed around women

Sue   You are attractive to them because you are a
fortress
    Pat was attracted to you and don't tell me she was just
after your money

Ed   She forced the door open

Sue   And it's up to me to walk in
    Rub my feet some more Ed
    It feels good when you do that
    Besides I suit you better than Pat did
    She was too dynamic she would have led you around
by the nose

What was your wife like?

Ed   Sylvia was very dynamic too
You've got the wrong impression of me
Sylvia was dynamic but I gave the orders
In GH's financial division I am known as the bulldozer
If I do become the CEO you can be sure the sparks
will fly
I know a few people who will have to wake up from a
nap that's lasted several years or they'll have to leave

Sue   Still asleep?

Ed   Even if we have to shove them out
Bob made a lot of noise but he pretty much let things
hum along

Sue   Bob didn't like you

Ed   What difference did it make
He needed me

Sue   From the minute we took off I could feel
That he disliked you intensely

Ed   He liked his own creations
The men he made
That's normal
At the beginning there were three of them
Tannenbaum Green and Lamb
Green and Lamb eliminated Tannenbaum who had the
original idea
After that there was a deadly duel between Green and
Lamb Green was the technician Lamb the salesman
I was on Green's side his right-hand man
Green thought he could get rid of Lamb by letting him
embark on the European project
Green believed that Europe would bury Lamb but
Lamb opened up the European market and Green was
eliminated

Sue   That's how it works?

Poor Tannenbaum
Poor Green
And you stayed?

Ed　I had to eat
Sylvia had just gotten sick and the drugs cost a fortune
Lamb did everything he could to make me quit he took away my vice-presidency and stuck me in some subordinate job
I got my chance after Watergate Carter got it in his head to reform the business world
Over a five-year period Lamb had handed out one hundred and eighteen million dollars to politicians of various countries to facilitate contract negotiations
He remembered that I was there as he had to have someone explain things to the Justice Department
Lamb had every reason to be pleased with the results not only was I made a vice-president again but in addition he put me in charge of administration and finance with the title of senior vice-president

Sue　I can't help thinking of poor Tannenbaum

Ed　Oh Tannenbaum was remarkable

Sue　And the unfortunate Green?

Ed　A Don Quixote and I was his Sancho Panza

Sue　You are a patient man

Ed　And loyal
Bob Lamb did recognize that by the end

Sue　I am so happy Ed
Jack never told me anything
You tell stories as well as
My old Mayan chief
Where did Jack fit into all this?

Ed　He was to Lamb what I was to Green
Lamb couldn't do anything without Jack

Sue   From a mouse's ass
The birth of Mighty House
His story and his end

Ed   This isn't the end Sue
It can't stop
We have to continue
Bob didn't really understand a great deal about
management but he was an authentic visionary
Seated in his chair on the twenty-ninth floor he could
see
He could see with his own eyes all those little houses
going up all over the world
The shovels being passed around
Then the debris being removed from the slums of the
city centres and around them
He saw the three elements that make up the capital H
above each door the symbol of a more dignified life for
millions of people
Above all he saw the flourishing of Latin America
Chile was a miserable piece of earth today they call it a
Renaissance Pinera the Chilean minister proclaimed it one
The regime's objective is to turn Chile into a country
of small landowners
Thanks to foreign capital and they have issued a
Foreign Investment Charter that encourages industry to
come there fully confident of success
Not to mention Brazil but in Argentina
You heard General Viola say on the radio last week
that all honest people have the right to live better
We are on the crest of the wave Sue
I will meet General Viola I will see Pinochet

Sue   Ed it's obvious
You have taken over
What did you write your brother?

Ed   That he can't be sure
That he'll get his cheque for Christmas

Sue   A lot depends on this mountain
And on what's behind it
You can take Jack's stick with the loop
Also his handmade socks
There's no sense in hanging around here

Ed   The sleeping bag

Sue   I dug it out

Ed   Food

Sue   I packed enough for ten days
That's all we can carry

Ed   Sunglasses

Sue   I've got them
And the lighter to warm up our fingers
Shall we go?

Ed   Sue were you serious
About marrying me?

Sue   I was serious about the dollars

Ed   I have a favour to ask
If I get dizzy

Sue   Close your eyes
Hold on to me

Ed   Are you sure?

Sue   When we storm the mountain
Just walk where I walked

They put their shoes on, get dressed, packed and leave the cabin to go outside. We see their backs as they slowly get further away and disappear.

The Neighbours

Les Voisins

translated by PAUL ANTAL

Characters

Blason
Alice, *his daughter*
Laheu
Felix, *his son*

The work is played without an interval.

The first and third acts are in real time. The second act covers a period of one year and consists of ten sequences which are played without interruption except for a lowering and raising of the stage lights in one movement like the dropping and rebounding of a ball. No other music except the Andante of Mozart's *Divertimento* K. 563, and this only during the changes between acts.

The Neighbours was first performed in the UK at the
Orange Tree Theatre, Richmond, on 4 November 1997,
directed by Geoffrey Beevers.

Act One

The backs of two identical houses. In the foreground, their common patio. **Blason** *and* **Alice** *are setting a table for four. A summer evening. The two houses are symmetrical, each with a double french door leading to the living area and another door leading to the kitchen.*

Blason Missing
A little over eight hundred thousand francs

Barely perceptible sound of a bell.

It's theirs isn't it?
Their telephone ringing?

Alice *hesitates, rushes into the house at right. She returns calmly a few seconds later.*

Alice Felix

Blason It's for Felix?

Alice For him
Personally
One of his customers

Blason Daphne?

Alice You're right she again
Urgent
Remind me to tell him to call her back

Blason Take a piece of paper and write down Felix return Daphne's call
When they arrive we'll all be so upset we might forget the champagne glasses they should be rinsed out since they've been sitting so long in the china cabinet up to the last gasp
He stroked her

Alice (*writing*) Felix

Blason   Is still reeling

Alice (*writing*)   Return Daphne's call

Blason   You can add it up the first two thirds of his life
put to rest today seeing that we celebrated his twenty-
fourth birthday last month
    And she was born on this patio sixteen years ago

Alice   Oh I remember and that? Those black beads
that's caviar? Real caviar?
    Elsa

Blason   Put on your glasses and read what's printed on
the label
    In tiny letters Alice on the right at the top

Alice   Imported from Iran
    Felix and I terrified
    We were crouched down on the ground in this corner
holding hands while Suzanna was delivering
    That red stuff what is it?

Blason   Salmon roe relatively speaking it's not as rare
some people find it tastier
    As it's half the price I took twice as much

Alice   And you brought out the old pink napkins edged
with lace

Blason   Embroidered by your mother
    A year before her accident

Alice   You always say her accident you were there so
was I

Blason   The difference is you and I are still here today

Alice   Today yes
    And yet
    Isn't it our accident?
    They're almost twenty years old

Blason   The plates with the ivy garland in the centre

are maybe a hundred
   The service came down from my great great-
grandparents it's genuine Limoges
   Give them a little wipe Alice before setting them down
   The little knife to the left of the big one

Alice   When Felix and I have our restaurant
   I'd like the food to be served on plates
   Not anything like this precious china but pretty
porcelain all the same
   A service with character

Blason   Something classy exactly
   If you want to attract the proper clientele you'd better
   But in any restaurant even supposing you have a high-
volume dishwasher as you'll no doubt want
   However careful you both will be the problem is the
amount of handling you have no idea how much breakage
does occur
   You have to count on an eleven-month turnover

Alice   What does that mean?

Blason   That each plate has an average life of eleven
months

Alice   How do you know that? Do you have that many
restaurants among your clients?
   I didn't know that restaurants also take out insurance
on dish breakage

Blason   Theoretically you can insure against anything
just a question of cost
   In practice I mean in day-to-day circumstances of
running the business breakage of dishes is not in fact
something that the companies insure against
   You see I regularly go through twenty or so trade
periodicals so whenever a new client calls I know in
advance what his problem is
   Statistics will tell you a lot if you know how to read
them

Butter dish next to the toast it's beyond me

Alice   You do love figures

Blason   They're part of me
Percentages stick with me
Look here

Laheu *and* **Felix** *enter. Sudden and long silence.* **Blason** *smiles.*

Blason   Laheu take him for example
Statistics are not his cup of tea figures make him cringe
He says they suck the life out of things

Silence.

Laheu   Take Blason as far as he's concerned things
become real only when he puts them in columns
For him they just don't come to life otherwise

Blason   Consider Laheu
Now Laheu's only interested in something if it's unique
But a unique thing just doesn't exist
Things only exist insofar as they form series
And the man knows it full well

Felix *and* **Alice**, *holding hands, observe the pair of men.* **Laheu** *smiles.*

Laheu   It's simply unbelievable
In order for him to get a grasp of something it has to
stop existing in itself has to dissolve in the magma of big
numbers

Blason   A particular case is nothing more than a
particular case

Laheu   An average is nothing

Blason   God almighty just listen to him
This man is supposed to be the quality control manager
at Universal Biscuit
Dare I ask what method you use at your job?

Laheu   I suppose when the day's over at the factory I switch off whereas you
   Felix look at what they've laid out for us here

Blason   Or is it that you control one cookie after another?

Laheu   You've never tasted such things have you?

Alice   Me neither

Felix   Well there you have it

Alice   Felix he says there you have it

Felix   I've taken my largest order

Laheu   Caviar champagne for us Felix all these delicacies just think

Alice   Largest ever?

Blason   When a loved one departs leaving us in sorrow

Laheu   And not an ordinary one either
   Moët et Chandon Felix

Felix   The largest since I've been travelling for Christophle an order for 65,000 francs from Madame Daphne
   She's on her way to doubling the floor space of her store

Alice   Makes me think about it Felix

Blason   Didn't I tell you to jot it down?

Alice   Return her call

Blason   Don't let's call it a banquet
   However rather than crying

Felix   Madame Daphne called?

Blason   Just call it a small celebration

Alice   We can celebrate his big order too

Felix   Well I better attend to it

He goes into the house on the right.

Laheu   Felix is still in shock

Blason   Where did you bury her?

Laheu   A corner of the woods she used to love covered with pine needles and cones

Alice   I know the place

Blason   Well now help yourself

Laheu   Yes
   He used to go there all the time with her and Alice
   He'd throw a pine cone she'd leap at it bring it back you could have come along you know

Alice   Felix said no he said it was something between father and son
   Besides I thought that Papa would need me to get everything ready

Felix *returns.*

Alice   Having to do with men it's a question women keep asking
   Should we listen to them?

Felix   She called to add four Trianon fish services eighteen hundred each
   That amounts to an order of nearly 70,000 if I add in the fish services

Blason   And you planted something? No? The punch this Daphne has
   Particularly if you consider that young people today tend to marry less and less forty-three per cent of couples under twenty-five live together casually compared to twenty-eight per cent just ten years ago if it were only marriage as an institution but everything is going to pieces wherever you look they've uncovered

An 800,000-franc gap in the books at Macassin
Brothers
A firm dating back to 1873
I suppose you think that surprises me?

Laheu We dug at the foot of a stone that had a flat
surface
Felix engraved her name on it

Blason One day or another it was bound to happen

Alice Elsa

Felix There you have it

Alice Felix he said it again there you have it

Felix Madame Daphne says so she says that young
people are going back to marriage bridal registries are
picking up
She says the trend is reversing better days

Blason On the horizon?

Laheu Like the two of you talking about going down to
city hall if I understand correctly

Blason I keep telling them go out and look just to be
sure not to make a mistake why those two have never
known anybody but each other

Alice The grave Felix
Will you take me to it?

Felix It sure is visible today
Your scar

Alice Whenever I've been crying
It comes out and you know yesterday I finally asked
him for it Monsieur Fabre
My raise
Monsieur Fabre it's been two years my pay hasn't
budged
If my performance has been unsatisfactory please say so

Alice   why certainly dear I must think of doing
something about it
   The problem is all he thinks about is Monsieur Delorge
   Monsieur Fabre I said to him my salary's actually
decreased with inflation
   Listen Alice he says Delorge has practically planted his
tent in the lobby of the Ministry of Trade fortunately I do
have a few friends myself at the top closer friends possibly
   However never underestimate your foe Alice he wants
my project torpedoed I smell a machination
   What I'm being paid is not an executive secretary's
salary Monsieur Fabre it's an entry-level typist's salary
   Of course Alice do remind me next week won't you?
But all he thinks about is how to get Delorge to hit the
dust

Laheu   Scare him Alice
   I'm slamming the door in your face Monsieur Fabre

Blason   I'm going over to Monsieur Delorge

Laheu   With all your secrets

Alice   He'd kill me

Blason   Serve him right

Laheu   The swindler is asking for it

Blason   He's no ordinary crook though
   He's a hot shot

Laheu   I'll help myself to seconds with your permission

Blason   Champagne? Felix what about you?
   Doesn't hear a thing stands there like a stick of wood
with his empty glass

Laheu   A swindler all the same

Blason   A winner
   Drink Felix come what may

Felix   Alice and me we're off I'm going back

Blason   To the grave?

Felix   I left my pocket-knife there

Felix *and* **Alice** *exit.*

Laheu   An exploiter
Anything in order to win or make a fast buck
Shameless ruthless
Yet you admire them
You should've been a serf in the Middle Ages

Blason   Hit hard to get to the top is what he's done
Fabre is a great man whichever way you look at it
Not only in the Middle Ages throughout history great
men have always

Laheu   Trampled everything on their way

Blason   That's the way it goes that's the way it should
be

Laheu   You saying this? Scrupulous as you are?
Come off it
Thirty years we've been living side by side Blason

Blason   The fact is I'm no entrepreneur
I move slowly
But I do move
Have a look

Laheu   What's that?

Blason *gives him a small package which* **Laheu** *starts to
unwrap.*

Blason   Heavier than it looks eh?
I acquired it yesterday
Haven't said a word to Alice yet

Laheu   Wasn't Felix real proud
With his huge order?

Blason   Nor is he Laheu
Nor will he ever be an entrepreneur

An ingot a kilo Laheu my fifth
Give me a hand will you we've got to lift this

Laheu   I see you're persevering?

Blason   The savings of the last three years lucky thing
you're there
Without you I'd never be able to lift the damn trapdoor
you know I've never been able to do anything with my
hands

Laheu *takes a crowbar out of his toolbox, goes about lifting a flat
slab in the patio floor.*

Laheu   All the same who'd believe it? You dealing with
financial matters all day long ought to know
Money is made to bear fruit

Blason   You're the one who says so you haven't got any

Laheu   If I did

Blason   Which will never happen

Laheu   I'd have it bear fruit

Blason   The future isn't worrying you simply because
you never think about it I can't get it out of my mind
I have this house I have Alice and I have you as a
neighbour but everything else is going to pieces
Insecurity's gaining ground all around so much so that
I can't shut my eyes at night
You have the privilege of being blind and deaf to all
that's going on in this world

Laheu   I beg your pardon not that way at all I read the
papers
We're rolling in a cart and there's always been bumps
but the world's still there more than ever right there and
you just need to equip yourself with a good pair of shock
absorbers
One front one rear

Blason   No hope of ever understanding one another

At least admit that to start out in life one's got to pay an admission fee

Laheu   I don't know what you're talking about

Blason   Since they've got this restaurant thing in their heads I've been thinking that just shy of half of what's there under our feet could buy them a roof

Because no matter what you think Laheu it really does bear fruit down under there

The first kilo when you helped me bury it remember fourteen years ago today it's worth twenty times

Neither stocks nor bonds nor real estate has brought in a better return

It bears fruit quietly and war can break out and banks can fold

Laheu   I think you're mad as a hatter

Blason   It's beyond me how dense you can be

Laheu   Maybe you're right maybe I'm the one that's cracked

Blason   No doubt I'd be happier if I were you

Laheu   The fact is

In your business you're bound to look at everything from the point of view of the risk involved

Blason   You think it's just by chance I'm in insurance? There's no such thing as chance

Laheu   You think everything is determined? The accident?

Blason   Everything

Laheu   And your wife's death? You think it was predetermined that she'd be killed in the accident?

Your fatalism is monstrous

My wife dumped me because I gave her good reason to do so and to fall in love with somebody else

Why don't you drive any more? If everything's

determined couldn't you drive again?

Blason   It's written somewhere I don't know where
That my driving days are over

Laheu   Not so
The car stirs things up in you and frightens you
Suppose there was a robbery tomorrow?
Suppose Felix found another girl?

The two men burst out laughing and touch wood. **Alice** *and*
Felix *have reappeared. They are still far off, standing in an
embrace. They approach and look in the trapdoor with curiosity. A
wink passes between the fathers. Night falls.*

Lights out.

Act Two

Same set but with this difference: a good fourth of the patio has been dug up – in the area where the trapdoor was located – and presents a disordered appearance. **Laheu** *and* **Felix** *are setting the table for four. Late afternoon.*

Felix   Another order from her an even larger one
   Eight complete Pompadour settings six Anthony and Cleopatra lunch settings four silverplated Chambord ice buckets four trays three cut crystal salad bowls two vases from the House of Daum four pairs of Chenonceau chandeliers twelve plate liners and just the tureen you figure a Beauharnais tureen by itself not counting tax

Laheu   Felix

Felix   Three thousand eight hundred twenty francs

Laheu   Come off it my boy
   Knives on the other side you should know better
   To the right it's the basics of the trade
   How do you account for the fact
   That we heard nothing?

Felix   If only Elsa had still been there

Laheu   Blason prefers Bordeaux
   I brought a bottle up from behind the woodpile
   But what scares me

Felix   She'd have barked

Laheu   But look it must have made a hell of a racket
   They couldn't have done it without making a terrific noise
   Why
   But even harder to understand
   How did they know?

Alice *enters.*

Alice   Papa's late

Felix (*with a laugh*)   She's put slippers on

Laheu   But how could they have known

Alice   At least they left me my slippers

Laheu   Your papa stayed calm Alice I admired him
I really did but what I fear is
Oh I can't make it out

Alice   I wonder why they didn't take away this pair of slippers
They took my suede boots my white leather Italian sandals right down to my last pair of shoes
All of Papa's shoes all his suits his shirts all my things my underwear my comb my little clock *Gone with the Wind* I had just started it it was open on my bed

Blason *enters.*

Laheu   Dinner's ready

Alice   They tore my mattress apart

Blason   They call that taking your deposition

Laheu   Look Blason first things first a seventeen-year-old bottle
This is an area where your expertise beats mine Felix says it should be decanted do you think that's right?

Blason   Absolutely you decant it after an hour and a half answering their questions
I'll be damned not an ordinary wine this Laheu
You still had that in the cellar? One just doesn't find the likes of them any more
Trouble is they don't believe you

Laheu   Felix made boiled chicken with rice

Felix   The last one I cooked

Blason   I remember

Felix But this one is a new recipe

Blason Is that so?
They end up making you believe

Laheu You wonder if it isn't you who've done it

Blason You're the guilty one that's right

Laheu Yes you're the one

Felix Madame Daphne placed an even larger one with me

Blason Don't say
They'll come and ask you to testify too
You'll have to loosen that tongue of yours a little bit

Alice That's going to hurt won't it Felix?
You're under suspicion Felix

Laheu You and I we're the prime suspects
Monsieur Blason kept no secrets from us did he?

Blason That's what they asked me and that's what I told them

Laheu Sure
Pass me your plate
I had the key I knew of the existence of a hideaway

Blason You knew about the slab and what was underneath
You knew

Laheu Where it was located on the patio

Blason And how to lift it
I myself couldn't for the life of me

Laheu You? Too clumsy to do it yourself

Laughter.

Blason your glass

Blason An army of vandals has been through the place

Laheu   One day or another we'll find out

Alice   All the same

Laheu   Alice your glass too

Alice   As if madness came over them that urge to destroy

Felix   They had axes I'm certain of it it looks like they went in swinging axes

Alice   Breaking everything they couldn't carry off

Blason   Apart from what she's got on her back
You're naked Alice and have nothing left

Alice   The hideaway if they hadn't found the hideaway but they found it didn't they Papa they got what they wanted
Then why
Tear apart the drapes rip up the carpeting?

Blason   Who knew?
Tell me who?

Alice   You too
Not a shirt left not a pair of pants

Blason   No shirt no pants
No breach of domicile the insurance

Laheu   Won't pay?

Blason   No chance

Laughter.

It's what's called total loss and not a single clause you can base a claim on
Forwards and backwards I can recite them to you

Felix   Bell rang

Laheu   No doubt come for me we'll each of us have our turn to be grilled I guess

Look Blason don't you have some idea? Not the slightest?

He enters the house on the right.

Felix   In the meantime Monsieur Blason Alice and you
Papa said you move into our house all we have is yours
the money you know where it is take what you need to
replace whatever's necessary
I'll sleep in the attic Alice is taking my room and Papa
got his ready for you he moved his things into the study
Elsa would have barked if she had been around

Fade out and in 1.

Blason *and* **Laheu**, *seated at the table, are having breakfast.*

Blason   Mind you to get her raise she had to resort to
heavy artillery she handed him her resignation in proper
form at which point he must have said to himself

The two men chuckle.

Laheu   She's switching to Delorge

Blason   Pretty good don't you think
This blackcurrant jelly

Laheu   And she finds time to make preserves I tell you
you won't see me complaining 'cause it's a lucky chance
for that boy but Felix isn't up to her level

Blason   Nonsense you shouldn't talk that way you made
him after all and now you look down on him he feels it
so he folds up
The bird's not quite out of the shell you wait and see
he's going to surprise us he's going to fly high

Laheu   Every year you tell me
For twenty years now

Blason   We parents tend to get impatient besides a girl
steps out faster it's a well-known fact

Eighteen per cent and she got it retroactive to the first
of January if it had been me
I don't think I'd have had the nerve to ask him for it
Monsieur Fabre yielded on all fronts
He must have feared

The two men chuckle.

Laheu   She'd switch to Delorge

Blason   Privy to all his secrets
By the way Fabre has just made a fabulous coup
Haven't you heard?
Delorge had obtained the official permit to construct
now the permit has just been cancelled

Laheu   You mean the eight extra storeys to his hotel?

Blason   You're way off Fabre couldn't care less about
the hotel extension
I'm talking about the shopping centre

Alice *enters.*

Blason   Because you know that was his great dream
from the beginning right Alice?
That there be a shopping centre downtown with his
name flashing in big letters on top of it
And here comes onto his own turf this former bicycle
racer
Winning the Tour de France two or three times is one
thing intruding into Fabre's territory is another
Alice we're going to be able to move back to our place
I don't mean to say you can't be a champion and also
a clever businessman

Laheu   There's no hurry

Blason   Not that we haven't enjoyed sharing your home
No matter tomorrow the repairs are completed

Laheu   Alice I want to congratulate you

Blason   You sure as hell got us out of this pinch

Laheu That raise you deserved it all right
Just ask Felix
We'll miss you
Yes

Felix *enters.*

Blason Yes it all goes to show ordeals can be of use
you find out the kind of man your neighbour is

Laheu Come on what you really find out is who you
are yourself because with regard to your neighbour you
knew didn't you?

Blason Alice and you my boy?
Coffee?

Alice Love one thanks
And you Felix?

Felix My best customer took a dive

Laheu Daphne?

Felix She was overdue in the remittance of her last
invoice
Didn't worry me too much

Alice You didn't answer if you wanted coffee

Felix The store is under legal seal and she
They arrested a gang of teenagers in the midst of a
break-in red-handed and one of them ratted
Clean sweep that's the headline in this morning's paper
they confessed a series of burglaries and that Madame
Daphne

Blason Well

Silent pause.

Well well

Felix She was the brains behind it and that's how she
financed her expansion because she got twenty per cent of
every take

They've locked her up

Blason   Well then

Fade out and in 2.

Toward evening. **Blason,** *alone, sets the table for four.* **Alice** *and* **Felix** *enter.*

Alice   You know I think we've found it

Blason   I didn't expect this of you Alice you left me to get everything ready by myself
  You haven't kept your word

Alice   Our little restaurant

Blason   Hadn't you promised?
  We tell Monsieur Laheu there will be a celebration and you were supposed to make the souffléed potatoes

Alice   Dear Papa when you hear the reason why

Felix   Sorry the fault is mine Monsieur Blason I'm the one that drew her out there
  The little farmhouse you see the one I mean? The one up on the hill after the turn right at the outskirt of the woods

Alice   Where Elsa is buried

Felix   We didn't think it would take that long we went on our bikes

Alice   From up there you take in the whole countryside this morning Felix as he was going to visit her grave he went by it and they had just put out a sign 'For sale'

Felix   I went and picked up Alice when she got off work we went up and asked to visit it

Alice   There aren't two like it for twenty miles around it'll be grabbed up
  You have to act fast

Laheu *enters.*

Laheu   Hey what's everybody so worked up about?

Blason   Dinner's going to be late
   That it should happen on the very day of the
celebration of Monsieur Laheu's hospitality
   Laheu I'm sorry
   No matter tell about it

Alice   The dream

Blason   But not a cent to pay for it

Alice   I can borrow
   Monsieur Fabre often told me he'd be glad to help me

Blason   And you'd put yourself in his claws? Laheu you
tell me if I'm right or wrong these kids are losing their
marbles Felix
   Pop this cork for me the last bottle of champagne we
had together was in honour of poor Elsa's memory
   Open the fridge Alice bring out the foie gras Monsieur
Bordier Laheu you recall don't you? I've spoken to you
about him sometimes and always in the best terms

Laheu   Your old head accountant, isn't he?

Blason   Has been with us for thirty-five years Monsieur
Macassin fired him without notice and he committed
suicide none of which explains the missing eight hundred
thousand francs

The telephone rings. **Alice** *goes into the house at left.*

Blason   They wanted a scapegoat
   And light the oven
   Foie gras filet mignon souffléed potatoes the
Chambertin's at room temperature mind those potatoes
   She does have a knack for making them crunchy
   Felix what are you waiting for? Tell us about it
   Cheers
   Well really this is to thank you

Laheu   Who's to be thanked? You've given us a lesson
in courage
  Cheers
  You didn't flinch under fire

Blason   Now let's not let these kids do anything stupid
  I drink to the example you set

Laheu   Your health

Blason   Your health

Alice *returns.*

Blason   The foie gras Alice

Alice   The gold Papa

Blason   Well
  What? The foie gras I'm telling you

Alice   And I'm telling you the gold
  They've recovered part of it
  At Madame Daphne's they've conducted a search
  The police chief wants to talk to you

Fade out and in 3.

Night. **Blason** *and* **Laheu** *seated, glasses of beer in front of
them.*

Blason   Because in the first place if you want my
opinion the police are a bunch of morons
  Look here put yourself in Daphne's place
  Now you're not a detective story reader are you?
  They find a gold ingot at her place they identify this
gold ingot it belongs to Blason at Blason's house there's
been a burglary OK
  What's she got to lose? She's already admitted she's
running this gang of youths doing all the burglaries in the
area
  The key fits the lock hard for her to pretend she

doesn't know anything about the burglary at Blason's house

The police put the heat on her she must have had an informer no breach of domicile and how would she have known there was a trapdoor in the floor of the patio?

So she thinks of Felix who calls on her from time to time to take an order

Felix who's the son of Blason's neighbour you follow me?

And the cops gobble it up

Laheu   Put yourself in their shoes

Blason   Why sure
Couldn't suit them more nicely

Laheu   Because the story does hang together

Blason   Considering their mental make-up it does

Laheu   So you don't believe it?

Blason   Laheu you and I look we have to keep our heads clear

Felix is innocence itself a boy who thinks the world around him is as pure as he is and Daphne was handing him hefty orders

The smile in his eyes when he was bragging about it
Stop looking like the bottom's dropped out

Bordier committed suicide you know why? The cops push their pawns they have to fill in each little square and Bordier I can tell you he was integrity itself

The trouble with him was he trusted people too much

You think I don't know what pocket the eight hundred thousand francs landed in? Come on

Like father like son you're just simpletons you don't see what's staring you in the face you're made out of the same clay

At least one of the five ingots is being retrieved which is what I wanted to talk to you about

That little farm up there on the hill what do you think?

Monsieur Fabre's money smells avoid it like poison

Fade out and in 4.

Early afternoon. **Laheu** *alone.* **Felix** *enters.*

Felix   It's been sitting vacant for eight years when you roam around inside

Laheu   Nothing surprises you does it

Felix   Like what?

Laheu   For example that Madame Daphne
For once I want you to listen to me

Felix   The smell stays in your nose
Goat or cow by the way when the last of the animals were gone it wasn't even scrubbed
The scrubbing will have to be done never mind all four of us could get at it together
The beams are going to be quite a job they'll have to be scraped bare

Laheu   You listening to me?
The lock wasn't broken and who had the key?

Felix   I don't know
Alice wonders too
If the cow shed would better be turned into the dining room or should it be the horse stable
Assuming it's the horse stable
Because restaurant guests really enjoy it if they have a view to look at between courses
Leisurely
Alice says
Or even between mouthfuls while they're eating if it's the cow shed we'd put in two large bay windows
It's a big beautiful shed it could accommodate business seminars and be used as a banquet room they'd find it attractive

Laheu   At the police it lasted all that long did it?

Felix   All morning
At four I have to go back it isn't over
In the courtyard there's a huge tree a maple in fair
weather we can serve outside
Corporations we'll be aiming at primarily
They appreciate a country setting for their meetings
and you can charge them a good price
Between the cow shed and the horse stable there's a
barn not that big
Our minds are almost set Alice and I the kitchen
We're thinking of installing the kitchen in the barn right
between the shed and the stable

Laheu   Your mother was the same way
She wouldn't answer
What's got hold of you Felix?

Felix   I'm explaining

Laheu   The gold you and I knew that there was gold
nobody else
The slab you and I we knew where it was and
Monsieur Blason hadn't told anyone else
The key you and I

Felix   You playing police too?
Let them do their job we do ours

Laheu   Why you have to go back?

Felix   They want to confront our testimonies me and
Madame Daphne

Laheu   You know what she testified
She testified that you often called in at her place
Not just in her store but in her apartment
She stated
So they're going to confront you
What's got hold of you Felix what's got hold of you?
How could you have

Listen
Deny
Even if they claim you've got your fingers in it deny
understand?
Play dumb like you know how
Like your mother used to do
Dumb right to the end
Deny

Felix   I'd rather you didn't talk to me that way

Laheu   I'd rather you hadn't done that

Felix   What have I done?

Laheu *goes out.* **Felix**, *alone, makes a very special kind of whistle.* **Alice** *enters.*

Alice   That's the way you used to call Elsa

Felix   She was born here right in this corner

Alice   I remember we stood right here you and I
First there was a stillborn one then another and then
that little moving tuft of hair

Felix   Elsa

Alice   You said Elsa and it stuck
Elsa
It sounded like Alice I thought

Felix   Didn't really think

Alice   But suppose it had been a male dog?
You're beautiful Felix
I can't stop thinking you're as beautiful as a dog
Yesterday your father asked me what I saw in you
He's at a loss he can't understand it
Now I can tell him now I know
You are beautiful and now I'm going to tell you that a
thousand times
Even if you say nothing
No matter

Stroke me
The way you stroked Elsa's belly I was almost jealous
that evening though I realized she was dying I was a little
jealous nonetheless
Stroke me here

Blason *enters, visibly distraught.*

Alice   I can die now

Blason   There's got to be an explanation but now you
have to tell me Felix
Look it's a photocopy of a sheet of graph paper they
found at Madame Daphne's
With a map of this patio on it
A cross where the slab is
An arrow pointing at the cross and the word 'treasure'
In your handwriting at least they say they've ascertained
that it's in fact your handwriting

Felix   A minute ago it was Papa
Now you too?

Felix *backs away slowly and leaves.* **Alice** *follows him.* **Blason**
remains stymied. **Laheu** *enters.*

Blason   You were right
It's him

Laheu   What do you mean I was right?

Blason   This map look it's all there

Laheu   So what?

Blason   It's in Felix' handwriting

Laheu   Felix' writing really?
Is that what you're telling me?

Blason   You saw it all clearly before I did
I didn't believe you

Laheu   What am I supposed to believe?
I don't understand you

Blason   Now I've come around I'm with you

Laheu   Absolutely nuts

Blason   Who? me?

The two men, still facing one another, step apart. They look at one another, bewildered.

Fade out and in 5.

Early morning.

Felix   If we'd only left a deposit right away
Now it's been sold

Laheu   It's no loss

Felix   Alice and I had drawn up plans
It was bought by Monsieur Fabre

Laheu   Nothing in life is ever a loss Felix

Felix   To make shade

Laheu   It can all turn around to our benefit

Felix   I don't know of any other tree in the region I could compare to it unless it's the oak at Monsieur Viaux's
I know the surroundings well

Laheu   Because one has to defend oneself and that's what you've done
A lot of things we took for granted have blown up now our eyes are wide open yours and mine
The Viaux property has been put up for sale Delorge picked it up for a song
All becoming clear
Daphne Blason
Your beautiful Madame Daphne and our neighbour Monsieur Blason

Felix   He's going to set up a foundation the Fabre

Foundation
He's planning to tear down the shed the stable the barn
and put up a small office building in mirrored glass

Laheu   I have it on good authority
That there was a long-standing affair between these two
You follow me?
Ha ha one by one all the threads come together

Fade out and in 6.

Evening.

Blason   A scheme Alice
You wouldn't imagine it

Alice   You didn't keep your promise

Blason   Never mind the little farm

Alice   With the maple tree
Sold

Blason   What time is it? What's he doing?
There's a light in his room
Will he have the nerve?

Alice   You're in such a state

Blason   Delorge is in that house
There aren't a dozen orange Mercedes around and
there's no mistaking his chauffeur's silhouette

Alice   Even if he were there

Blason   The two of them are in collusion and Delorge's
got friends in the right place
The order to dispose of the case came from high up
Matter closed
Forget it all

Alice   It's better that way
For Felix it was hard

Blason Oh it was hard for Felix was it?
But don't you realize what it all leads to?

Alice Things I see

Blason Those two are parading now
The field is theirs

Laheu *enters.*

Blason Has he gone?

Laheu Who?

Blason Your visitor

Laheu Since when are you interested in who visits me?

Blason You do me a favour so I do you one that's the
way friendships are knitted and maintained
I had no inkling that you had such excellent and
intimate relations with Delorge
Maybe even Monsieur Fabre is unaware of them
What do you figure Alice?

Laheu In point of fact I was coming to ask you

Blason By the way didn't you race bicycles years ago?

Laheu Just out of curiosity
Is it a fact that Daphne used to be a dance hostess in a
bar in Pigalle called Hot Nights in Madrid
At the time you met her and never up to this very day
have you strayed far from her tracks
Then what a lucky idea you had to entice her to come
and open a gift shop in this very city
China silverware bridal registries and the like all by
chance of course
But then there's no such thing as chance am I right
Blason everything is determined isn't it? Fate

Blason As fate would have it
Too bad for you Laheu
Sometimes what a person says comes back to haunt

them
    Fate had me see his chauffeur walking back and forth
    I've got friends too
    It's just possible that a journalist might want to
investigate the circumstances in which a judge signed an
order of nonsuit
    Whereas the dossier was
    Rarely has there been a dossier so utterly crushing and
I know no more than you do about Madame Daphne's
background she may have been a bar hostess as I've also
heard people say that she's been a shepherdess watching
sheep
    What clearly emerges is the wretched gesture of a
father taking advantage of the fact that his son is a little
bit backwards

Alice   Felix?

Blason   You pushed him into the sticky sheets of that
woman

Laheu   What is it you're saying?

Blason   Knowing that woman has a weakness for young
boys with peach fuzz she initiates them starts their
apprenticeship teaches them the elements of the trade
    Then when they're ready for service

Laheu   That's an interesting theory allow me Blason I
have another
    We could sit down

Blason   Fine
    And drink something
    Alice suppose you bring us a bottle

Felix *has entered without being seen.*

Felix   I can bring you one if you'd like

*He goes out, returns with a bottle and two glasses. The two men
take their first sips of wine in silence.*

Laheu   We've been through a lot together Blason I think I know you

You've been thick with that woman Daphne since before your marriage you were her first sweet young man her first trooper

Getting married was a good management decision on your part since you had no capital and your wife had just inherited this house

The shared patio bothered you but we'll see later

Madame Blason dies very conveniently in an accident about which nothing is known except that you were behind the wheel with no traffic ahead or behind straight line then all of a sudden the car swerves a few barrels as a souvenir on the pretty face of Alice who was four at the time a scar

But you couldn't stand this common patio you figured that out of these two houses side by side it was possible to make one you knock down the adjoining wall open up a large living area

Only thing is there's Laheu and his son Felix so with Daphne you figure she's the one who comes up with the idea

The gold the slab the break-in the map of the patio in Felix's handwriting carefully faked

The Laheu family is trusting we must profit from it

Blason *is on his feet, livid.*

Blason   You rotten swine

Laheu   A rat
   You
   Period

Fade out and in 7.

Night.

Felix   Their differences are getting deeper

Alice   It's just a stage

Fade out and in 8.

Early morning.

Blason   What were you doing last evening?

Laheu   I was washing my car

Blason   Really?

Laheu   The windshield after that storm
Couldn't see out

Blason   Like something to drink?

They pour drinks.

Alice quit her job with Monsieur Fabre

Laheu   She resign?

Blason   Something wasn't ticking

Laheu   I've noticed yes
She's not her usual self
Felix is having his share of problems at Christophle's
his sales are down

Blason   Well sure
Since Daphne's place closed
You're going to face a surprise soon Laheu
I'm not entirely without a hand in it

Laheu   All the better
You know I often think about the suicide of that poor
fellow Bordier
I have a notion about the missing eight hundred
thousand francs

Blason   You do?

Laheu   You said one or two words too many

Blason   Too much talk ruins
   Universal Biscuit doesn't do all that well right?
Competition is getting just a little too rough
   This size of operations is no longer viable now that the
business is getting more and more concentrated in the
hands of a few conglomerates you explained this to me
   One's got to diversify and of course you know that
Monsieur Fabre has already made a few acquisitions in
the food industry
   He's gone a long way just think his father had this tiny
butcher shop on Market Square and now lo and behold
   In two months' time the Fabre Shopping Centre will be
opening its doors two hundred and ninety thousand
square feet
   I thought it was right for me to call his attention at a
Rotary meeting one evening to the situation at Universal
Biscuit basing myself on what you had told me about its
potential and its plight all the inside dope
   That didn't fall on deaf ears
   Fabre has taken over Universal Biscuit it'll be in the
papers today
   The first thing he'll do as he usually does is to draw up
a list of employees he can do without
   You know for certain you've got nothing to worry
about
   Now if by chance something did happen to you you'd
always be able to get a job at Delorge's wouldn't you?
   However in the event some bad luck should come along
   The house you occupy I'm the taker

The two men glare at one another.

Fade out and in 9.

Early evening.

Felix   The personnel manager called me he told me
maybe I wasn't cut out for this line of work

Alice   Not cut out for

Felix   Yes he said these two things
Not cut out for
And
Lack of punch

Alice   I didn't say anything to Monsieur Fabre
I who never missed a day
One morning I didn't show up
I knew I couldn't go back

Felix   Let's do something together Alice

Alice   Let's
A franks and french fry stand

Felix   Franks and fries

Laheu *enters.*

Alice   Today's the anniversary of Elsa's death
It's nice on the patio this evening

Laheu   Hours after the inauguration
The shopping centre burned

Blason *enters.*

Alice   I thought we might eat a little something together
this evening

Laheu   Fabre suspects Delorge

Blason   It would take more for a man like Fabre to give
up I can tell you

Laheu   So you got fired?
Did you go back?

Felix *and* **Alice** *set the table.*

Felix   Just now

Blason   The stone is still there?

Laheu   With her name engraved?

Alice   Cold chicken
It was her favourite meal she would grovel until you
gave her the leftover bones

Blason   Some bread please Felix

Alice   Don't you think it's nice here together?
Wine?

Laheu   That's true it's nice

Blason   From secretary to secretary information gets
around
Mine found out that there was a letter from you in
Macassin's mail

Laheu   Beg your pardon I didn't write
I phoned to ask for an appointment with Monsieur
Macassin

Blason   You phoned?

Laheu   Just so
The secretary wanted to know the subject of the call I
told her I had data that might interest him relating to the
gap in their books

Blason   What? What have you dreamed up now?
Without so much as a shadow of proof

Laheu   He kept me in his office for an hour yesterday
I told him I had no proof
Circumstantial evidence only

Blason   Macassin is a gentleman
Waste an hour of his time listening to sheer nonsense

Laheu   He took notes he seemed to find it of interest
Especially the story of the gold and Daphne
A little more chicken? Filet?
Frankly I'd be surprised if he felt he could keep on
someone who had done what I told him you'd done

Blason   Wait till Monsieur Fabre

Laheu   I'm not worried

Blason   I spoke to Monsieur Fabre about you in considerable detail

Laheu   The suicide of a fine man like Bordier ought to weigh on anyone's conscience

Blason   In turn Monsieur Fabre asked me one or two questions he particularly wanted to know how Delorge uses you

Laheu   Monsieur Fabre is a not a man to give credence to a tissue of inanities the circumstances of the death of your wife especially struck Monsieur Macassin

He impressed me as an extremely upright sort

Blason *overturns the table, yelling.*

Blason   The spite

For years you've been dying of spite and envy

You don't bother to put away a penny in the meanwhile I save

I trust you I show you everything and I let you share

But pride has a grip on you you think you're smarter than I am so you have to strip me clean

You're an engineer you know how to devise a booby trap

Before you skin me what do you do? You strip and humiliate your wife you kick her out on the sidewalk

Look at Felix this boy with his lips sewn shut it's because he hasn't forgiven you

You think I haven't figured out why you're trying to get him to marry Alice? It's so she'll belong to you it's to take her away from me

You're smart all right but you're lazy and therefore a failure one solution destroy me ruin me

Laheu   The hideous snare you've set the fool I've been to let myself be caught in it

Blason   You have the nerve

Laheu   You wanted a victim

Blason   What didn't I do for you

Laheu   The shame

Blason   Shut up

They fight.

Lights out.

Act Three

In the background the backs of two sheds side by side and in the foreground an area of beaten earth with an irregular surface. An old mini-van. It is spring. Daybreak. No one on stage. Bird songs and sounds of insects against a backdrop of leaves stirred by the wind and the occasional passing of a car in the distance. Suddenly a small dog barks. Pause. **Felix** *enters.*

Felix Shush
Wretched

He whistles in his peculiar manner.

Where are you?
Gone
Obviously
You rush in and wake everybody up then run off on a spree

Alice *appears.*

Felix Wretched animal

Alice I slept like a log and you?
Shall I bring you coffee?

Felix Runs like a devil now
His paw's fine

Alice The week's receipts Felix I've added it all up
It was a big week

Felix People are beginning to know about us
Alice an idea I had during the night

Alice Two thousand four hundred this is the first week
we've gone over the two thousand franc mark

Felix Now that they've opened this new building site
Franks aren't popular with the North Africans
Alongside the franks we could sell merguez an

additional source of income

He whistles.

I don't know if you agree anyway the thought occurred
to me

Alice   Have you noticed? A clientele of elderly people is
starting to form
    Suppose we make a bench a lot more of them would
be attracted

Felix   And lovers too

Alice   Two benches then

Felix   Easy
    You're always going too fast Alice

Alice   Having worked that long for Monsieur Fabre it
rubs off on you

Blason *has appeared.*

Blason   True you went to the right school

Felix   He runs you'll notice

Blason   Besides
    You're a born entrepreneur Alice
    Go go

Felix   Like a rocket he plunges every which way didn't
you say we shouldn't keep him he'd be better off dead
you used to say
    I can tell you his paw is like new

Blason   Wasn't five in the morning when he burst in
yapping in my ears no way of getting back to sleep

Felix   You got back late didn't you?

Laheu *has appeared.*

Blason   Past midnight ninety miles driving just to bring
back this heap of wood

Laheu   It's quite clear the used furniture business is
nothing but your excuse for eating up the road miles

Alice   You could spend the rest of your life hanging on
the steering wheel

Laheu   Blason the new gasoline addict

Blason   On and on she couldn't stop talking
   This woman they were forcing her to move over to that
nursing home
   And she'd go on and on till the middle of the night her
son was dead and her husband it had been thirty years
since he passed away the grandchildren held a family
council they decided she was insane
   It was so they wouldn't have to pay her monthly
maintenance so they got a medical certificate
   How can you fight that? She told me it was a medical
accommodation certificate one of her grandchildren is a
member of the city board and the mayor is a physician
get it? But me she said I'm just fine right where I am and
you tell me if I'm incapacitated or senile or crazy I'm not
afraid of dying but I'd like to die with my furniture
around me and I don't bother anyone but it quite
obviously bothers them to put those eight hundred francs
each in my account every month

Alice *has brought in the coffeepot, mugs, bread. They eat while
they unload the mini-van.*

Blason   Not exactly what you'd call fine merchandise
   Laheu what I've brought back is mostly work for you
have a look see what I mean? It's falling to pieces
   It held together in her rooms so long as you didn't
touch it except for Madame Ufize mornings with the
feather duster
   She waxed
   Not a speck of dust

Alice   A lot of character
   This sideboard door has

I think so anyway

Felix Look
A bench Alice

Laheu The whole works
How much?

Blason I offered three she wanted ten I said to myself
five maximum and I got soft
Six

Laheu Six thousand francs?

Blason I pictured her there in that nursing home with
the canteen where you can buy sweets for a little extra
and the little gifts you have to give to the aides if you
want to survive for a while

Alice Monsieur Fabre would have stuck by his first offer
he would have hauled the whole works away for three
thousand
Three thousand three hundred he would have yielded
ten per cent and she'd have felt proud to squeeze a
concession out of him

Blason I'm not Monsieur Fabre

Laheu That's not a bad cargo Blason not by a long
shot
Quite a bit of work has to be done on it to be sure
once restored we could get fifteen to eighteen thousand
out of it
Figure I've got a week's job

Laheu *has already started with it.*

It was just about time too
How much was there left in the till?

Blason Six thousand

Laheu You should have stopped at five thousand five
What are we going to live on this coming week buddy?

Blason   Alice told me that she and Felix had a good
week

Felix   We'll give you an advance Monsieur Blason

Laheu   Make a note of it Alice
I don't want the accounts mixed up
A handsome piece of furniture that sideboard it's made
of solid walnut
All by itself
Shining new
Go for five thousand or so

Felix   We're off Monsieur Blason

Alice   We're going to the grind Monsieur Laheu

Alice *and* **Felix** *exit.*

Laheu   Accounts are something we'd better have a talk
about you and I

Blason   Precisely what I was telling myself driving back
such matters better not be left vague

Laheu   Driving really does you good

Blason   I seem to recall you used to suffer from
conjunctivitis didn't you? You've gotten rid of it since
you've been working with files and hammers all blessed
day

Laheu   Let me tell you something
At Universal Biscuit there was air conditioning
It dries out your mucous membranes

Blason   At Macassin Brothers after years of bickering
Monsieur Macassin made a decision windows could not be
opened in the summer except on one side of the building
on account of the fact that papers would fly all over the
place so that settled the problem except that the office air
became unbreathable

Laheu   You do what you have to do you forget what

you love to do

Blason   I used to think I loved what I was doing

Laheu   Felix and Alice now they knew what they wanted

Blason   A maple

Laheu   Can be planted
  Would you please lean forward so I can tip the back of this sideboard your way?
  I want to see underneath
  Something intrigues me
  As far as arrangements between you and me are concerned

Blason   Half and half on the profits
  That's how I see it
  I buy and I sell I'm in charge of marketing
  You disassemble and reassemble you put together a piece with a chairback here and a legframe there you give it the finishing touch
  You're in charge of engineering and manufacturing

Laheu   There's also the financial and administrative function
  You mind getting down on all fours for a second?

Blason   We could take charge of it jointly
  The general management function likewise

Laheu   Have to think about it

Blason   Yes think carefully

Laheu   Seems to me you've got it all figured out already

Blason   I'm not trying to impose it's just an idea to start with it's up for discussion
  The important thing is for each one to do what he knows best

Laheu   Regarding the profits

Blason   And
Have enough to eat
Do the sort of work he's cut out for

Laheu   Do what he loves to do

Blason   And have enough to eat

Laheu   You know what?
Step back from there look underneath
There's something strange that I can't make out
When I push this drawer it reaches all the way to the
back
The other one is shallower and so doesn't go in so far
and yet it hits
Somewhere in there there's an empty space
An inner space unused

Blason   Maybe a secret hiding place

Laheu   Half and half I wonder if that's fair
For example this piece is going to cost me a good
week's work and it's my labour that ups the value from
six to eighteen thousand

Blason   Suppose you tried lifting?

Laheu   I thought maybe by forcing a little
But it doesn't give an inch

Blason   Once the cabinetmaker got to his last drawer he
must have run out of wood
Maybe pressing on it

Laheu   Let's try
Nothing

Blason   The oak bed I brought in last week
How much time did you spend on it?
None or just about
Is it fair to say
That it was resold as is?
And for double what I paid for it?

Laheu   I rubbed it down polished it
  I added fresh lustre to it

Blason   Hardly worth mentioning but see it's typical of
you drawing conclusions out of a unique case

Laheu   It's hollow can you hear? I knock and there's a
resonance

Blason   Circumstances do vary but on average
  And on the side

Laheu   On the side?

Blason   Try to shove it a little on the side

Laheu   There you go with your averages again
  You do have a bee in your bonnet

Blason   You want us to be rational about it?
  Then the matter has to be addressed statistically there's
no other way
  Let me try

They change positions.

  Say
  Inside the empty space there's something
  Hear it?
  If I hit it there's something flies around inside
  One times one week one times two hours and you take
the average let's suppose fifty operations in a year to form
an idea you take the average
  The point is as a buyer I might spend a month two
months to locate a potentially worthwhile seller feel him
out overcome resistance negotiate a good price
  That aspect of the business is something a
manufacturing man usually fails to size up
  And with regard to selling
  Two months three months can go by at our stand in
the flea market before I hit upon a customer who makes
up his mind and meanwhile the number of times you miss
a sale the young couple comes around they argue they

bargain she wants to he's not sure he wants to she no
longer wants to

Laheu   How did you do it?

Blason *is holding the secret draw in his hands.*

Blason   It pivoted in my hands

Laheu   I did try to get it to turn

Blason   I must have given it a slight push here in the
left-hand corner
  Suddenly the back rotated

Laheu   A hidden spring
  Feel it's incredible all shiny
  Still moist with the original grease

Alice *comes in.*

Laheu   The absolute beauty of it

Alice   When I hear a thing like that
  Here are your franks and fries

Blason   Felix has to see this too

Alice   The stand can't be left unattended especially this
time of day
  Business is booming with the men on the building site
admittedly the fries sell better than the franks
  By the way Felix had an idea
  Help yourselves

She gives each of the men a frank with fries. **Laheu** *gives her the
object that was in the drawer: a ball of loose wool.*

Laheu   Here

Alice   What's this?

Blason   Take it apart

Laheu   Open it

Alice   A woollen sock

She catches gold coins in her hand.

Come what may I'm going to get him Felix has to see this

She places the gold on the hood of the van which has been the lunch table, wraps the sock around her neck and disappears on the run.

Laheu   What do you think it's worth?

Blason   You still have that old scale?

Laheu *disappears around the shed on the right and reappears with an old fashioned beam scale. While they carry out the weighing procedure* **Alice** *returns, followed by* **Felix**.

Blason   Three hundred eighty grams assuming the scale is still accurate
   The price per gram is in the area of one hundred francs that would make thirty-eight thousand francs

The atmosphere has become thick. None of the four seems able to break the silence.

Felix   I closed the stand
   But I'd better go back
   The customers wouldn't understand

Laheu   Half and half I reckon

Alice   Felix wait

Blason   Would seem fair to me

Felix   Why wait?

Alice   You might have your say

Laheu   Are we sure it's ours?

Blason   According to law it belongs to us

Laheu   According to what would it not belong to us?

Blason   Law decides

Laheu   So it's ours?

Blason   Nobody else's

Laheu   The old lady?

Blason   A thing is sold with everything it is deemed to contain

Laheu   Deemed?

Blason   Deemed or not deemed

Laheu   The old lady was not deemed to know

Blason   Somebody died without having the time to tell Madame Ufize her husband her father her grandfather maybe Madame Ufize's father didn't know even her grandfather didn't know in the event it was the great-grandfather

The atmosphere starts to relax.

Felix   I'm going back

Alice   Wait Felix

Blason   One can share and not share
I mean we share but each leaves his half in the common pot

Laheu   That becomes the capital of the business

Blason   With two shareholders at fifty per cent

Laheu   And that constitutes the working capital
Felix have you seen?
The spring the bottom pivots *ffft*
It could have stayed inside another thousand years

Felix   That wouldn't have been a bad thing

Blason   The spurt this gives to the business

Felix   I'm going back

He goes out.

Laheu   Everything's picking up speed

Blason   With this additional cash I buy

Laheu   The more we buy

Blason   The more we sell
Cash snowballs
Laheu

Laheu   Yes

Blason   No

Laheu   What no?

Blason   I find it hard to come to terms with it somehow

Alice   I'm going back too
Something wrong with Felix
I'm worried about Felix

She runs out.

Blason   Makes me dizzy
If Madame Ufize had it

Laheu   Something wrong Blason
With you too?

Blason   We don't need that

He climbs into the van, starts the engine.

Laheu   What are you doing?

Blason   Going back

Blason *sits still, hands on the steering wheel.* **Laheu** *puts the coins back into the sock, slowly, one by one.*

Laheu   One thing I didn't tell you Blason
You're worth your weight in gold

He brings the sock over to **Blason**.

Blason   Suits me fine
Being here with you
I thought I'd tell you

Laheu   Suits Alice one can see that

Blason   How many times have I told you about Felix
That one day he'd break out of his shell not a single
morning he doesn't wake up with some new idea
Did he tell you of his idea about the merguez?

Alice *appears bearing* **Felix** *on her shoulder. He is bleeding.*

Alice   His pocketknife he always carried it in his pocket
Didn't manage to drive it down into his heart I don't
think so anyway

First aid. Barking of a small dog.

Portrait of a Woman

Portrait d'une femme

translated by DONALD WATSON

Characters

Sophie Auzanneau
Xavier Bergeret
Cornaille } *medical students*
Lachaud
Claudette
Colonna, *on the teaching staff of the Faculty of Medicine*
Monsieur Auzanneau
Madame Auzanneau
Madame Guibot, *Sophie Auzanneau's landlady*
Dr Bernd Schlessinger, *surgeon*
Gerbier, *gunsmith*
Francine, *Xavier Bergeret's fiancée*
The President of the Court of Assizes in Paris
The Public Prosecutor
Maître Lubet, *Counsel for the Plaintiff*
Maître Cancé, *Counsel for the Defence*
Dr Haudebourg, *expert*

The following parts are played by one performer:

– **M. Auzanneau, The Gunsmith, Dr Schlessinger**
– **Mme Auzanneau, Mme Guibot**
– **Lachaud, Dr Haudebourg**
– **Cornaille, Colonna**
– **Francine, Claudette**

The world première of *Portrait of a Woman* was given at the Orange Tree Theatre on 8 February 1995 with the following cast:

Sophie Auzanneau	Lucy Tregear
Xavier Bergeret	Simon Day
Claudette/Francine	Nicola Fulljames
Madame Auzanneau/	
Madame Guibot	Jan Waters
Cornaille/Colonna	Graeme Henderson
Lachaud/Dr Haudebourg	Christopher Staines
Monsieur Auzanneau/	
The Gunsmith/	
Dr Schlessinger	Colin Farrell
The President of the Court of	
Assizes in Paris	John Baddeley
The Public Prosecutor	Roger Llewellyn
Maître Lubet	John Hudson
Maître Cancé	Ian Angus Wilkie

Directed by Sam Walters
Designed by Su Bentinck

A circular or oval stage with no fixed décor. A stagehand, in constant attendance, is ready as the action unfolds to introduce, remove or change round the portable items of the setting. These are of two strongly contrasted types. On the one hand the chairs, tables, beds, doors etc. belonging to the outside world . . . monochrome, undifferentiated, inexpressive and interchangeable, blending together to serve various functions, brought on or taken off only as the need arises. On the other hand the ultra-realistic representation of the Court of Assizes in Paris in 1953; or rather a fragmentary suggestion of it, isolated pieces of an unfinished jigsaw puzzle, each one executed in trompe-l'œil. *Human figures can be represented in these items (assessors, clerk of the court, guards, jurymen, photographers, journalists, the general public), which never leave the stage though they are subject to continual rearrangement, by sudden changes or by smooth transition, to create an impression of constant movement.*

A soundtrack intermittently reproduces the mutterings, laughter, exclamations and disruptions from the public.

Eleven actors take seventeen parts. The changes of appearance (costume, hairpieces etc.) needed for the five actors playing more than one role are made swiftly and perfunctorily in full view of the audience.

The play is continuous and is performed without an interval.

It opens with the appearance of the stagehand, who brings on a landing door and installs it in the centre of the stage. On one side of the door is the staircase of an apartment block; on the other, where the stagehand places a chair and an armchair on either side of a table, is **Xavier***'s bedsitter, 25 rue de l'Abbé Groult, Paris XV',* *on the seventh floor.* **Xavier** *comes and sits in the armchair.*

Pause.

Sophie *appears on the landing.*

President   She walked up to the seventh floor
   Why didn't you use the lift?

Mme Guibot   Forewarned is forearmed

What's more the boy was warned twice two telegrams the same day one from me and one from his dad

President   Your telegram despatched from Lille on the 15th of March was couched in the following terms 'Sophie gone to Paris stop avoid meeting urgent'

Mme Guibot   Better safe than sorry Mr President so I warned his dad as well

President   And the same day the father sent the following telegram to his son 'return immediately Saint-Omer'

Sophie *rings at the door.* **Xavier** *waits for a time, stands up, moves to the door, hesitates, then opens it.* **Sophie** *enters the room.*

Xavier   What are you doing here?

Sophie   I had to see you

Sophie *moves quickly forward and sits on the chair.* **Xavier** *returns to his armchair.*

Xavier   I told you we shouldn't see each other any more

President   Several remarks were exchanged more or less in the same vein

Sophie   I couldn't not see you again things I've got to explain

Xavier   There's nothing left for us to say you know

Sophie   I can't help it you've got to hear me out Listen

Xavier   What difference will it make?

Sophie   I can't

Xavier   Listen Sophie that's the way it is

Sophie   What way?

Xavier   It's all over

Sophie *takes a revolver from her raincoat pocket and fires to hit him in the forehead.* **Xavier** *collapses over the table. She stands up and shoots him in the back. Then she fires a third time, into his ear.*

Sophie   I walked up to the seventh floor because I needed time to think out what I had to tell him find the right words to use I hoped if I knew how to talk to him I could make him feel sorry and win him over

President   And failing that put an end to him and then commit suicide?

She nods her head slowly in confirmation.

Only you forgot
In your disturbed state
To turn the weapon on yourself

Maître Lubet   Understandably Monsieur le Président what else can one expect? In the heat of the moment one can't think of everything

Sophie   Face to face I couldn't say any of the things I wanted to
He seemed so distant
Almost a stranger

Lubet   So you might as well have taken the lift

Sophie   It happened so quickly
It was over before I realized
I was so worked up

President   You know how to fire a gun
One bullet at zero range the other two point-blank

Public Prosecutor   Yes he collapses the first time you fire but do you then put your arm around him and cry 'Xavier speak to me what have I done?'
No you aim a second shot into his back do your nerves get the better of you?
No you fire a final bullet at zero range into his ear

And this Sophie Auzanneau and I'm appalled to have to say it to a young girl like you

This is what you did and didn't do

Lubet   How did you deliver the fatal shot? What position was he in? Head slumped over like this? Or like this?

Sophie   I can't give you the details sir if I could remember I'd tell you

Lubet   Hm and after that?

You were found on the kitchen floor with the gas turned on

Oh yes a revolver's too brutal you prefer gas you know all about that from your medical studies that there's not so much risk lying flat on the floor and you hadn't forgotten

Maître Cancé   I deny the implication that between the three shots there was breathing space to think

That was a mean suggestion

Cheap and cruel

It was murder that's true she meant to kill and she did isn't that enough for you?

No you have to turn it into a novelette distort the facts and serve them up like a fisherman's yarn

Mme Guibot   Still he had been warned

President   Forewarned as he was how do you explain that he opened the door?

Mme Guibot   He was a young gentleman none better nice as they come

Well brought up good manners

President   He knew he was at risk

Lachaud   He was on his guard but perhaps deep down he wasn't

He passed the telegram on to me and said 'here take it if anything happens to me you can prove there was malice aforethought' but whether he believed it or not

President   He didn't follow his father's advice which reads more like an order 'return immediately Saint-Omer'

Lachaud   Xavier was anything but chicken

Cornaille   But those telegrams were on his mind he spent the last two days of his life rather like someone on the run

Lachaud   He stuck close to his friends either sleeping at their place or persuading them to come to his

Cornaille   She managed to catch up with him she wanted to see him tête-à-tête he put the meeting off made a date in the Place de l'Odéon for the 17th at 9.45

President   But persistent as she was she posted herself the previous evening in a café opposite No. 25 rue de l'Abbé Groult

Public Prosecutor   Sees him come home walks up to his apartment with the revolver in her coat pocket

President   Sophie Auzanneau after you recovered consciousness when the police questioned you you declared 'all I know is I took my revolver out to kill myself in front of Xavier but I can't remember anything that happened from the moment the first shot went off'
   Do you still stick to this version of the facts?

Sophie   No

President   And what is today's version?

Sophie   It's not a version sir
   I wanted to kill us both yes at the time
   I meant to bring him down with me both of us together

Lubet   You no longer maintain you killed Bergeret by accident?

Sophie   No

Lubet   So you lied to the police?

Sophie   Yes

Lubet   Yet today you're indignant if we cast doubt on a single word you say on this matter Monsieur le Président I have nothing more to add
  Except that in your shoes Sophie Auzanneau I'd show a little less indignation and a great deal more remorse

Sophie   You're not in my shoes

Lubet   For you will have noticed Ladies and Gentlemen of the Jury that nothing the defendant has said so far

Cancé   I protest Monsieur le Président

Lubet   Betrays the slightest trace of remorse

President   I must have order in the court
  I will not hesitate if the need arises to suspend this hearing
  I will ensure come what may that these proceedings be conducted in an orderly manner
  I ask the defendant

The terrace of a café in Lille.

Sophie   Me? What do I like?
  To be always changing new situations like a boy following you when a lecture's over

Xavier   That's not very new
  There aren't hundreds of new situations
  You can count them on the fingers of one hand three or four at the most
  Each with a number of variations

Sophie   The number of situations is infinite
  And each time the world begins again

Xavier   A world like that would be unthinkable

Sophie What good does thinking do?

Xavier To grasp things

Sophie To let them grasp you

Xavier To be passive?

Sophie To drift

Xavier Anywhere?

Sophie Wherever

Xavier That's what you believe?

Sophie Chance and fate are two sides of the same coin

Xavier I believe one can and should take control of one's life

Sophie What for?

Xavier To get somewhere

Sophie Are you serious?

Xavier I don't mean a career or happiness maybe what I mean is the image you have of yourself

Sophie My elder brother was drowned in his submarine
The younger one died in his fighter plane a few months later on an exercise it crashed

Xavier What's that got to do with it?

Sophie There's such a gap between us

Xavier Perhaps that's why I wanted to follow you

Sophie What about cats? Do you like black cats? A black cat stalking through the long grass?

Xavier Where are you from? If you don't mind my asking?

Sophie My family live in the suburbs of Dunkirk I was

born in Dunkirk a town that was a fort
  Inert they talk about the force of inertia don't they?
You're very polite
  Do you like long beaches?
  I love pebbles all kinds of stones
  I pick them up fill my pockets with them
  I'd like to break them open to see what's inside

Xavier   Shall we have supper together this evening?

Sophie   Do I interest you? I must find out about you
what you like I bet you love kicking a ball about you
look like a striker you do play football? Where's your
family from?

Xavier   My father's a vet at Arras
  I'm not a bad cook you can come to my place

Sophie   All the boys I meet want to cook for me
  It's a stroke of luck because I
  But I've got some revision to do

Xavier   We'll revise together

Sophie   Will you ask me some stinkers about the
cervical vertebrae?

Xavier   Or the iliac bone

Sophie   It's such a huge subject

Xavier   Colonna does his best to make a shambles of it

Sophie   Oh him and his urinary tract he's fanatical
about it
  The urethra I ask you and the bladder what a bore I
easily get swamped

Xavier   All depends on the prof Colonna's hard to
follow
  I'll grill you some sardines

Sophie   I hate sardines
  Specially oven-grilled with mustard my mother's

favourite dish the smell lingers in the house all year round

At the **Auzanneaus**' *house in the suburbs of Dunkirk.*

Mme Auzanneau   That storm's played havoc with the garden

Sophie   It doesn't really matter you know

Mme Auzanneau   Reminds me of the storm we had when our little girl left home and we only found out later she'd gone to the hospital to become a nurse

Xavier   You're on bad terms with her?

Sophie   This all sounds like the start of a novel

M. Auzanneau   And a tart

Mme Auzanneau   How do we know what went on? She wasn't even seventeen and he was at least fifty-five

M. Auzanneau   What are we eating?

Mme Auzanneau   A nice tail-end of cod
Fresh from market this morning
At least that Schlessinger was a decent sort of chap who made sure she had proper meals

In a bar in Paris.

Francine   I've been so scared

Mme Auzanneau   She hadn't even stopped growing

M. Auzanneau   A disaster for the beans

Mme Auzanneau   And those hailstones
The tomatoes all peppered with them

Francine   You you're always so punctual
Oh Xavier I imagined all sorts of things I thought she must have tracked you down

M. Auzanneau   She was sixteen when she took off and that was the start because you put up with all her shenanigans
   I must go and prop up that pear tree

At the gunsmith's in Lille.

Sophie   How much is that one?

Mme Auzanneau   It would be the one with the best pears
   But she'll settle down again
   It's the times we live in
   The war

Sophie   And that one?
   I know nothing about them you know
   To fire it

Gunsmith   First you load it

Sophie   Yes of course you load it

Xavier   Poor darling
   But I don't want to keep you in the dark
   She found me and I'm sure it wasn't by accident she knew my movements
   It's hopeless you get the feeling you can't get through to her with words

Francine   And then?
   After that?

Xavier   I told her about you and me

Gunsmith   Take a good look

Francine   When you're jealous you don't listen

Xavier   To be jealous you have to be in love she doesn't love me

Francine   I'm not so sure all I know is that you don't

love her because you love me
  You do love me?

Xavier   Sure as this table's a table

Francine   Fancy comparing

Xavier   I'm not comparing you to the table

Francine   You're comparing our love to a table

Sophie   And what does one do next?

Xavier   All I mean is our love is as real as this table
  My love

Francine   I thought it was stronger than that
  Never mind what did she want?

Gunsmith   That's it then you take aim

Sophie   Nothing too complicated

Gunsmith   What matters is how you look after it
  If you want it to give you good service
  You make a weapon last by taking good care of it
  This pistol here see made in 1780 it's always been in
the Bonachon family we've been gunsmiths since 1720

Sophie   Are you a Bonachon?

Gunsmith   Yes and no I married a Bonachon
  My name's Gerbier but Bonachon's still the firm's name
  You've got a licence?

Sophie   You need a licence?

Gunsmith   I'd advise you to choose this one
  It's easier to handle

Mme Guibot   She showed me her revolver sir oh she
never kept nothing from me not a bit sly no almost the
opposite

President   Meaning what?

Mme Guibot   If she had a bee in her bonnet she went

overboard

President But she didn't go over the top for this boy

Mme Guibot Not to start with

President At the start it was Bergeret who was mad
about her

Mme Guibot Yes

Lubet The fact that she wasn't so keen on Bergeret
 Didn't stop her slipping between his sheets
 But she didn't mind changing her sheets did she?
 It's even said she could do without sheets
 The oilcloth on a kitchen table would do

President Order

Lubet I have here a letter addressed to her by one of
her former lovers in which allusion is clearly made to the
corner of a kitchen table covered with a pink and white
oilcloth

Cancé All is grist to my learned friend's mill even if he
risks contradicting his own argument
 If there had been intent wouldn't my client have taken
care before committing the crime to destroy this intimate
correspondence the contents of which could clearly be
used against her?
 The bare facts speak for themselves but you no you
have to spice them up and so mask their authentic flavour
 Too spicy by half
 It's unfair to single out one sentence
 What I want you to arrive at Members of the Jury is a
total view of a complex human being of a whole live
person who merits your understanding however guilty she
may be but you must remain cool and curb your
abhorrence if you are to listen attentively to the innermost
promptings of her heart
 Hard as it is for you to enter this emotional arena here
alone is there a chance some answer may emerge to the

fearful question you have to resolve
Why did she do it?

Lubet   Self-interest as I shall demonstrate
For want of any argument he can get his teeth in my
esteemed colleague is riding a fashionable hobby-horse in-
depth psychology which as we know will permit him to
make any claim he likes even to call a black cat white
Why do I speak of a black cat? We have evidence
according to which the defendant had a passion for a
black cat
No doubt her one and only genuine passion
But apart from that my learned friend we know how
predisposed you are to dredge everything up from the
vertiginous depths of the soul
Petty of me perhaps but I'm concerned with the facts
I stick to the facts

Sophie's *room in Lille.*

Mme Guibot   Like the butcher fr'instance he's all upset
waiting for his bill to be paid
'Course *I* don't complain about you only you owe me
the last two months' rent
My sunniest room I only have one per floor with two
windows and you've got the top one looks over the trees
The one everyone asks for
You must say if you want to stay

Xavier   She threatened to kill me I mean she made a
scene

Mme Guibot   If you're staying it's all right by me

Francine   Did you love her very much?

Mme Guibot   I've got used to you

Xavier   For me she was a demon

Mme Guibot   Even if you've got lots of things on your

mind and not all of them nice ones
   You mustn't forget to pay me

Francine   More than me? Did you love her more than me?

Mme Guibot   If you're staying
   You're always tearing from place to place

Xavier   It hurts me that love can come to an end

Mme Guibot   No good tormenting yourself like this

Francine   Hers?

Xavier   Mine
   'Cos she never loved *me*

Mme Guibot   You ought to empty your head of this rubbish for good an' all

Xavier   When I broke with her she was annoyed not upset
   That's what my friends told me

Francine   One day you might stop loving me too?

Xavier   With those big round glasses of yours
   My sweet angel

Francine   Aren't you scared?

Xavier   You know I'm not
   I ought to be
   Cornaille thinks if I don't clear off abroad for six months without leaving an address

Sophie   No I can't marry you

Xavier   Why?

Sophie   Deep down I'm sure of it you you're so positive

Xavier   So what?

Sophie   So stable so clear
   I'm staying Madame Guibot I'm staying

Mme Guibot Just as well just as well you're in no state
too much running through that head of yours and you
can't go on like this on an empty stomach
    Two days you've gone without food

Xavier I try to reason myself into being scared

Mme Guibot You must eat

Sophie I can't

Xavier But you know

Mme Guibot A cup of tea and some chocolate biscuits
I bought you

Xavier It's my weakness I believe everyone is naturally
good

Sophie I can't marry you

Francine Go away if you have to
    Don't give your address even to me not to anyone I'll
wait a year for you two years

Xavier It was Lachaud slipped her my address
    She was waiting for me outside the Faculty she'd
checked up she knew what time I came out

Mme Guibot For two days now you've been shut in
your room
    Curled up in a ball on your bed

Francine Xavier oh Xavier listen
    All sorts of ideas are rushing through my mind

Mme Guibot Shut him out of your heart Mademoiselle
Sophie once and for all if you'll take my advice

Sophie I can't

Mme Guibot And in three or six months you'll see
you'll be a different person

Sophie He's dug his claws into me

Francine   When you come back we'll open your surgery can you see me in a white coat? I'll note down your appointments you'd like me to be your assistant? At the start we'll be living from hand to mouth but then

Sophie   I feel as if I'm sinking

Francine   You'll see and even
   When we've had time to build up a practice

Mme Guibot   You like them these little biscuits? Come on it'll all work out in time

Sophie   I can't hang on any longer I'll end up doing something dreadful

Mme Guibot   That's what she said

Sophie   I don't care if I'm not a good loser I don't love him enough to watch him walk off with somebody else

Mme Guibot   And she showed me her gun she held out her arm

Cancé   Do you think of her as a cold-blooded criminal?

Mme Guibot   And she went and took it from under her pillow
   And brandished it in my face and she told me
   If you want my opinion she's not all there maybe she does put on an act but she gets too caught up in the part she's playing and then she overdoes it

Sophie   What fate decrees that must we blindly obey

At the **Auzanneaus'** *in Dunkirk.*

Mme Auzanneau   It's no use
   Your answer's always the same

Cancé   She's meant to be hard-hearted

M. Auzanneau   Because it's always the same old story

Mme Auzanneau   When we first met it wasn't like this

Cancé   But underneath the armour she's built up

M. Auzanneau   It was exactly the same

Mme Auzanneau   You saw me in a different light
It's no use

Cancé   A poor heart was desperately beating

M. Auzanneau   If we've got to go back that far
I saw you as the sweet little darling you were

Mme Auzanneau   Like the sweet little darlings you ogle
today when they walk past under the window

Cancé   Locked away in prison

M. Auzanneau   Haven't you done enough nagging?
What is it you want?
For us to go out dancing? We'll do some jiving ha ha
ha
Tomorrow for our little girl's birthday
Any of that stew left over?
You ought to give us sardines
It's a long time

Mme Auzanneau   Tomorrow

M. Auzanneau   Our little girl loves them

Mme Auzanneau   What about the present?

M. Auzanneau   How many years has she been telling
us not to put ourselves out for her

Mme Auzanneau   It's true with her we could never get
it right

M. Auzanneau   What we did last year three thousand
francs in an envelope she never turns her nose up at that

Mme Auzanneau   This year Louis you could make it
five thousand everything's so expensive

At the gunsmith's in Lille.

Sophie   How much does it cost?

Mme Auzanneau   It's her brothers she's missing you know

Gunsmith   Four thousand eight hundred

Sophie   Oh I've not got enough

A bistro in Lille.

Cornaille   Cut your losses

Lachaud   The bloody fool's blubbing

Gunsmith   How much have you got without indiscretion?

Sophie   Two thousand five hundred

Gunsmith   If you cross the road there's a toyshop where they sell water-pistols

Cornaille   What good does crying do? Belt her one
   Take your choice either you belt her give her a beating she won't forget or you say cheerio hello and goodbye Sophie best of luck with Colonna

Lachaud   Give her the push

Xavier   But I'm crazy about her

Cornaille   A damn good hiding then
   Because she's taking you for a ride

President   So it was then you set your cap at Xavier Bergeret
   A decent young man clever and ambitious
   From a close-knit family well regarded in Saint-Omer
   Answer me

Sophie   Yes Monsieur le Président

Lachaud   The way she flaunts herself

Cornaille   The three of us'll gang up and bash her
about

Lachaud   Like a tart

President   His father was a vet a man of means

Lachaud   Beat her up

Cornaille   If you let it drag on

President   A good choice
A comfortable prospect for you gilt-edged no?

Sophie   Yes Monsieur le Président

Lachaud   She plays the field to get up your nose

Cornaille   It's not Colonna she's after
What she wants is to watch you getting all screwed up
while she makes a play for Colonna

President   In other words you had everything to make
you happy

Lachaud   For the whole world to see

Sophie   I don't know

President   Nor presumably do you know the reason
why
When you had found someone to love you
You gave in to this Monsieur Colonna?

Lachaud   That's the way she loves you

Cornaille   She'll be the death of you

Lachaud   Stop being a boody fool Xavier

Xavier   It would be easy if she was only aiming this at
me
For some reason I don't understand she's doing it
To hurt herself

Sophie   I don't know

Cornaille   A good hiding

Xavier   I don't think

Cornaille   That's what she's asking for

President   You don't know?
  Let's say it's a classic ploy for a woman
  Jealousy fans the flames you can find examples of it in
all the best authors can't you?

Xavier   To drift

Sophie   I don't know

President   But you've told us you devoured all kinds of
novels perched up there in your pear tree

Xavier   The first time I met her she told me that's what
she liked to drift

Lachaud   What she needed as a kid was
  A proper dad
  I'm not sure but you can imagine
  If he'd given her the odd spanking she was after

At the **Auzanneaus'** *in Dunkirk.*

Mme Auzanneau   You look peaky Sophie
  You getting enough to eat?

Lachaud   That's what she wants from you

Cornaille   She's dying for it

Mme Auzanneau   Since last year you've lost weight
  But as we only see you on your birthday

M. Auzanneau   You tell her that every time

Mme Auzanneau   You don't take enough care of
yourself

M. Auzanneau   Off we go again

Mme Auzanneau   What?

M. Auzanneau   It's no use

Sophie   I've been working hard Mum

Mme Auzanneau   If we saw a little more of you

Sophie   I paid you a visit in September did you forget?

Mme Auzanneau   A flying visit

Xavier   It's not in my nature

Sophie   To pick up my winter things

Lachaud   Later will be too late

Cornaille   It's now or never

Xavier   The moment's neither here nor there it's not like that with her

Mme Auzanneau   You don't look well
Do you get enough sleep?
You should come and spend part of the summer here to build yourself up again

Lachaud   The shrew's asking to be tamed

Sophie   They failed me in my exam

Cornaille   Tame her or chuck her out

M. Auzanneau   And you say you've been working?

Sophie   Looks as if you've redone the roof

Xavier   Sophie's beautiful inside and out

M. Auzanneau   The gale blew half of it away

Xavier   She's fighting against God knows what

M. Auzanneau   Nothing left of the beans
The pear tree

Mme Auzanneau   And the tomatoes

Xavier   Struggling against something inside her that's
breaking her up

M. Auzanneau   The storm split the pear tree in two

Xavier   It's got nothing to do with her nature
Sophie's not a nympho she hasn't got it in her

Sophie   My pear tree?

M. Auzanneau   To say nothing about the others

Cornaille   You must snap out of your dreamworld

Mme Auzanneau   And you're still seeing that boy?

Lachaud   She's screwing with Colonna

Sophie   Xavier he got through

Cornaille   Colonna's a better bet than you are

Sophie   I'm sitting it again next session
In the spring we're getting married setting up in Paris
Doctor Xavier and Doctor Sophie Bergeret
Sound good?
I want to go and see the pear tree
You didn't cut it down?

Mme Auzanneau   Well say something why don't you
tell her?
Dad managed to save it the trunk was split all the way
down he put a clamp round it

M. Auzanneau   We'll have to wait till spring

Mme Auzanneau   Give her the envelope
Oh Louis why don't you tell her for once?
For your twenty-fourth birthday here's an envelope you
really deserve it because you've worked hard

M. Auzanneau   So hard they failed her
Ha ha ha

Mme Auzanneau Don't pay attention to your father's little jokes you know him if you get married
There'll be something else on top of it of course

President At that precise moment Sophie Auzanneau did you love him?

Sophie I don't know

President I doubt it will do you any good to retreat into silence

Sophie I say what I know

President The court is trying to understand

Mme Auzanneau That way when we're old *you* won't forget *us* in our old age

President You're anxious for us to believe you
So give us an exact account of how your relationship with Xavier Bergeret began

Sophie He followed me
He suggested we went for a drink
He invited me back to his place to have some fresh grilled sardines
I told him I wasn't too keen on his sardines

President At your very first meeting a certain pattern was established in the contact between you
You switch him on then you switch him off in a game of cat and mouse

Sophie I was talking about sardines
He was quite put out he didn't know what to do with his hands so I pressed them over my breasts and then we went to his place to go to bed

President Was it he who proposed this?

Sophie I don't remember

President Whichever way it was you weren't embarrassed? Spending the night with a young man you'd never seen before that day?

Sophie   It was pleasure

President   Pleasure comes easily to you
I insist on order in this court
You take your pleasure with Bergeret pleasure with
Colonna then with Legouit and I pass over the others
I suppose when you were sixteen Colonel Schlessinger
the doctor in the German army gave you pleasure just as
easily

Mme Auzanneau   Your papa has sacrificed a lot for
you and you've never given him a single word of thanks
He doesn't ask for much
When he patched that pear tree together who do you
think he did it for?
Who does the work that pays for your room in Lille
your registration fees your dissecting instruments and all
those books and dictionaries?
When we sent your elder brother to university he wrote
us this letter I've always kept and I must have read it to
you a hundred times

The bed in **Xavier**'s *room in Lille.*

Sophie   It was the tree I used to climb when I was
small I'd stay there for hours curled up in the fork where
the three big branches met
My cat used to come too when she felt like it and
snuggle down in my lap I'd tickle her behind the ears and
when *I* felt like it I'd pick a pear that still wasn't ripe and
dig my teeth in
There in my nest I was invincible

Xavier   Invisible you mean

Sophie   Invincible because I was out of sight

Xavier   You've always like to remain unseen
Yet you'll get up to anything to draw attention to

yourself?

Sophie   It's bliss
To hide myself away
No Xavier
I don't love you as much as you love me

President   He insisted you should marry him

Xavier   You play hide and seek with yourself
You hide from your own feelings
I can see what you refuse to see

Sophie   What do you see?

Xavier   That you love me
I'll make you see it
We'll get married and you'll see

Sophie   I don't know

Xavier   The ice will melt

Sophie   You'll be my tree

Xavier   Will you then?

Sophie   And the storm will come

Xavier   You're devastating

Dr Haudebourg   She betrays a particular form of
instability which is the signal characteristic of an
unbalanced mind she's impulsive irascible and if you add
to that strong signs of degeneration on the maternal side
of her family

Sophie   I don't want to make you unhappy

Dr Haudebourg   The concomitance of these two
observations has led us to the conclusion that this is a
case of diminished responsibility

Xavier   I want to make you happy

Public Prosecutor   She has told us Doctor that she

fired in cold blood you speak of her 'irascibility' how did you get that idea?

Dr Haudebourg   Let's call it 'an irascible state of mind' it makes no difference she is irascible by nature but may still maintain a certain coolness in any given act
   Psychiatry anyway is not a mathematical science

Sophie   You're so terribly tender and gentle with me

Xavier   And you don't like it?

Sophie   I'm not used to it
   Are you taking me to a film
   I want to smooch at the flicks

Xavier   You're still not giving me an answer

Sophie   Afterwards we'll see

Lubet   So we can see Members of the Jury that even before the fatal act of physical liquidation
   There was a deliberate attempt at psychological degradation the breaking down of a human being whose one weakness was an attachment to certain values
   A precious metal that will be attacked insidiously by an acid which will prove fatal to it

Mme Guibot   She was a chilly mortal too
   Not a mollycoddle I mean there's a difference she used to roll herself up without a stitch on in three thick blankets even in the summer
   Her cat in bed with her
   And giggle

Colonna's *bedroom in Lille.*

Xavier   I'm intruding on your privacy Monsieur Colonna

Colonna   What can I do for you Bergeret?
   At this hour I must say

Mme Guibot   Sometimes there were two or three
people in her room peals of laughter and hers was the
loudest

Xavier   Is Sophie here?

Colonna   I'm sorry Sophie who?

Xavier   Sophie Auzanneau

Colonna   Auzanneau? What an idea

Xavier   It's about her I've come to see you
  She's been seen with you quite a lot she doesn't hide it
  I'm interested in her it's not a secret we've been
together for over a year I want to know what's going on
  I have a right to know

Colonna   Ask her

Xavier   She says she's a free agent

Colonna   If that's what she thinks

Xavier   But you see it's not what she thinks she tells me

Colonna   What can I do about it?

Xavier   You can tell me if you love her if you're
thinking of marriage

Colonna *smiles and holds out his hand. Handshake.* **Xavier**
leaves. **Sophie** *emerges from the cupboard, naked, wrapped in a
blanket. Roaring with laughter. She stops laughing abruptly and
shivers.*

Sophie   I'm cold warm me up

Colonna   But it's quite hot in here

Sophie   I'm always cold

Colonna *wraps her in two more blankets, lifts her up and lays
her on the bed. Then he lies down beside her.*

Sophie   Shall we make some tea? Piping hot
  I think I love him

Colonna   Yes

Sophie   You think so too?
At least *you* don't love me that's a relief
And you're not wanting to marry me

Colonna   I haven't exactly said I don't love you

Sophie   It would be a relief if you did

Colonna   China Tea? Ceylon?
Darjeeling?
You crying?

Sophie   I feel so miserable

Colonna   You didn't answer
Darjeeling?

Sophie   Is that what you asked me?

Colonna   Just now

Sophie   I don't know anything any more
Oh I don't know what I want

Colonna   And I made some Darjeeling
My relationship with Mademoiselle Auzanneau went on
for three weeks perhaps a month it was some time before
the tragedy I wonder what I'm doing here I really didn't
know her well enough to be able to pass judgement on
her
The news was such a shock I may have made certain
remarks but I realise now time has passed that they have
little bearing on the truth
For me she was a good companion rather too intense
at times it's been said it was self-interest that made her
turn to me
Nothing could be further from the truth
To be in my good books as her examiner no truth in
that at all I have never been a member of any board of
examiners

Cancé   What were you feeling?

Colonna   Feeling for her?

President   I must have order in the court

Cancé   About her

Colonna   About her? An unlucky sort of girl

President   I must ask the witness to be good enough to wait until public order is restored before proceeding with his evidence

Colonna   She chased after a love she was never able to find it's undeniable she was thrown off course by some of the men who also chased after her and indulged in blackmail to win her consent that also helped to influence her behaviour

Cancé   Thank you

President   Are there other witnesses for the defence to call?
   You were born?

Sophie   On March 11th 1927 at Dunkirk

President   Your father ran a plumbing and roofing business and your mother just kept house

In front of the Faculty of Medicine in Lille.

Claudette   Coming?

President   Though she helped to keep her husband's accounts

Sophie   Where?

Claudette   For a walk

Sophie   I'm in the dumps

President   You appear to have been your parents' favourite child yet you'll tell us you lacked affection
   Your father thought you were too brainy your mother

didn't understand you is that correct?

Claudette   But you don't mind do you?

Sophie   He got through and I got a resit I won't put up with this separation I'm going to see him

Claudette   He's determined to go to Paris?

Sophie   I'll tell him I'm going with him

Claudette   Sure you know what you want to do?

Cancé   Sometimes up in your pear tree you took a book with you?

Sophie   I always kept a book in the pocket of my dungarees

Cancé   Do you remember any of the titles?

Sophie   *Gone with the Wind*

President   Came our defeat and the ensuing Occupation it seems your father was not unduly affected by these events

Cancé   Romances? Novels?

Sophie   *Pride and Prejudice For Whom the Bell Tolls*

President   In 1940 you were thirteen years old two of your three brothers were killed one on the submarine he commanded the other during an airforce exercise in 1941 when you were fourteen you were seen on the terrace of a café wearing a bathing costume in the company of German sailors

Sophie   *The Sun Also Rises* usually American novels

President   And before you reached fifteen you went horse-riding with the Commander of the Occupation Forces one evening you go out for a walk arm in arm with a soldier of the Wehrmacht and you're stopped by a policeman who makes out a report the headmistress of your school is stirred into action

Discreet measures were apparently taken which led to the defendant's expulsion after which she seems to have pursued her studies at home

Cancé   I have proof that this assertion is incorrect Monsieur le Président and I herewith submit the deposition of the headmaster of the school not you notice the so-called headmistress according to which Sophie Auzanneau was never excluded from his *lycée* during the Occupation

This is by no means the only example in this case of what would appear to be manipulation of the facts

President   I will not allow these proceedings to break the tradition of calm deliberation alone conducive to the pursuit of justice and the uncovering of the truth

On a pavement in Lille.

Sophie   Did you treat yourself to a new suit? It must be a must

When one's going to make one's first appearance in Paris

Turn around take a few steps it changes the way you walk

A bit loose round the shoulders

Xavier   It was agony choosing it

Sophie   You should have taken me with you

Oh no that back's no good at all

Xavier   What?

Sophie   The jacket doesn't hang straight

Xavier   Sophie

Sophie   What?

Xavier   You're doing this on purpose we were meant not to meet again

Sophie   Maybe I am maybe I've been too hard on you
I didn't know how I stood with you it took me time to
find out
Now I know

Xavier   Now it's too late

President   All your friends have said you were more
annoyed than upset by this break-up

Sophie   Words I don't know what they mean

Cancé   Sophie Auzanneau fell in love with Xavier
Bergeret at roughly the same moment as he stopped
loving her

Sophie   I was in despair

Lubet   A black comedy of despair

Cancé   Since a man died I'd call it a tragedy

Lubet   A comedy at the first I repeat
A sinister comedy fabricated from start to finish out of
pique
A carefully rehearsed performance inspired by blighted
hope and by egocentric malice of the most savage and
contemptible kind

Sophie   I'd like to try and say I'd like you to believe me

Lubet   In despair let's see what you did in your
desperation
You went by train to Austria and as soon as you set
foot in Vienna in great despair you find the real thing a
love affair this time with a Monsieur Legouit a French
engineer on assignment

Sophie   I'd like to try and explain I'd always lived at
home with my mother and father afraid to show my
feelings
I never found it easy to talk about my personal
problems to people who took no interest

President   But surely your mother would have noticed something

Sophie   Those who are closest to you sir may be the last ones to know you really well
In my home somehow we always lived cut off from one another you'd never imagine how cold my father was

Lubet   How I ask is this relevant to your idyllic Austrian romance?

Sophie   When I was small I thought he didn't love me at all so whether I felt happy or not I'd got into the habit of keeping it all to myself

Sophie's *room in Lille.*

Claudette   Why yes I promise you

Sophie   And he talked about me?
He hasn't forgotten me?

Claudette   Goodness I can hardly believe how you look
What a transformation

Sophie   Hang on I'll ask Madame Guibot to make us a cup of tea
What did he say Claudette tell me everything he said

President   In 1944 you were seventeen it was the end of the war the Allies had surrounded Dunkirk

Claudette   He was worried about you how things were going for you
And what you'd drifted into
He was hoping you hadn't been left on your own that there was someone to take care of you

President   The German authorities had all the civilians evacuated but you stayed on with your father

Sophie   No I had a room in the military hospital

Claudette   He was afraid you'd go to pieces

President   The hospital for the Wehrmacht

Sophie   He didn't say he'd like to well I don't know

Claudette   See you again? Oh no he said
It was over well and truly over he told me he'd got
engaged to a girl called Francine
It seems to be a practical arrangement you know not a
shattering affair
He'd had his share of grand passion he said
Settling down I guess

Sophie   Tell me his address

President   There you come across a colonel in the
Medical Corps Doctor Schlessinger a man of fifty-five you
were seventeen and you became his mistress

Claudette   I don't know his address

Sophie   You're lying

Claudette   Perhaps you'll meet again in a few years'
time
You'll both have settled down and you'll be swapping
notes about the kids you've each had
But now if you take my advice pack it in

Sophie   You do know his address

Claudette   He usually confides in me he's fond of me
but I could tell he was on his guard he knows I'm your
closest friend

Sophie   His address

President   The Allies' final onslaught brought the
conflict to an end

Claudette   Normally he would have told me his address
We mustn't let our paths cross again

Sophie   He said that

President   But you are never to lose sight of your
Doctor the Colonel you write to him and you go and see
him at Ulm in August 1950

Lubet   Only a few months before the crime

Sophie   I've simply got to see him Claudette

Lubet   A crime that's presented to us as a crime of
passion

Claudette   It's a bit late to wake up to him now

Lubet   What did she want from him?
  Money no doubt

Sophie   I didn't realise

Lubet   It's all one to Sophie Auzanneau which lover she
pursues

Sophie   Can you lend me two thousand francs?

Lubet   Young or old German or French

Sophie   For the train fare
  I'll pay you back in a week I'm going to my parents for
my birthday there's an envelope waiting for me with some
cash

Lubet   She never returned the loan of course

Claudette   I'm sure she would if events had turned out
differently

Sophie   Let me have the two thousand francs

Claudette   Now you've got this other bloke after what
you tell me he's a decent sort he's got a good position
and he wants what's best for you
  Go and live abroad for a while
  Vienna's a lovely city
  What's his name?

Sophie   Legouit
  Just now I can't think about Legouit

Claudette He's in love with you and you say you love him
  Turn the page

Sophie I get my pages mixed up
  I need that address

Claudette You never stopped telling him you weren't the wife for him
  You made him believe it in the end

Sophie On my knees I'll go on my knees to him
  Oh Claudette today I'm ready to agree to anything
  I'll be the wife he's dreamed of

President You arrived at the Gare du Nord
  Then what did you do?

Sophie I went straight to his place

President You hadn't seen him for

Sophie Eighteen months

Lubet I note Monsieur le Président that the defendant contradicts herself in a previous statement she made it clear it was not until the morning of the following day that she charged in on Bergeret having spent the night at a hotel

Sophie I hadn't the money for a hotel room
  I went straight to his place

President And then what?

Sophie He let me in

President What happened next?

Sophie We had supper

President In his room?

Sophie Yes

Public Prosecutor The events leading up to this

bloodbath have now been pieced together
It was all worked out in advance down to the smallest
detail the admissions made at this hearing?
All calculated
A bloodbath and a torrent of lies
There may be talk of other affairs but I tell you no
affair is quite like any other and Members of the Jury you
weren't party to them anyway so let us stick to our affair
and ignore all the rest

The hospital in Dunkirk. **Sophie** *is wearing a white coat.*

Dr Schlessinger   What is there to eat?

Sophie   You look tired

Dr Schlessinger   You're my one consolation
Today they arrived in droves badly wounded

Sophie   Young Wolfgang died spitting blood
I held his hand

Dr Schlessinger   There should be more little French
girls warm-hearted like you
Now you can come and hop on my lap
So I can give my little kitten a cuddle

Sophie   Gently now
You're going to lose this war

Dr Schlessinger   Never

Sophie   And I shall lose you
Will you take me with you?

Dr Schlessinger   What would Frau Schlessinger say?

Public Prosecutor   I oppose and reject any plea for
diminished responsibility or extenuating circumstances our
distinguished experts have made much of her
temperamental character but I tell you these experts have
misread the motive

Sophie was hell-bent on destroying any chance of happiness because Sophie is a monster

Wasn't she a monster already as an adolescent when she linked up with our invaders?

Between them and her there was a great affinity

And isn't she still a monster when the day before her trial is due to start in the very last moments before her feigned attempt at suicide she makes out a will in favour of who you may ask? In the name of a woman sentenced to hard labour for life

A woman who had killed her first child aged eighteen months and five years later a second one and in both cases claimed that their death was accidental

Once again Sophie Auzanneau found a great affinity with this odious woman

Not without reason did Xavier Bergeret say she was devastating

So this death that she brought upon him

Xavier's *room in Paris.*

Xavier   God
What are you doing here?

Public Prosecutor   I now call down upon her

Sophie   Can I sit down?

Xavier   Sit

Public Prosecutor   Not in the smallest measure

Sophie   It's nice for you here

Xavier   Think so?

Sophie   It's cheerful like you

Public Prosecutor   Can I find it in my heart to forgive her

In defence of humanity and our feeble hopes of happiness I demand for this monster the ultimate penalty

Cancé I stand up alone
To face these extravagant allegations
For this is all wild exaggeration and the very enormity
of it weighs me down like a cloak of lead

Sophie Have you got a bathroom too?

Xavier See for yourself

Sophie All you need eh you haven't changed

Xavier Nor you

Sophie I have

Xavier Still got your cat?

Sophie Madame Guibot looks after her
You don't hear too much noise from the traffic is this
new?

Xavier This kit
A friend in electronics put it together for me

Sophie Do you listen to lots of music?
Do you still believe there are only three or four possible
situations?

Xavier With variations

Sophie Did you learn in the end
How to do your own ironing?
Can I take my shoes off?

Xavier Where have you come from?

Sophie Gare du Nord

Xavier Who gave you the address?

Sophie Are you cross?

Xavier No
It's just that we agreed

Sophie I know
You want me to go?

Xavier   You've taken your shoes off
  So stay for a while

Sophie   Can I invite you to supper?

Xavier   I'm inviting you there's leftovers in the fridge

Lubet   Lies lies lies a barrage of lies

President   If you don't mind Maître I have not yet
finished the cross-examination

Lubet   On the morning of the 7th of March she took
Xavier by surprise at No. 25 rue de l'Abbé Groult
  The address she'd wrung out of her friend as we heard
  Some minutes later she left having realised the break
was beyond repair
  As she went out she made the following remark 'if
that's the way it is all I can do now is disappear'
  We know because next day Xavier repeated it word for
word to his fiancée Francine
  These Monsieur le Président are the facts

President   For heaven's sake Maître let us take things
one at a time
  You took a room in a hotel

Sophie   I took the métro at the Gare du Nord and went
straight to his place
  We had supper in his room

President   What did you talk about?

Sophie   Nothing of importance

President   You hadn't seen him for eighteen months
you say you were madly in love with him and you spoke
of nothing of importance?

Sophie   Yes but we spent the night together

President   I will have order in this court

Lubet   So when you were asked by the police why
didn't you mention this before?

Sophie   I didn't want to tell anyone about it
I just said he'd kissed me the way he used to

Public Prosecutor   I rather think you kept quiet about
it because you weren't sure that Bergeret was dead and
you felt he might have denied it
Only when you found you really had killed him did it
occur to you to fabricate a story to make it look more like
a crime of passion
So this night you spent together is pure invention

Cancé   Who is inventing making up stories now?
Public Prosecutor sir you reduce me to despair your
legal procedure is so finely tuned in such good working
order that it would leave me defenceless were it not for
my open mind my probity
So I am uneasy
In the course of my professional career I have tried to
come to terms with the clients I defend get to like them
for what they are try and understand them
And you Members of the Jury should make an effort to
understand too
By looking closely into yourselves at your own faults
your own misgivings
And if it so happens you can find none
Then by considering the failings and misfortunes of
others

President   And you returned to Lille?

Sophie   Yes the day after

President   This time it is Madame Guibot your
landlady's evidence which enlightens us
Madame Guibot was more than a landlady to you
Someone you could confide in? Not unlike an
accomplice?

Mme Guibot   Me an accomplice sir?

President   Don't misunderstand me I know you sent
that telegram and warned the boy's father by telephone

you did the right and proper thing
    But you felt some sympathy for your tenant a sort of indulgence almost motherly
    You understood her as it seems her own mother had never done

Dr Schlessinger's *surgery at Ulm.*

Dr Schlessinger   What an absolutely wonderful surprise
    My little ray of sunshine

Sophie   My cavalier my first one

Dr Schlessinger   Problems?

Sophie   Bernd
    I simply had to see you

Dr Schlessinger   Some special reason?

Sophie   I miss you terribly
    Every single day

Dr Schlessinger   I'm an old quack an old Boche unappetising at that
    And you're a splendid young woman of twenty-three
    My kitten's grown into a tigress

Sophie   Don't joke about it
    If the world was a better place
    We'd be living together

Dr Schlessinger   Recognise this pebble?

Sophie   The doctor still keeps it in his pocket

Dr Schlessinger   Now you're a doctor too?

Sophie   No

Dr Schlessinger   Married?

Sophie   No

Dr Schlessinger   What about that boy who wanted to

marry you and you wouldn't

Sophie   Now he doesn't want to and I do

Dr Schlessinger   So the world is a pretty awful place
Let's change it

Sophie   We'll rub it out and start again

Dr Schlessinger   Where have you just come from?
Lille? Paris?

Sophie   I'm living in Vienna with a very nice man who
says he never fell for anyone like me before
   Bernd I want to stay here with you for a day or two

Dr Schlessinger   That won't be too easy with Frau
Schlessinger around

Sophie   I don't mind a hotel if I can see you for an
hour every day
   You've nothing to fear from me Bernd
   I'm not wicked or mad
   It's just that I must

Dr Schlessinger   And your Viennese gentleman?

Sophie   Do you know Vienna Bernd?
   A gingerbread city a long way from the sea
   A part of it's subsiding and my gentleman's got the job
of underpinning it
   He wants us to get married I told him I needed a few
days away to think it over

Dr Schlessinger   You haven't learnt much

Sophie   I don't know anything Bernd any more

Dr Schlessinger   My tigress can't decide which way to
jump next

Sophie   Any nice forests round here?

Dr Schlessinger   I've heard tales of woods in Vienna

Sophie   Not even a tree just one tree?

President   Right in front of him

Why did you throw yourself under his very eyes into the arms of Monsieur Colonna a man you didn't love?

To taunt him? Or just out of cruelty?

Sophie   Can you know in advance if love will come?

President   Xavier knew he was in love with you but you didn't love him you told us yourself what you felt for him was not love but affection so why keep him on the hook for so long?

Sophie   It's true my feelings weren't the same as his I thought at the time we couldn't ever be happy together

At least I didn't realise we could

But then I came to see I was really in love

President   All the more surprising then if you were so fond of him

All the more surprising that you should get involved with this engineer this Monsieur Legouit in Austria who you then walked out on to go and spend a few days at Ulm with your former lover Doctor Schlessinger

One can't help wondering who you're in love with

A little order Ladies and Gentlemen in this courtroom

Sophie   If there was no hope for me with Bergeret I had to get fixed up with someone else I'd got it wrong once already

It had made me very unhappy I didn't want to make another mistake I wasn't sure I was in love with Legouit

President   That is not the impression one gets when reading your letters to him let me quote from one

'This is the first time making some man happy or seeing that he's happy for some other reason

Has meant more to me

Than my own self-gratification'

Sophie   I never realised

Anyway it didn't stop me thinking about Bergeret

Public Prosecutor   Didn't you say that with patience your fidelity would bring Bergeret round?

One can't help wondering what you understand by fidelity

Sophie   It's hard to explain

President   Laughter in this court is out of place

Mme Guibot   And then I put my hand in her bag and pulled out the bottle that contained the fatal concoction

Your young gentleman's all of a piece I told her he's straight as they come

He was in love with you you put him off so he broke it off

President   A good summing-up

Mme Guibot   And I pointed out there were other fish to fry

She knew there were others all right

That all happened a fortnight after they broke up and he moved to Paris he came back to Lille for a day or two she found out and wanted to talk to him he agreed to meet her but he refused to take up with her again and she threatened to poison herself Monsieur Xavier got into a state and came in to warn me I rushed upstairs fast as I could with my rheumatics

Sophie's *room in Lille.*

Mme Guibot   Where's your handbag?

Sophie   Here

Mme Guibot   What is it?

Sophie   Cyanide

Mme Guibot   Better have a good cry than swallow this muck

Sophie   They say it's got a nasty taste

I've no choice it's all too much for me there's no way out leave me alone

Mme Guibot   I don't remember what I said next but her tears started so I stroked her hair and she fell asleep with her head on my shoulder

Lubet   Obviously a put-up job a sly bit of blackmail

Cancé   That no one should remain in ignorance
When Monsieur Auzanneau heard what his daughter had done he took his own life he was found with a gas pipe in his mouth his body full of ether
Earlier on he had sent Monsieur Bergeret a letter of excuse and condolence

Sophie   In my family no one ever seems to die a natural death

President   You can judge for yourselves how genuine were her attempts at suicide
May I recall the report drawn up by Doctor Paul following the attempt which forced us into an adjournment
Sophie Auzanneau made good use of her medical knowledge first she applied a tourniquet to her left forearm then with a needle or a piece of broken glass we're not quite sure which she cut clean into the radial vein
She lost about a litre of blood and was found comatose in her cell at six o'clock this morning when I saw her at ten she was still in the same condition
Pulse rate impossible to count blood pressure under six
But next morning she had recovered enough of her strength and her mental faculties to compose a letter she addressed to me which reads as follows
'I am obliged to write this letter in the dark as I don't want to switch the night light on
I hope Monsieur and Madame Bergeret will forgive me if they can and take pity on my mother I'm sorry for all I've done

I bitterly regret that I killed him
But I will not submit to a system of justice devoid of all
dignity I refuse to be tried in public in front of a crowd
that reminds me of the howling mobs of the Revolution
my trial ought to have been held *in camera* I'm glad I've
been able to thwart the officials who set the stage for this
masquerade'
I shall not ask you Sophie Auzanneau whether you
have had second thoughts about this scurrilous attack on
the law

Public Prosecutor   To slow the law down that above
all was your strategy Sophie Auzanneau to drag it all out
Thanks to your squalid performance you have gained
seven weeks

Cancé   I object to this interpretation from the
representative of the State I too have received a letter
from my client
A heart-rending one
Which with your permission I shall not make public

President   In the moments that followed the crime
because we have to return to that
Did you Sophie Auzanneau really intend to put an end
to your life?
Or was it rather
To use your own words?
An attempt to set the stage?
Would our expert like to throw some light on this
point?

Dr Haudebourg   For Sophie Auzanneau there seems to
be something normal and logical about suicide she was
brought up to think like this
In our psychiatric report we specifically referred to it as
a theatrical suicide and yes we chose the expression with
care
We called it theatrical to draw attention to its
flamboyance and not to say it was simulated

The bed in **Xavier***'s room in Lille.*

Sophie   Xavier

Xavier   Yes

Sophie   I feel sleepy

Xavier   Relax with my arms round you

Sophie   In your arms yes
   And not wake up again
   Why is everything so difficult?
   Why does it hurt so?
   Why do I hurt you so much?
   How long is this going to last?

Lubet   I'm not going to muddy the issue
   When a spade is a spade
   I'm outspoken enough to say so
   The defence is engaged in a subtle manoeuvre designed
to trap you into understanding while at the same time
befogging you in clouds of mystification

Xavier   You're all snuggled up but you're tensed up too
   How can you
   If only you could let yourself go

Sophie   Let myself go
   Yes
   If you knew how I'd like to
   But then you know I can't
   I can't   .

Lubet   The defence prefers to dwell in that somewhat
disturbing twilight zone where the line dividing what is
from what is not becomes blurred

Sophie   Can you hear
   The storm
   About to cause havoc in the garden
   Papa had to get up in the middle of the night
   I'm afraid

Xavier   Afraid of what? I'm here

Sophie   Of myself
Of everything
I should never have told you about the sardines
The trunk splits and the branch gets broken
My cat has slipped under the netting
Gone a-roving
Do you love me? And do I love you?
Words that don't come neat in their little compartments
But go rolling rolling on

Lubet   Understanding what escapes all understanding of
course so you are no longer able to pass judgement
Because judgement ah Members of the Jury judgement

Sophie   Like a pebble
You ought to break me open to find out what's inside

Lubet   Judgement as André Malraux said is clearly the
negation of understanding
Never mind if I break the spell and drag you back to
earth
There one can understand and pass judgement in the
full light of day

Sophie   Break me with your teeth
Bite me
Hard
Where am I? Who is it?

Xavier   It's me
And it's you
Here

Sophie   Where?
One day you know I'll kill you
To simplify

Xavier   What will that simplify?

Sophie   Do you know why you love me?

Xavier   I know how it all began
   I loved your laugh before I loved your face
   In the large lecture-room I could sometimes hear this
laugh coming from a bench behind me

Sophie   When did you find out which face it belonged
to?

Xavier   One day I followed a girl out of the lecture-
room she was beautiful and on the boulevard between two
rows of plane trees she said to me chance and fate are
two sides of the same coin
   It stuck in my mind you see because then she laughed
and I recognised the laugh I'd heard behind me
   A laugh that has nothing to do with a sense of humour

Sophie   She doesn't have a sense of humour?

Xavier   None at all

Sophie   So she can't enjoy a joke
   What if the whole of her life was a joke?

Xavier   She blew hot and cold
   Is that what I loved about her?

Sophie   Look
   It's going to be fine today
   It'll be the most beautiful day
   To learn how to love loving perhaps
   I hope one can learn how I do so want
   To be able to love

Lubet   You don't need to make up your minds about
whether a crime was committed or who the guilty party is
the admissions already made by the defendant have
relieved us of this obligation
   You only have to resolve two problems premeditation
and mitigating circumstances and your response will
depend upon the personal conviction you have each of
you formed concerning the motives for the crime
   What the defence puts forward is woolly and obscure

Attempting to lead you astray
Whereas I shall demonstrate

Xavier   That's what I like you're the one I want

Sophie   But I hurt you

Xavier   The first night you spent with me
You said I was hurting you

Lubet   I shall prove that the one and only motive for
the crime was self-interest

At the **Auzanneaus**' *house in Lille.*

M. Auzanneau   You're not going to like this much
Though with you one can never tell
Henri is dead

Sophie   I'm often like that
Henri who?

M. Auzanneau   Your brother

Mme Auzanneau   She was always at loggerheads with
her elder brother

M. Auzanneau   His submarine has been sunk

Mme Auzanneau   With the other one it wasn't the
same
She seems to have grieved for him

M. Auzanneau   She showed nothing

Sophie's *room in Lille.*

Claudette   Why?

Sophie   Yes why do you think he wanted to know who
was sleeping with me?

Claudette   His affair with you may be at an end but

that doesn't stop him you know still taking an interest in you

Mme Auzanneau   Our little girl was precocious emotionally

M. Auzanneau   The war didn't help

Sophie   Did you feel he was jealous?

Claudette   Of course a touch of jealousy it's a natural reaction
Anyone would think it's good news I'm bringing you
But Sophie no he won't see you any more he's getting married it's over

Lubet   Self-interest
The crime of an opportunist a money-grubbing woman set on marriage
Whose interest in men is stimulated only by their status
A fortune-hunter
If she got Xavier in her clutches it's because Xavier was the most desirable and if she left him later it's because he wouldn't have her any more
The men she tried to seduce after that also appealed to her only because of their money or their position Colonna Legouit
She discovers that the first man is not the marrying type and the business prospects of the second didn't equal her expectations
Then she wants to go back to Xavier Bergeret
But the young man is unshakeable he has made up his mind he gets engaged to Francine no hope left there
So she reached her decision
Every avenue is closed to her and she will not allow this man to seize his chance of happiness
She will shoot him down
With a revolver in her pocket she waits for him in the entrance to his block of flats
Like a killer
Is this your drama of love?

She has thought it all out
She fires the first bullet into his back he collapses she
walks all round the body
Fires a second time at his forehead
Then the *coup de grâce* at zero range into his temple
Of course it's only a hypothesis

Public Prosecutor   On a café terrace in her bathing
costume in the company of German sailors

A café terrace in Paris.

Cornaille   Don't let her in

Xavier   You mustn't all drop her completely or she'll
just let herself drift

Mme Guibot   I wouldn't say I'd had a premonition but
I'd use a cup of tea as an excuse
    At odd times I'd go upstairs and suggest a cup of tea
    On her bed I saw a will a paper anyway and on it
she'd written will

Cornaille   He was an honest frank straightforward
fellow incapable of deception

Lachaud   A gentleman that's the word from a united
family his father was a vet at Saint-Omer

Mme Guibot   She must have tiptoed down the stairs I
never heard her come down
    She'd been lying up there all depressed for a couple of
days and then suddenly no one there not even her
shopping-bag

Claudette   It was as if something had made her happy
    Yes at that moment there was a change in her
character

Mme Guibot   I sent my telegram off

Claudette   She didn't seem so strange to me not so

hard
   I was much more drawn to her

Mme Guibot The telephone call to his father too
   To Saint-Omer where he had his clinic

Cornaille He loved her "tis pity she's a whore' he said
to me one day but that remark should be taken sir as
typical of a student for us
   It didn't have the same literal meaning a policeman
would give it

Lachaud Though he really had grown away from her
there was a lingering trace of compassion

President Your past life is what one might call erratic
tempestuous even

Mme Guibot I used to do her washing for her
   One morning when I took her clean clothes back there
she was starkers in bed she always used to sleep in her
birthday suit even in the winter with ten below freezing
outside
   Someone came in without knocking it was Monsieur
Xavier he slipped into bed beside her fully dressed the
two of them never took no notice of me
   She asked me if I'd bring up two cups of tea

Public Prosecutor So now we can trace in ghastly
clarity the emergence of this blackguardly scheme in
which every step was calculated
   She didn't take the lift
   She climbed the stairs from one floor to the next with a
brief pause perhaps on each landing
   In order to rehearse every move she was about to make
   With him unbeknowing upstairs
   And her
   With her foot in the door in case he should reject her
once more
   It's terrifying

At least let us not be afraid to call things by their
proper name this is the unscrupulous perfidy of a woman
who had worked everything out weighed up all the pros
and cons

Cornaille   He had warned me never to give her his
address

Lachaud   We were on our guard

Cornaille   We knew she was proud intelligent romantic

Lachaud   But we never thought her capable of this

Dr Schlessinger's *surgery at Ulm.*

Sophie   I feel tired Bernd

Dr Schlessinger   I told Frau Schlessinger I had to
perform an operation this evening
   Till late at night

Sophie   Say something nice to me

Cornaille   Xavier was a great guy and Sophie
Auzanneau wasn't the kind of girl a fellow like him could
take as a wife

Dr Schlessinger   In the hospital at Dunkirk there was
a little parrot do you remember?

Sophie   My cat used to prowl around him ferociously
   While the bombs were dropping

Lachaud   Sophie Auzanneau wasn't good enough for
Xavier
   Xavier reproached her with what we all blamed her for
betraying him making a fool of him over Colonna and the
rest
   All she ever wanted was to do her own thing

Sophie   Maybe in my whole life I've never been happier

Sophie*'s room in Lille.*

Xavier   Just over a year ago I asked you to be my wife
  In spite of all that's happened I'm asking you again
today

Francine   He told me at once that he'd known this
woman but it was over
  Since he first got to know me I'm sure absolutely
positive he hasn't seen her again

Lachaud   It's true I never had much sympathy for her
myself

President   So I'd like to ask you whether in your
concern for justice this feeling of repulsion for her has
been moderated?

Sophie   No Xavier don't ask me that

Xavier   Is this your last word?

Lachaud   Did I mention repulsion?
  In any case I'm sure even Xavier
  Wouldn't approve of all this

With a slight gesture around him.

Public Prosecutor   Wouldn't approve of all this? Aha
  But he must have foreseen it all and that must be right
if I'm to believe your own evidence for that telegram was
passed on to you with the words
  May I ask you to repeat them?

Lachaud   'If anything happens to me'

Public Prosecutor   And in fact didn't something
happen to him?
  Something premeditated

Lubet   The life of this young man

Public Prosecutor   Can there be any doubt about it?

Lubet   Like all those who are really strong he was

honest and upright

The happiness of that united family yes who had everything going for them

Has all been swept away destroyed annihilated by Sophie Auzanneau's criminal act

Death broken lives indescribable suffering and it's all due to you Sophie Auzanneau though you seem hardly aware of it

Obsessed as you are with yourself

Hour after hour month after month we've been hanging on your lips for one word of regret or excuse hoping for a hint of repentance in your eyes

But your mouth has been silent your eyes have shown nothing but the glint of a hard heart

So don't expect either pardon or mercy from us

Sophie You'd laugh at my landlady Bernd she watches over me with a gruff kindness I never knew at home

She does my washing for me and brings me tea

Dr Schlessinger You let it get cold you always have you always say you like it piping hot

Then you leave it for hours to get cold

At the **Auzanneaus***' house at Dunkirk.*

Mme Auzanneau She's twenty-four an age when one should think about marriage it's time she settled down

A postcard from her she's all right and she'll be here as usual for her birthday

Sophie She loves telling me off when are you going to stop chasing around like an Amazon?

She's convinced the Amazons are natives a tribe of wild women who are cannibals in South America

M. Auzanneau We spent enough on her education didn't we?

Sophie Yet at the same time I get the feeling she'd

protect me if anyone tried to hurt me

Mme Auzanneau   We did all we could the same as we
would for the others

Cancé   But there you have it she'd been told never to
show her feelings in her face she was taught to distrust
people's faces

Dr Schlessinger   I never met a girl I fancied as much
as you

Sophie   Shut up Bernd

Dr Schlessinger   No let me tell you
  I've a fancy to give up my practice and carry this girl
off to a place where we could go native she'd hunt for
game and I'd roast it
  Somewhere far away near the Amazon

M. Auzanneau   It's like we never existed except to
cough up when she comes collecting for her birthday

Mme Auzanneau   Aren't they all like that these days?

M. Auzanneau   Never a word of thanks no gratitude

Cancé   Monstrous
  The influence of a family whose chief aim was to come
out on top
  Choke any sign of affection and then you can savour
your success such was the appalling upbringing yes
monstrous the Prosecutor found the right word inflicted on
this girl who was encouraged to be proud and arrogant
  A murderess yes Members of the Jury but a victim as
well a victim not a torturer unless it be to torture herself
  The psychiatrists who were rather hastily discounted by
the Prosecutor are may I remind you experts you chose
for yourself
  If you made a bad choice why don't you dismiss them?
You usually have faith in them don't you? It just seems
  That in this case you ignore anything you find
embarrassing

You ignore everything that might tend to demolish your theory of premeditation

A highly improbable theory but gifted as we know you are you make up for your failure to prove it by pursuing it with a ruthlessness which in all my career I have rarely witnessed before

One of the three shots fired was at zero range and you thought fit to label it the *coup de grâce* the death-blow it's so easy to say but

How was it fired? Suddenly as his body crumpled it must have fallen against her and set the revolver off and this turns out to be your *coup de grâce* a set of facts can be interpreted in any way you like

Claudette   There are so many crossed lines Monsieur le Président

I'm not sure that there wasn't a time when he was still in love with her and she had started to love him

We all went to Antwerp once the three of us together to visit a museum

Cancé   If after the attempt to take her life last month my client was able to write 'I believe there's a curse on my family and on me as well' if she was able to understand that the time had come to make a confession

The Fine Art Museum in Antwerp.

Sophie   Look at that character

Xavier   Which one?

Sophie   Leaning out of the window the sporty-looking type with something on his mind up there in the right-hand corner I like that picture

He looks like you

Xavier   And the girl with the red scarf on the other side of the road who seems to be gazing at him she looks like you

Cancé   If she was able to write 'I hope Monsieur and Madame Bergeret can forgive me and take pity on my mother' doesn't this suggest she realised the time had come for her to redeem herself? So on her behalf
And with her own words
I ask you to forgive a girl whose real sin was pride

Sophie   She's horrible

Xavier   I think she's not bad

Sophie   Are you serious?

Xavier   If I met her in the street

Sophie   With that green nose and her yellow hands
I never realised

Xavier   I'd follow her

Sophie   And I'd go for the sporty young raver with something on his mind I don't think the girl has treated him all that well look you can see she's going to eat her heart out

Cancé   And I believe I can ask you to forgive all those parents who think they know how to bring up their children and who make them into a replica of themselves living cheek by jowl with them without learning to know them at all I ask you to forgive the manner in which she defended herself and the blunders she made

Sophie   I wonder if the painter let the red paint run down the canvas on purpose
It looks as if her heart's been bleeding
I never realised

Cancé   Forgive her too for having chosen to defend her
A feeble servant of the law
Who if he refuses to give way to tears can only appeal to you with all the dignity he can muster

Claudette   You're taking your time

Sophie   Come and see and tell us if you think
   If those two got together
   It could lead to anything?

Claudette   It's an enormous picture

Sophie   Who painted it?

Xavier   James Ensor

Recorded voice   Sentences Sophie Auzanneau to penal
servitude for life

The Television Programme

L'Emission de télévision

translated by DAVID *and* HANNAH BRADBY

Characters

Pierre Delile, *53*
Rose Delile, *his wife, 50*
Paul Delile, *their son, 24*
Nicolas Blache, *52*
Caroline Blache, *his wife, 46*
Hubert Phélypeaux, *juge d'instruction (translated as magistrate), 28*
Estelle Belot, *clerk, 25*
Béatrice Lefeuve, *TF1 journalist/researcher, 35*
Adèle Grandjouan, *TF1 journalist/researcher, 30*
Jacky Niel, *freelance journalist, 22*

No scenery, no music, no sound effects. The strict minimum of furniture: only those demanded by the acting. The lighting on the one hand and the form and construction of the tables, chairs, beds, doors and props on the other hand serve to differentiate between the locations of which there are six and whose place on the stage is not fixed.

The play is uninterrupted. It is played without pauses between the scenes. The positioning of the actors and of the corresponding furniture for a given scene is done in full view while the previous scene is finishing, allowing an instantaneous cut from one to the next. A little as if the spectator, provided with a remote control, was zapping in front of the playing space.

The Television Programme was first performed in the UK in July 1992 at the Gate Theatre, London, with the following cast:

Pierre Delile	John Muirhead
Rose Delile	Di Langford
Paul Delile	Toby Whithouse
Nicolas Blache	Alistair Cording
Caroline Blache	Joanna Bacon
Hubert Phélypeaux	Guy Burgess
Estelle Belot	Anastasia Malinoff
Béatrice Lefeuve	Devon Scott
Adèle Grandjouan	Esther Turnage
Jacky Niel	Marva Alexander

Directed by Kim Dambaek
Designed by Kathy Strachan
Costume Designer Bernadette Roberts
Lighting Designer Johanna Town

Author's note

According to French judiciary procedure, once a crime is committed, a magistrate, called *juge d'instruction*, is assigned to the case with the mission of investigating it prior to the trial. His job includes the following: he summons and hears under oath, as witnesses, and outside the presence of lawyers, whoever he deems fit; he has the power to charge (or indict) a suspect when he considers the evidence of guilt is sufficient. Only when a person is charged (or indicted) does their lawyer come in and have access to the dossier. The role of the investigating (or examining) magistrate ends when either the case goes to court or the charge is dismissed. He is assisted in his work by a clerk whose main task is to type under his dictation, and in their presence, the summary statements made by the witnesses, who are then asked to sign them.

Scene One

Examining magistrate's office. Morning.

Mlle Belot *is standing holding a duster, the magistrate is sitting amongst his files.*

Mlle Belot   And there I was
Stuck
I didn't understand a thing
This gurgling kept getting louder I had to escape I
couldn't although I wasn't tied up
I heard the word 'of course'
I wondered if it was him saying it or me I was sure
that it wasn't me and at the same time it couldn't have
been him because blood was streaming from the top of
his head as if he had his skull split in two and rushing
into his wide open mouth
'Of course' again and then I knew that it was my
mouth which uttered the word 'of course' it was him I
recognised him
The blood was clouding his eyes and cascading down
into his open mouth it was him
He was there
Sheepish
Arms wide apart
The one you heard yesterday and who said it wasn't
him
I knew that it was him

Phélypeaux   Enough of your dreams

Mlle Belot   Sometimes they put you on the right track

Phélypeaux   Mademoiselle let's sort out this morning's
agenda
Who do you mean him?
And stop flicking around it isn't your job you are a
clerk of the court not a charwoman

Mlle Belot   Madame Bordet's sick leave has been
extended Monsieur le Juge there'll be no one to replace

her for the whole week
    We can't let the dust cover everything here

Phélypeaux   Him? Not the redhead?

Mlle Belot   No of course
    He confessed his past
    The other his mate who didn't stop saying
    Me rape? But since I wasn't in there
    In the ladies' toilets of the New York
    But since I wasn't in there
    Me rape? Not me
    The one who fiddled with the chain around his neck
with a cross

She shakes out the duster.

    Just look at that dirt

Phélypeaux   Cleaning's not in your job description
    I insist

Mlle Belot   You look quite exhausted if I might also get
personal

Phélypeaux   Nonsense I'm absolutely fit
    We don't make the same use of the night you occupy
yours with dreams me I wander about

Mlle Belot   Go on at that rate and you'll burn yourself
out

Phélypeaux   One sleepless night wears you out whereas
two in a row propels the mind into a state of extreme
wakefulness
    At Bussard's the food is good and the people talk I pick
things up there
    You've never been? Get your boyfriend to take you
there and say I sent you Yvonne is an old-fashioned cook
and her prices are amazing yesterday she had a whole
cooked salmon on the bone some Pouilly to wash it down
    She gets her wine from a little producer who saves her
one third of each vintage we were five at table twelve

bottles were passed around until about three o'clock when
she wanted to close
   There was commissioner Gémier with two of his
inspectors Golet and Mérolleau there was Baron the
deputy public prosecutor at other tables were girls from
the New York they poured out their stories as if they'd
never finish and then I went walking
   I walked by the river between three and five o'clock the
Loire is quite magical the dawn was just coming up when
I found myself in front of my door a warm bath a shave
   Get me the Blache dossier

Scene Two

Kitchen. **Delile** *villa. Evening.*

Delile   Do I swim?

Mme Delile   All the same you can swim a bit
   You manage in the water

Delile   My case how did you hear that
   How did my case

Adèle   Come to our notice?
   It's our job

Béatrice   It's what we're paid for

Adèle   Being on the look-out

Béatrice   Keeping our nose to the ground

Delile   Can you swim? Can you go on a flying trapeze?
   Enough of this farce

A silence.

   Leave me

Mme Delile   He can swim a little like everyone
   But you must excuse him

Delile   Shut up Rose

Mme Delile   Living the way we do not seeing anyone turned in on ourselves for all these years
You can't understand
One loses the ability to converse
Like the chain on his bike which had gone rusty since he hadn't touched it for so long
One day I said to him Pierre what if you went out to get some fresh air with your bike

Delile   Rose shut up

Mme Delile   He didn't even reply
I tried it again

Adèle   So you go cycling?

Mme Delile   Does he go cycling?
His bike was the only thing
After he was made redundant he continued to do some but less and less and then no more
Two and a half years went by without him touching it and he got a paunch even though we were counting the pennies for our food our son Paul told him one day Dad you are getting a spare tyre they shouted about it because Paul never says the right thing at the right moment and my husband couldn't put up with anything he'd got irritable
Isn't that true Pierre? One day you startled me I had lost hope a bit and then I catch you with your oil can greasing the chain of your bike

Adèle   He got over it then?

Mme Delile   That's saying a lot
There were ups and downs
At least he wasn't just a couch potato stuck there from morning to night

Adèle   Summing up Monsieur Delile you had been out of work for

Mme Delile   I told you two years and six months

Adèle   Then you got on your bike
Did you ride it every day?

Mme Delile   Tell them Pierre
Tell them that it saved you
Tell them like you told me that to get up at seven to
do your thirty kilometres in the morning
If nothing else it chased off those ideas of topping
yourself

Adèle   So you did thirty kilometres every morning?

Mme Delile   Even in heavy rain he went out
Returning he'd find lunch laid out on the table and you
know what he'd start to talk a bit

Adèle   Because he'd stopped talking?

Mme Delile   Except rehashing the same thing over and
over

Béatrice   Your kitchen's nice just right wouldn't you say
Adèle?
Spacious really is it here you spend most of your time?
Rather than in your living room?

Mme Delile   Endlessly reviewing the technical details of
each and every solution like shoot himself or the beam in
the attic or tie a rock around his neck or set fire to the
house and so on setting fire to the house is what he came
back to most often and I had to tell him whether I
wanted to consider Rose I am not forcing you

Adèle   To stay with him?

Béatrice   Inside?

Mme Delile   If you do that Pierre

Delile   Finished?

Adèle   Quite the contrary perhaps Monsieur Delile
Apologies if this is all too painful to you

But perhaps quite the contrary for you
It's all beginning

A silence.

Delile   How did you learn about my case?

Adèle   A bit of luck a bit of nous

Béatrice   Antennae

Adèle   You have to be able to take off

Béatrice   Chance

Adèle   The art of guiding it

Béatrice   Glide with the wind

Adèle   Love people

Béatrice   That is important

Adèle   From the top of the sky

Béatrice   Wings spread out

Adèle   With the help of providence

Béatrice   Dive

Mme Delile   Like angels?

Laughter.

Adèle   It's their job to love

A silence.

Béatrice   Your story is a happy story
   The way that we conceive this programme there will be
a certain number of tragic cases as varied as possible
which will be linked by a common theme unemployment
and the destructive effect that it produces on the fabric of
the family but also on the profound inner self of the
individual
   And then there will be a happy story
   The story of a man who has passed the fateful age of

fifty unemployed for years and who finds a way of making
a new start
    Assuming that your case is taken on you will be in a
real sense the star of the programme your brightness
alone will pierce the rather gloomy mass of the whole
picture
    Do you swim?

Mme Delile   He can swim a bit

Béatrice   You stand on the beach hesitating for a
moment and splash you throw yourself into the stream
    Then we see you do a few strokes

Mme Delile   Excuse me
    Didn't you say the programme would be made live in
your studio?

Béatrice   That's right and you will both be
    You Monsieur and you Madame
    Live on the set of TF1 among all the long-term
unemployed people of over fifty invited to take part
    Vincent Bonnemalle will be among you he will go
round and shoot questions
    To you just as to all the others
    But the whole point of a programme like this is to
incorporate inserts
    With a stroke of Vincent's magic wand the picture of
the set fades and the television audience finds itself here in
your kitchen you sitting at the table with your wife or
inside Bricomarket where we see you starting in your new
job or on the beach beside the Loire
    Woven into the talk show there will be flashes of real
life
    Short films which must naturally be shot before the day
of the broadcast

Adèle   And whose heroes are at the same time present
on the set

Béatrice   Exactly

You will be at the same time inside and outside
Inside I mean on the set among the other unemployed
people
Outside that is at home at your work or on the beach

Delile   On my bike?

Béatrice   Well why not?

Adèle   Standing on the pedals climbing a hill

Delile   You said among the other unemployed people

Béatrice   Yes live

Mme Delile   Why yes Pierre it's clear excuse him

Delile   You said among the others didn't you?

Béatrice   Why yes

Delile   The other unemployed people? As far as you are
concerned I am one unemployed person among others?

Béatrice   The unemployed people stop I withdraw the
word other

Delile   Mixed in with them?

Béatrice   Perhaps a bit apart
Vincent Bonnemalle sees to sorting out the studio
placing

Delile   So you're mixing everyone up
In the same bag the unemployed and those who aren't
any more?

Mme Delile   Would you like a cup of tea?
We've had no visitors for so long and so many things
happen in one go they know what they're doing Pierre
they will put us wherever is proper

Béatrice   And I'd love a slice of lemon
Can't you see? The inserts will single you out

Adèle   You'll have been seen pedalling

You'll have been seen on the job at Bricomarket

Béatrice   What is it exactly do you do there?

Delile   I come and go

Mme Delile   Explain calmly Pierre

Delile   A certain proportion of clients aren't satisfied
That's because there are more and more people who start on DIY having no idea of what they're up to
That means they buy materials which aren't right for the job
Then they want their money back
The management is trying out the idea of having a customer advisor patrolling in each of their superstores
I have to be all over the shop and go up to anyone who looks uncertain

Adèle   That's excellent it's very good

Béatrice   So you'll be seen doing exactly that

Adèle   Then fade to an interview of your boss

Béatrice   For what reason Monsieur le Directeur did you choose to hire someone over fifty for this job?

Adèle   All things considered we gave preference to a seasoned technical expert

Béatrice   Age means experience I see only advantages in it straightaway the client is reassured

Adèle   This prejudice against age in my opinion is nothing but a type of racism
Surely you have come across people past the age of fifty who're still in their prime?

Béatrice   At Bricomarket we react against this form of discrimination which prevalent as it may be

Adèle   Is destructive to the individual

Béatrice   Harmful to the whole framework of society

Adèle   And tell me Monsieur le Directeur this Monsieur Delile is he up to it?

Béatrice   Listen of course it's an extra salary
But it's apparent already that this cost is more than offset by the growth in turnover attributable to his activity amongst the shelves

Adèle   His presence has been felt very quickly

Delile   You know I have only just started

Béatrice   Oh but it didn't take you long

Adèle   When is it you took up your duties?

Mme Delile   Yesterday he started

Adèle   Oh yesterday?

Mme Delile   But it went well
Didn't it Pierre? You were buoyant when you got back home last night
Tell them

A silence.

Delile   When you've turned into an animal
The bike I couldn't
I didn't want to be seen
An animal goes into hiding

Béatrice   But you are happy

Delile   You can't put yourself back together at a stroke
They can make me wash floors on the night shift if they want anything they want
But anyway I'm sure it won't last

Béatrice   Why?

Delile   It's too good to be true

Mme Delile   Yes can you believe it?

Béatrice   I believe it absolutely

Delile   Yes you

Mme Delile   Pierre listen to them

Adèle   For the programme it's vital that everyone sees
that you believe it

Béatrice   Yes and yet
Wait let me speak
The feeling not altogether gone of being an animal
That could be rather interesting

Adèle   All the others are going to be heart-rending
This man must be radiant

Béatrice   It can be a mixture of both
The radiance still faltering

Adèle   We need the maximum contrast shade and light

Béatrice   We'll get it
We must count on the dynamics of the programme
If you are selected to represent hope
Something within you will change Monsieur Delile

Delile   Yes
That doesn't mean that they're going to keep me

Mme Delile   It's not your nature to doubt
Between you and Blache you're the one who always
thought that things could only go right
Pierre
Pierre things can turn around
Listen to them
You know that my husband even in his difficult
moments only saw the good side of things always a
cheerful word
They are the ones who go under the quickest because
they believe that nothing can happen to them
The doctor said so when it happens to them they
crumble whereas the likes of Blache
Blache was always worried about the next day even

though everything was going well for him

Delile   You'd better not mention Blache

Mme Delile   What's up with you? Pierre
You did tell me that it was well over

Delile   And that's why you're mentioning him again?

Mme Delile   Sure since it's over

Delile   It's over we won't talk about it again

Mme Delile   I'm talking of those silly ideas you once
had
Oh Pierre that can't be

Delile   Can't be what?
Over?

Mme Delile   For twenty years it's been over

Delile   And you're harking back to it

Mme Delile   We must explain to these ladies
I can't believe that that should resurface

Delile   There's nothing to be explained

Béatrice   Even so

Mme Delile   Blache was his lifelong colleague and his
best friend
Both were made redundant on the day that the
company closed down the division they were running
You'd think that misfortune brings people closer to each
other but it's the other way round
Pierre no longer wanted to see anyone and even less
those who were closest to him
I thought that once he'd found another job

Adèle   Blache found work?

Mme Delile   Oh him? Yes six months back

Delile   They should go and see Blache
He'll do for them
He's landed a permanent job and he's in his old trade
He'd revel in your tomfooleries and swimming is his
favourite pastime

Mme Delile   Pierre
There's no question that people who always expect the
worst when it happens they're not hurt half as badly
Blache didn't suffer the same

Delile   Go ahead and say it

Mme Delile   The same degradation

Delile   He'll deliver the kind of story you want in the
morning when I shave I can hardly look at myself do you
expect me to show that on telly?

Béatrice   This strain showing all over your face
The marks of suffering
It's good stuff because it says an awful lot

Delile   The telly I don't know what the telly is like any
more we sold the set a year ago after the car the washing
machine the silver because to live on eighty six francs per
day once you've reached the end of your benefit and you
have no more right to anything because you aren't worth
a thing I am tired of seeing you tired you understand
that? Tired

He leaves abruptly.

Mme Delile   If you take Blache instead of him
He won't get over it

Adèle   As we told you he is not the only candidate
Vincent Bonnemalle wants us to offer him at least two
candidates for him to make a choice

Mme Delile   I got that all right
But not Blache

If Blache were to be picked

Adèle   Who's suggested we look him up?

Mme Delile   Can't you see
It's part of all he's been at to destroy himself
Because he's not a man any more in his own eyes
Because society has rejected him and so there's nothing
left for him but to reject himself
See our living room he can't sit there any more for
three years we've confined ourselves to the kitchen
Oh but
I know him well enough you can be sure your
programme would make him the proudest man in the
world and you have nothing to fear oh you won't be
disappointed
Of course this whole thing frightens him because he's
got to come to terms with himself again and that doesn't
happen in one go I mean recouping the feeling of being
someone
He is scared of not being up to it that's all
In this programme myself I've got things I want to say
as well you know
Things I can say better than anybody oh I haven't told
you anything yet
One day he came home with a flower that he had
bought a red rose with a long stalk the most expensive
when we hadn't even enough to buy ourselves potatoes
because I am called Rose
And we stayed in each other's arms
A long time as if dead it was like death
No one nothing around us no more shame
Monsieur and Madame Blache that's something else I
can guarantee that they were not destroyed like we were
there wouldn't be the same emotion
I'm positive and you've said it yourself this programme
would
And as a swimmer he's as good as the next man you
don't need a champion do you?

Scene Three

Magistrate's office. Daytime.

Papers are flying off the desk.

Phélypeaux   Mademoiselle Belot how come
All these draughts?

Mlle Belot   One and the same draught always the same
When the wind blows from the north
That pane that they haven't replaced
I reported it upstairs

Phélypeaux   Verbally?

Mlle Belot   I wrote a maintenance note

Phélypeaux   Pester those morons
Your name

Delile   You know it as you summoned me

Phélypeaux   Nevertheless Monsieur Delile
Your surname first name age marital status profession

Delile   Delile Pierre fifty-three years old married one
child customer advisor at Bricomarket

Phélypeaux   Place of abode

Delile   Two Turret Way Orleans

Phélypeaux   Are you related to Nicolas Blache or have
you been in his service?

Delile   In his service? He was in mine

Phélypeaux   Please reply yes or no

Delile   No

Phélypeaux   Swear that you'll tell the truth and nothing
but the truth

Delile   I swear

Phélypeaux   I hear you as witness to the affair of the murder of Nicolas Blache which took place on the night of the fifth to sixth of June

Delile   I wasn't witness to anything

Phélypeaux   But you knew the victim well and for a long time
   I want you to talk to me about him
   Will you tell me what you know of him and also retrace your relationship with him
   Anything the matter?
   And tell me of the fluctuations in this relationship

Delile   When his affairs were going so brightly
   That it should happen
   I can't get over it

Phélypeaux   To the point

Delile   I hired Blache

Phélypeaux   Be specific where how and for what post

Delile   As engineer

Phélypeaux   You were

Delile   Director of manufacture of the paper division of the Grange company at Orleans we made diaries

Phélypeaux   Your age at that time?

Delile   Thirty-two I started at Grange straight after military service as a packer in the warehouse

Phélypeaux   And you climbed up the ranks
   All the way up?
   That's remarkable

Delile   Monsieur Grange quickly noticed that I was inquisitive
   I poked my nose in everywhere and gave him ideas of how to bring the costs down
   He promoted me to head of operational methods and

then production manager

Phélypeaux   You recruited Blache who was a qualified engineer and who found himself reporting to you
That may have been awkward

Delile   We complemented each other
His skills were in product development he had a knack of anticipating changes in consumer tastes
There was friction sometimes because modifying design necessitates the acquisition of new equipment before the old stuff is written off
The excess costs must be offset by an increase in turnover
Most of the time the introduction of a new design produced a jump in sales for fifteen years we succeeded in frustrating every effort by our competitors
Even though most of them were ten or fifteen times our size
But we formed a flexible close-knit team

Phélypeaux   You and him?

Delile   Yes

Phélypeaux   There's never been a problem?

Delile   Professionally no

Phélypeaux   And in your private lives?

Delile   He built himself a villa close to mine
We saw each other a lot

Phélypeaux   You were friends?

Delile   You could call it that

Phélypeaux   And then there was a cooling off?

Delile   Nothing unusual these things happen
No consequence

Phélypeaux   Woman trouble?

Delile After a while we sorted it out

Phélypeaux Will you give me the details of this break-up?

Delile These things fade
One forgets

Phélypeaux Really?

Scene Four

Living room. **Blache** *villa. Evening.*

A bottle and three glasses. A dog.

Adèle And so now?

Blache Now I consider that this long ordeal has had a positive impact on my personality
Perhaps you are free to have dinner with us this evening we could continue this conversation couldn't we darling over a small meal and take our time
You can't imagine how valiant my wife has been all along I will spare you the humiliations of all sorts we went through
Realising that we used to have everything

Mme Blache The way people looked at us

Blache They wouldn't even look at us

Mme Blache People we knew

Blache Avoided us

Mme Blache We'd become a nuisance
All the same there were some who were taking it upon themselves to ask well how is it going
Their way of addressing someone who's going under to be on the receiving end of that

Blache Me old? Well yes my poor Blache at fifty a

man is through won't you stay then? No frills

Mme Blache   Pot luck

Blache   Chronologically
First the shock

Mme Blache   Indeed
Disbelief

Blache   Then a period of euphoria which lasted a few
months a combative phase answering all the ads
I was going to bounce back
Find a position at least the equivalent

Mme Blache   Typing fifteen letters a day
Following them up
Waiting for the replies

Blache   There were no replies
Or it was no

Mme Blache   And progressively panic set in

Blache   Absolutely yes you can say that
Doubt grows and turns into certainty
You're not worth a fart

Mme Blache   I saw him dissolve before my very eyes

Adèle   That seems just fine to me
Do you swim?

Blache   I jog I swim yes and I play tennis
Some people go in for armchair sport in front of the
telly
I only watch the telly for the documentaries and some
of the talk shows

Adèle   I imagine you follow *The World and I*

Mme Blache   Does he follow it

Blache   I wouldn't miss one I was fascinated by last
month's what was it on?

Mme Blache   The return of faith

Blache   Right there was one sequence I don't think I'll ever forget
   Among the palm trees the collective suicide of I can't remember which sect
   Wasn't it taking place on some island?

Adèle   Not exactly but never mind
   We did carry an insert on the carnage in Guyana
   Now tell me
   How did you get yourself out of this predicament
   There are so very few of you who have

Blache   You know my wife and I often wondered how Vincent Bonnemalle manages to find participants who are usually so outstanding I suppose the answer is that he's got super-stars among his scouts

Adèle   One tip leads to another

Blache   Superb really

Adèle   We get the scent

Blache   I won't ask you how you found me I think it's marvellous
   So to your question

Mme Blache   Come take a seat
   Be careful the plate is boiling

Blache   The reply lies in the two syllables of the name Crusoe

Adèle   That smells good

Blache   Crusoe on his island triggered it in my forced idleness I had set about arranging my books in alphabetical order
   Imagine one of my childhood favourites in its red binding
   I skimmed through it and then I suppose it worked on my mind all night when I woke up I said to my wife

Adèle   This is delicious

Mme Blache   A very simple recipe he said to me

Blache   Stupid as it may seem
Tell her

Mme Blache   He said to me I'm Crusoe on his island
not an oldie but a castaway who has succeeded you hear
Caroline succeeded

Blache   In setting foot on a desert island
What does a castaway do? Organise his survival even if
the wait is long a sail will finally appear
In the meantime facing the expanse of emptiness
remain active scrutinise the horizon ready to send signals

Mme Blache   He started to go through the whole
economic press once again

Blache   I stumble across a short article about a bright
little outfit whose fault was they wanted to go too far too
quickly
Bankruptcy
I track down the number I insist on speaking to the
chief executive I propose my services asking no salary but
a commitment to hire me at the end if my intervention
bears fruit
Deal closed you can imagine that from then on

Mme Blache   Nicolas got stuck in

Blache   In six months the business was back on track

Mme Blache   Today he is the founder's right-hand man
with the title of Assistant General Manager

Blache   You know what?
I said to myself that one day it would be worth talking
about it on the telly but I never imagined
Even so to find oneself one day on the other side of the
screen Caroline

Adèle   And would Madame Blache accept as well?

Mme Blache   Oh Nicolas I don't know

Blache   You will have things to say more than enough
you too darling

Adèle   You'll be both at the same time inside
    Inside I mean live on the stage among the group of
long-term unemployed people of over fifty compèred by
Vincent
    And outside you know the system of inserts here in
your home at your desk and we'll have to get down to
the Loire on a beach your usual beach

Scene Five

Le New York Bar. Night.

A little round table. Glasses.

Jacky   You know I'm not bothered if that's what you're
after and if I get what I'm counting on
    But I'm not sure if that's what you want and for me to
sleep with someone as filthy as you
    And so confused

Paul   Come on

Jacky   And you stink

Paul   What are you counting on? You an accountant?

Jacky   I am a journalist   .

Paul   Sure

Jacky   You don't believe me

She shows him her card.

    I reckon you have things to tell me so I came here
where I was told I could find you
    If I'm wrong it's my problem
    Le New York quite a place

A major discovery I owe it to you I never would've
guessed a place as scuzzy as this exists in Orleans

Paul   And AIDS are you curious about that too?
You couldn't care less?

Jacky   Tell me what you like
Anything's possible
It seems to me you're trying to show off
Anyway there are precautions

Paul   And if I don't want any?
There are the delights of sharing

Jacky   I know
Hang on Paul

Paul   Aren't you coming?

Jacky   Not right away
Show me that arm you inject?

Paul   Sometimes

Jacky   Men?

Paul   Sometimes

Jacky   You lie sometimes as well
All the time perhaps
This won't get me anywhere

A silence.

You know

She gets up.

Paul   You're in a hurry? You're off?

Jacky   It's just my luck
Rotten sources of information always
I'm learning the hard way
Like it or not I must
I simply have to get a break just once
Tell me were you seeing Blache sometimes?

    If you are nice to me
    If you help me

Paul Will you be nice to me?

Jacky I have a good reserve of things to offer
    In exchange for which

Paul I have a stock of videos in my nest we could watch a couple and do nice things together

Jacky Later
    I have copy to hand in before two o'clock this morning
    I'll come back to get you if you're still around

Scene Six

Kitchen. **Delile** *villa. End of the afternoon.*

No one. Enter **Delile**, *in a white overall, white trousers and cap, on which is embroidered the words 'Customer Advisor'. A bandage on one finger. He stands for a moment. Sits. Gets up. Starts getting changed. Enter* **Mme Delile**.

Delile Where've you been?

Mme Delile How was it?

Delile You're out of breath

Mme Delile I hurried
    I wanted to be here on your return
    And then
    Paul has more problems I'll tell you about it but tell me first
    How was it?

Delile D'you know they don't have a cloakroom for the employees

Mme Delile But it went okay?

Delile What it amounts to is

You pace about between the shelves and address people
Sir ma'am can I be of assistance
Most of the time you can't they just wander about not
wanting anything in particular

Mme Delile   Soon you'll know

Delile   What?

Mme Delile   How to make out those who're really
looking for something in particular

Delile   Yes

Mme Delile   There's bound to be some who do

Delile   Yes

Mme Delile   You say yes
But you won't even listen to me

Delile   You aren't saying anything
Make me a coffee

Mme Delile   I've been going over and over it again I
went to see Helen and thrash it out with her
That finger

Delile   It's nothing
They don't have a cloakroom but they do have a first-
aid room
Demonstrating a circular saw for a lady in a fur coat
who wanted a present for her son
One false move

Mme Delile   It's such an extraordinary chance
The chance to be able to say what you had to hold
back for such a long time
Show who you are and that you exist
And that you're working

Delile   I don't want to demoralise you Rose
But this job's phoney they thought it up for the
occasion

It's an advertising gimmick they may even get paid by
the telly for hiring someone over fifty and then get lost
sorry good luck
   An arrangement between Bricomarket and TF1

Mme Delile   Helen thinks so too her cousin Berthier
runs the Bricomarket branch at Montpellier it doesn't cost
them much to make promises
   They hire and the next day they back out and it's
never anybody's fault because there are so many levels of
decision
   Which is why Helen is convinced that you must seize
upon this chance to get your message across
   Never mind if then they drop you Pierre

Paul, *blood-soaked face has entered, stands apart.*

Delile   They'll take Blache

Mme Delile   You shouldn't have talked about him

Delile   Who talked about him? You did

Mme Delile   How dare you say so?

Delile   You first

Mme Delile   But who told them that they should

Delile   Yes I told them
   Because Blache is who they need

Mme Delile   And you're the one who knows?
   Vincent Bonnemalle knows better than you
   Voice is the thing and yours carries well
   Blache swallows half his words
   Honesty's written all over your face
   You can't blame Blache but it's something that counts
when someone is on the screen and you feel what comes
out is genuine
   You've got more wrinkles than him but Pierre that isn't
a disadvantage
   Do you reckon those girls would have devoted that

amount of time to you if they didn't think that you are a good subject?

Now all you have to do is cross that bridge make it clear to them that you've made up your mind

Delile   Too late Rose

Can you see me do this

Mme Delile   Yes I can see you

Absolutely I see you saying what we have been through

And the end of the nightmare

Delile   Who says it's ended?

Mme Delile   Saying it will put an end to it

Delile   But I said no

Mme Delile   It was your first reaction

They must have expected that

They are waiting for you to call them back

They left a telephone number at their hotel

You must ask for Béatrice Lefeuve or Adèle

Grandjouan it's written there dial the number

Paul

How long have you been there?

I thought

Paul   Why they didn't even bother keeping me overnight at the police station those arseholes

Mme Delile   Paul

He's injured too my God

Paul   They were at a loose end they were hanging about they picked me up like I was a ball

They played football with me they were practising passes Golet knocked me over to Mérolleau

They had a bit of fun then they told me to bugger off

How's the job Dad?

Delile   Little shit

Mme Delile   Go and wash under the tap

I'll get you some disinfectant

Paul (*seizing the cap*) Customer Advisor Bricomarket
My Dad has a bright white uniform aren't I proud of
my Dad he won the battle of Bricomarket
Austerlitz and now Bricomarket General Delile takes
possession of Bricomarket
Fame and glory he is going to be on the telly

Scene Seven

Magistrate's office. Daytime.

Mme Blache It's stifling in here

Phélypeaux Your emotion is understandable

Mme Blache I'm having trouble breathing

Phélypeaux Your surname first name age marital status
profession

Mme Blache Blache Caroline forty-six years old widow

Phélypeaux Profession

Mme Blache None

Phélypeaux Place of abode

Mme Blache Fifteen Turret Way

Phélypeaux Are you related to Nicolas Blache or have
you been in his service?

Mme Blache He was my husband

Phélypeaux Swear that you'll tell the truth and nothing
but the truth

Mme Blache I swear

Phélypeaux I hear you as witness to the affair of the
murder of Nicolas Blache which took place on the night
of the fifth to sixth of June

Mme Blache   It was the first Wednesday of the month
Monsieur le Juge perhaps the murderers knew it
  That every first Wednesday of the month
  Because I am responsible for Tupperware sales in the
neighbourhood every first Wednesday of the month I
organise a Tupperware party in the home of one or other
of my clients
  When I got home that night the church clock was
striking eleven the front door was ajar that surprised me
and the rest you know I have already explained it so
many times to the police
  The lamp was on he was lying down like every evening
on the sofa it took a few moments before I realised I
thought he was sleeping but Azur our old dog was going
round him and then me and whining
  Nothing in the room had been disturbed
  He must've been asleep when the murderer came in so
he could come right up to him place the mouth of the
revolver right on the fabric of his shirt
  It was a shirt I had just bought him
  Shot in cold blood

Phélypeaux   With the barrel actually touching according
to the ballistic examination

Mme Blache   But then he must have crept in somehow
  We always bolt the door with the insecurity now in this
neighbourhood

Phélypeaux   And no evidence of a break-in
  Who apart from you and your husband had a key?
  No one? There were only your two sets of keys?
  Please do try Mademoiselle Belot could serve you a
little tonic

Mme Blache   I'd rather ask you to open the window if
I may

Phélypeaux   Sorry there are draughts which make the
papers fly about

Mme Blache   Those Wednesday evenings he usually waited for me at home and sometimes before I got back he dozed off
Returning from the office Monsieur le Juge he'd be washed out after three years of this suspension of activity he hadn't yet recovered his old punch
Almost the whole weekend he stayed slumped on that sofa he who'd been so keen on keeping fit

Phélypeaux   Any strains in your relationship

Mme Blache   We were a loving couple our bond became even tighter during those trying years
I can't describe to you Monsieur le Juge how deeply I shared his happiness when that job materialised
It's true he did become a bit absent irascible

Phélypeaux   Tensions accumulated

Mme Blache   Far from it he had mood swings
Dr Delalande told me you had to expect this for a while

Phélypeaux   Off and on your neighbours heard shouts

Mme Blache   I had to let off steam too

Phélypeaux   Naturally
Let's now consider the whole picture in outline Madame Blache
A man makes a success of his life and then whoops he trips up
Then what he achieves is remarkable indeed after the downward slide he climbs out of the pit
He's reinstated in the establishment
Do you know of anyone who could've resented this comeback?

Mme Blache   But who?

Phélypeaux   Bitterness

Mme Blache   I don't see

Phélypeaux   Vengeance?

Mme Blache   For what?

Phélypeaux   There must be a motive Madame Blache

Mme Blache   Was he telling me everything?

Phélypeaux   Try and concentrate on the few days prior
to the event
   Any exceptional circumstances?

Mme Blache   For a week Nicolas was going through a
period of great excitement
   He had been chosen out of I don't know how many
former unemployed people to be the star of a big
television programme

Phélypeaux   Take this down Mademoiselle Belot (*He
dictates, she types.*) Everyone around me knows that the first
Wednesday of each month I am out of the house being
occupied with an evening sale of Tupperware products
stop that Wednesday on my return it was eleven o'clock I
found my husband killed by a bullet in the heart on his
sofa stop I immediately informed the police stop you
didn't say it but you did it so I will add it to the
statement nothing disturbed in the place stop the front
door was ajar stop no one apart from my husband and I
had the key stop I did not know of an enemy of my
husband's stop six months ago my husband found work
after a long period of unemployment stop we made a
united couple and our arguments were superficial stop my
husband was feverishly preparing to take part in a
television broadcast when he was victim of this crime stop
have you anything to add? Do you accept this as a record
of your words? Would you like to reread them? Then
would you sign your statement?
   And now try to get a little rest Madame Blache
   I thank you

Exit **Mme Blache**.

Phélypeaux   Deceitful little woman
   Her discomfort was feigned

Mlle Belot   Women always think they must put on a
show of their grief
   Even when it's real

Phélypeaux   Often this sort of thing rejuvenates the
ladies
   She'll have a chance to make a fresh start
   Unless
   Turn around please

Mlle Belot   You're not ruling out

Phélypeaux   The blouse you're wearing
   You hadn't introduced me to it as yet

Mlle Belot   And for good reason
   A present received yesterday

Phélypeaux   Why the sigh?
   Your admirer knows you well and he has taste although
turn around the other way
   I'm not ruling anything out
   Although that low neck seems a little exaggerated for
the office
   Anything which might distract the witness must be
avoided

Mlle Belot   Or the magistrate

Phélypeaux   Next Mademoiselle would you please show
in the next witness

Scene Eight

Hotel room. Night time.

Béatrice *lying on the bed, in pyjamas, reading the* Radio
Times. **Adèle** *enters, undoes her jacket. A silence.*

Adèle   All right
I'm perfectly well aware I've pulled one over on you
So I went to see him

Béatrice   By yourself and without letting me know
Who is running this team?

Adèle   You are

Béatrice   Fine
I know there's no such thing as owing anything to
anyone

Adèle   I know what I owe you
You're sold on Delile and Delile is useless
I've done this for the sake of the programme

Béatrice   And did you have to blow me out too?
We were going to have a meal we could've talked it
through
You might even have convinced me

Adèle   You weren't going to let go
So I went for it

Béatrice   While I was waiting for you wondering where
you were
You really had me going
Have you had dinner?

Adèle   With Blache

Béatrice   Oh well done
Is she a good little cook?
I bring you into Vincent's fold I teach you the tricks of
the trade
Now you have to destroy Béatrice
Visit Blache alone
Certainly not consult Béatrice beforehand
Bypass Béatrice to make direct links with Vincent
For we've got on intimate terms with Vincent
We've spent a weekend with him
With cutbacks there's not enough room for Adèle and

Béatrice one will have to be ditched
   The ordinary course of things I suppose

Adèle   Time's getting short Béatrice and private life

Béatrice   Has nothing to do with it
   Oh no we keep that quite separate
   Vincent is so scrupulous your arse is one thing work
quite another
   The ordinary course of things granted no one owes
anything to anyone

Adèle   I know what I owe you
   I also know that you're as stubborn as they come
   Thirdly this programme has got to be a winner

Béatrice   Fourthly you want my position

Adèle   Fourthly using Delile the risk of going wrong is
too big

Béatrice   Fourthly sacrifice Béatrice

Adèle   Fourthly don't screw up the programme and
Vincent and us too
   For fuck's sake
   Audience ratings are a fact of life
   Three months of decline doesn't matter much don't
bother changing anything it'll sort itself out

Béatrice   Don't change anything except perhaps ditch
Béatrice
   Béatrice is from the old school
   Ideas which were good but not any longer
   Fortunately Adèle's on hand to help Vincent rise to the
challenge

Adèle   If you could stop talking such crap for a moment
   We could discuss this

Béatrice   Is it really worth the effort?

Adèle   So I got one over you
   Can we leave it at that?

Good
Another visit to Blache is a must we'll go together

Béatrice   Agreed

Adèle   Blache presents the opposite picture
Delile would offer more emotional potential because he's still up to his neck in it
With Blache we'd get a more striking scenario
Forceful
Telling
He'd project the image of a hero

Béatrice   Physically?

Adèle   Good posture
Less stature than Delile but more drive

Béatrice   His wife?

Adèle   The classic resilient spouse not as touching a leading lady as you'd wish but she's passable

Béatrice   The setting?

Adèle   Delile's kitchen has more character but then
Petit-bourgeois décor it'll do
There's a dog which is good
The problem with Delile is his story is shaky
Blache's story hangs together better
It's the kind Vincent can get hold of and turn into an exemplary tale
All the ingredients are there to enthral the audience
Whereas Delile's
His on-screen happiness
Who'd believe in it?

Béatrice   Did you go to your room before coming in here?
You called Vincent
Your jacket and bag were only to fool me

Adèle   I love you very much Béatrice

Béatrice   Yeah?

Scene Nine

Paul's *room. Small hours of the morning.*

A bed on which they are lying, eyes fixed on a television set, of which only the back is seen.

Jacky   How many times?

Paul   Three

Jacky   How long?

Paul   Two months plus three months in all five months
The first was a suspended sentence

Jacky   And you still have your pad in the family house
I don't lodge with mine any more finished

Paul   I've split a few times
I go back

Jacky   I have lunch there every Sunday
Because of the cat it's the same age as me
And then I do like them

Paul   How old?

Jacky   Twenty-two we were born the same month

Paul   That's old
For a journalist it's young

Jacky   I started two years ago
I'm crazy about the law I would have liked to be a judge but you need to have a degree

Paul   Don't you need one to be a journalist?

Jacky   I got in on cheek
I kept attending court hearings taking notes I started writing accounts and taking them along to the *Orleans*

Messenger none of them was ever accepted until that fateful day
It was a run-of-the-mill case pickpocketing but he had managed to stash a gun in his crotch he fired at the prosecutor and there were no journalists in the room
Except me

Paul   You didn't happen to see me being hauled up did you?

Jacky   I don't remember

Paul   There are so many
Aren't there?

Jacky   Yes now fate's just got to show up on my side once again to lift me out of this hole Orleans
It's choked up

Paul   To go where?

Jacky   Paris telly

Paul   Pretty reckless huh?
You come with a guy like me up to his room

Jacky   I simply must have a breakthrough

Paul   A guy that does all sorts

Jacky   No other way

Paul   For what?

Jacky   To get on
If you're not born into the upper crust
My father is a farmhand
I'm not afraid of you

Paul   You're on good terms with yourself
It's happened to me once or twice you know
This kind of feeling
The rest of the time

Jacky   What?

Paul   I don't know

Jacky   Better off dead?

Paul   Yeah but life sticks on

Jacky   And makes you do all sorts

Paul   Why do you say that?

Jacky   You said so

Paul   Yeah
Nothing matters

Jacky   What about girls?

Paul   Pick-ups I don't have the instinct
What graft do you need me for?
Don't tell me right away
We're just right

Jacky   Not necessarily graft

She takes his hand.

This hand needs to take your hand
This isn't graft
I need that breakthrough Paul

Paul   And I need to put my head here

*He puts his head on **Jacky**'s stomach.*

Jacky   Luckily for journalists people need news
I need to make my name as a journalist
If I could find the key to the Blache affair
There aren't many cases as sensational
It's making national headlines and the enquiry's at a
standstill

Paul   You think that I did it?

*She laughs. She lifts up **Paul**'s head. They change position. They
are head to toe. She puts one hand around **Paul**'s ankle, under his
trousers.*

Jacky   Not on your life
Even if you can do all sorts
Not that
I need you to tell me
I'd like to know your mother
How is it between you and your mother?

Paul   What for?

Jacky   My breakthrough

Paul   Are you going to ask me other questions?

Jacky   One other

Paul   What's in it for me?

Jacky   A surprise perhaps

Paul   She gets at me but it's okay

Jacky   And your father
How does he treat you?

Paul   He can't stand me he never could stand me

Jacky   Your pseudo-father

Paul   What did you say?

Jacky   Do you really suspect nothing?
Your mother and Nicolas Blache

Paul   What?

Jacky   One of two things Paul
Either you are the son of Pierre Delile or you are the
son of Nicolas Blache

He springs up.

Paul   Say that again

Jacky   In the neighbourhood amongst the old folk the
rumour has it that something happened between Madame
Delile and Nicolas Blache twenty-five years ago and that
you were born and the two men didn't speak to one

another for years

Working together and ignoring each other that's what the old people say if you manage to get a moment's privacy with one or other of them because otherwise it's buttoned up lips they sit tight on their little secrets

If there's anything in this story it gives one an insight into you Paul

A story that's not your making but you're the one who pays the penalty

Paul   Why do you tell me all this?

Jacky   Because you're a forlorn child and have nothing to lose

Nothing to lose and perhaps something to gain

Me too perhaps I have something to gain there

Pierre Delile and Nicolas Blache did they meet at any time in the last few days?

Recently did Pierre see Nicolas?

Scene Ten

Living room. **Blache** *villa. Evening.*

Blache *standing,* **Mme Blache** *sitting, in front of a large mirror. Close by, a tape-recorder. Azur, the dog.*

Mme Blache   That was good Nicolas

Blache   Not too long?

Mme Blache   I was captivated

See I've got tears in my eyes

Blache   For them it's always too long I'm desperate

The things I've got to say that are vital if I deliver them straight away it'll fall flat

If I start more softly like I just did and let the emotion progressively set in

The moment of saying what's vital my speech will be cut off

In all these broadcasts they always cut you off

Mme Blache   There is so much to say
Try to shorten it

Blache   What a nightmare

Mme Blache   Don't get yourself worked up sometimes
it's enough to say just one thing
Like the gas chamber
What you said about the thought of the gas chamber
crossing your mind many a time the thought of finishing
us both off

Blache   But it's disastrous if they interrupt me then can
you imagine

Mme Blache   And AIDS it was good the way you said
that it gnaws away at you inside
Unemployment AIDS the same calamity

Blache   Perhaps you should say that

Mme Blache   It wouldn't have the same impact
Only you should say it a bit more slowly you swallow
your words
You know how people watch

Blache   While eating

Mme Blache   Just like us

Blache   Wait let me listen again

He puts the tape recorder on 'play'. **Blache***'s voice, recorded.*

But it's whistling in the wind no one wants us any more
we are good for nothing our grey matter is put in the
cupboard we are left out in the cold the others have put
you on the touch line as time goes on

He presses 'stop'.

What a load of nonsense

Mme Blache   But it's true

Blache   Pure garbage let me try again

He presses 'record' and speaks.

   Old? A horrible tune sung by an insidious chorus of
pernicious voices like a virus attacking the bone marrow
   Old? Shelve that notion you're not old you're a
castaway and your business is to survive you're on your
desert island working for this single goal correction
   Working for this double goal keeping in shape and
sending signals correction
   Working for this triple goal keeping in shape sending
signals and being on the alert

He presses 'stop'.

Mme Blache   That's much better Nicolas why have you
stopped

Blache   Too long

Mme Blache   No no
   Vincent Bonnemalle will like the image of the castaway

Blache   Everything that I have to say hangs on that it
leads on to the rest

Mme Blache   Only you mustn't seem to be reciting

Blache   Blast it

Mme Blache   It must stay spontaneous
   As if it was coming to you on the spur of the moment
when you say it
   Maybe that's why they advise you not to rehearse too
much

Blache   If they cut off my speech Caroline
   I lose my thread

Phone rings. **Mme Blache** *lifts the receiver.*

Mme Blache   Yes? Oh
   Vincent Bonnemalle for you Nicolas

Blache   Hello yes it's me
Yes oh yes
But yes
Understood yes

He hangs up.

No time to say anything
Rendezvous with him in Paris you and me tomorrow
eleven thirty for a try-out

Mme Blache   Oh Nicolas

Scene Eleven

Magistrate's office. Daytime.

Phélypeaux   You know there is still something which
astounds me
At the time you were both thrown out on the streets
You had been reconciled hadn't you

Delile   We never fell out

Phélypeaux   You admitted there had been a rupture

Delile   A cooling off

Phélypeaux   A glaciation for that matter since not one
word was exchanged between you except on professional
matters for

Delile   Seven years Monsieur le Juge   ·
But with no adverse effect upon our service to the
company

Phélypeaux   A spontaneous glaciation you want me to
believe this do you?

A silence.

Delile   These things are hard to talk about

Phélypeaux   At last

Perhaps you're going to unbutton a bit

Delile   Blache and I it was more than just friendship we
were brothers
A cycle race cancelled at the last moment I return to
the house that morning unexpectedly Blache is sitting next
to my wife in the kitchen I see them from behind and
heaven knows what strikes me I feel like my legs have
dropped off in less than an instant I had imagined
everything

Phélypeaux   Let's call things by their proper name

Delile   Like lightning

Phélypeaux   Jealousy

Delile   One gets over it knowing it's without foundation
But slowly
Less than an instant for the damage to occur years and
years afterwards to recover

Phélypeaux   No sequels?

Delile   None whatsoever Monsieur le Juge except
perhaps that the child who was born at the time of the
crisis

Phélypeaux   Your son makes regular appearances here
But I'm not concerned with him today
Then you're made redundant this is the second big
crisis of your life and so what is remarkable is that the
blow that hits you and which hits your friend Blache at
the same time and in the same way
One would have supposed that reconciled as you were
this blow would have brought you even closer
But no here once again all relations break off
And reflecting on this second rupture
One must wonder if the loss of your job hasn't caused
a relapse into what you thought you were cured of
Hence a new glaciation with perhaps more pernicious
effects

Delile   You don't understand
You're a civil servant what happened to me will never
happen to you
Losing work is something special
I wish you'd hear me

Phélypeaux   That's what I'm here for Monsieur Delile

Delile   You were someone
Suddenly you're nothing
The trapdoor opens under your feet
You're stuck with your useless body you don't know
what to do with it
Except get it out of sight
Forget your acquaintances did you know that your
memory goes when you're out of work
While demonstrating a circular saw I couldn't
remember how to position my fingers any more

Phélypeaux   You're already preparing your defence
When did you see Blache for the last time?

Delile   I can't say

Phélypeaux   Did you meet him on the day of the
murder? In the days preceding? In the weeks? In the
months?

Delile   No

Phélypeaux   Not one single time since you're back in a
job? Try to remember

Delile   No

Phélypeaux   Do you know if he had enemies? People
who would wish him harm?

Delile   No

Phélypeaux   Would you please take this down
Mademoiselle Belot (*He dictates, she types.*) Came into the
Grange company self-taught as a packer I made my way
to becoming production manager as the aforementioned I

hired the qualified engineer Blache who became both my colleague and my friend one Sunday morning I surprised Blache sitting beside my wife I experienced an attack of violent jealousy and all relations between us except for at work were broken off for seven years the time I needed to cure myself after this we became friends again

I was made redundant by the Grange company aged forty-nine at the same time as Blache and other employees of the firm due to restructuring I had twenty-eight years of service and up until then my professional life had been without shadow the injustice of the blow which struck me as well as the uncertainty touching my future provoked a reaction of withdrawal and oblivion I note problems with my memory in my new work since quite recently after four years of unemployment I have found work I am still on probation and the preceding explains that from my redundancy I broke off for the second time and for good all relations with Blache I declare in particular not to have seen him in the course of the months weeks and days preceding the murder of the aforementioned nor on the exact day or night of the murder

Do you accept these as a record of your words? Have you anything to add? Do you wish to re-read it? Could I ask you to sign your statement?

I thank you

Exit **Delile**.

Phélypeaux   Strange sort of bird
Endearing really
There's class in the way in which
It flaps its wings
Struggles

Mlle Belot   Against who?
Strange that you speak of birds
You have shaken the coconut tree

Phélypeaux   Doubtful harvest

The nuts aren't ripe

Mlle Belot   Unless there aren't any
On that particular tree

Phélypeaux   Either he's done it

Mlle Belot   Or he hasn't done it
In my dream
You're in it it's embarrassing

Phélypeaux   I pursue you
Right into the night?

Mlle Belot   Perched on top of a rock
There you were surrounded by menacing birds who
were making a deafening row

Phélypeaux   That's reality

Mlle Belot   A cart passes pulled by an old man and the
cart's filled with worn-out ragged clothes he is going to
sell them at market you jump in
I want to warn the old man a huge bird spreading its
wings prevents me from getting near you take advantage
of it I don't understand why
You start to throw the old clothes overboard
I shout he doesn't hear me because of all these birds

Scene Twelve

Paul's *room. End of the morning.*

A basin. He is washing. She is in bed, writing.

Paul   This is exactly what Phélypeaux was telling me
that I have no character

Jacky   I am writing your portrait no character

Paul   Shit there's no soap left

Jacky   That box of Omo

Put a bit of Omo in the basin

Paul   That's my waste-bin
If I had had some character

Jacky   No character no soap no washing powder
A rather undeveloped sense of hygiene
Nothing but nots
Search
Perhaps there are things that you have

Paul   I've got art in my blood
I want to be a painter

Jacky   Ah
Artist's vocation

Paul   My father wasn't in favour he wanted me to study
result I didn't do either
I couldn't obey him or stand up to him

Jacky   No soap but there's a brush

Paul   So what?

Jacky   Scrub with that brush even without soap

Paul   Nothing left but the dream

Jacky   The hit to help the dream

Paul   What are you scribbling?

Jacky   I told you I'm doing your portrait

Paul   What for?

Jacky   Who knows?
Maybe to give you to read

Paul   You'll do a feature on it
Title
The disarray of a child of the end of the nineties of the
millennium's dying years
You sell the idea to the telly
You sell it to Vincent Bonnemalle for the next episode

of *The World and I*

Jacky You're on

Paul The millennium's dying years
What do you reckon?

Jacky Who knows?
The mess the waste the hopelessness of youth in the millennium's dying years
A nice theme

Paul Well worth it
Judging by the colour of the water

Jacky Feet as well please

Paul The next one's already bundled up featuring the agony of people over fifty thrown out of their job
My father's in it my mother too both participate
Their moment of glory
Shit
It's enough to make you want to top yourself

Jacky Your pseudo-father

Paul I don't know about that

Jacky Unemployed is he?

Paul Worse

Jacky Worse how?

Paul A flunky in a cap in a hypermarket that finally gets this post after four years of sitting on his arse doing nothing
Except working out a patience at the kitchen table
An example to prove one shouldn't get desperate
I watched them grooming themselves for it
It's worse than a porn film

He gets back into bed with her.

Blache would have been less grotesque

Oh well

A silence.

Jacky   You know
I'm hungry
We could make ourselves some breakfast
Put some music on
You could go get some croissants

Paul   Chocolate rolls

Jacky   You'd rather?
Would you have preferred it to be Blache?

Paul   They had settled on Blache
But then
Blache was no longer available

Jacky   Right

Paul   First they pick my father then they discover Blache
and give him preference because Blache
Ah my father couldn't stand that
Blache who owed him everything
I'm off he said
Where to? My mother asked
To his place
What for?
To have a word with him

Jacky (*springs up*)   So he did go round to Blache

Paul   Reunion of two friends falling into one another's
arms and melting after being lost to each other for four
years a picture I will paint one day it's all done in my
head a cylinder full of viscous scum spilling out not a
trace remaining of one or the other
Blache's death must have caught the telly people off
guard how fortunate my father was available as a back up

Jacky *has jumped out of bed and dressed instantly.*

Paul   Lucky for him too

He'll have a chance to show off his cap on the small
screen
    The coffee-maker's under the bed

Jacky   I'm not sure I've got time Paul

Paul   What are you always running off to?

Jacky   Breakfast the next time Paul
    Promise

Scene Thirteen

Kitchen. **Delile** *villa. Evening.*

Béatrice   All muscle no fat
    The first sequence will be you two here in this kitchen
    The way you always are
    Monsieur Delile but can I call you Pierre? Call me
Béatrice Pierre you hold the bottle of champagne
    Close up on your hands pulling the cork and bang you
pour out you say
    Today is a special day for me
    Rose you say
    Wonderful
    Pierre you wait a second and then you say
    I've found my way back to a job it's taken me four
years let's drink to it the occasion's worth it
    You can add
    And so the sadness is over now it's celebration time
    So Rose you look at him and you say
    There were some dreadful moments
    I won't be in the picture but you'll hear my voice off-
camera I'll ask you
    Did you think you'd ever make it?
    You nod your head in response to the question you
reply
    In my heart of hearts I thought so though I could see
everyone around me doubting it every day I consulted the

small ads a technical salesman was needed I'd send off my
CV no reply or regret does not fit requirements and
inevitably
  You take another sip of champagne you continue
  And inevitably I thought 'it's because of your age Pierre
you'll never find another job'

Delile   Because idleness you see is a terrible thing

Béatrice   You say that you say
  Idleness is a terrible thing it causes you to shrink

Delile   In your own eyes in the eyes of society

Béatrice   Very good Rose at that moment you also take
a sip you are seen smiling and you say
  Can it be true isn't this a fairy-tale after those four
years it's wonderful
  Still you you say
  Once we had the electricity cut off we had no light or
heating
  You say
  Our morale was at an all time low and we couldn't
watch our little telly any more
  Pierre you say
  That's right
  Rose at that moment you get up you say
  And then I got him back on his bike see in the old
days he went in for cycle races
  Pierre you say
  A good thing I had that I'd go off and ride fifty sixty
eighty kilometres I'd get high on it it cleaned my mind
  Rose you say
  If it hadn't been for the bike we would have done
something stupid he wouldn't have stood the stress you
have to have something to aim at
  Cut
  And we go on to the sequence without words you're on
your bike you go up the hill standing up on the pedals
  Next we centre on your little garden and the fence with

the road behind you've just driven along in your car

Delile   I haven't got a car any more

Béatrice   Ah
We'll provide one you've just started the engine you're
ready to go to work Rose you dash out of the house in
your nightie you shout
Pierre your sandwiches
He looks at you you come up to him and say
I've given you paté two bananas
Zoom on the white CX speeding away

Delile   A CX?
Really

Béatrice   Champagne CX they go together
We must avoid giving an impression of destitution
Following shot the inside of Bricomarket you are in
uniform and your boss is with you he is giving you his
instructions
Your sector Delile is from this shelf on

Delile   I am supposed to serve all the shelves

Béatrice   So he tells you that
Second to last shot the manager is centre he says
We could have hired someone young
But Monsieur Delile had experience
That makes the customer feel safe he has the know-how
Last shot return to you it's me out of shot interviewing
you
And so on this first day how does it feel?
You say
After four years of sitting at home I was a bit worried
but it took no time
I interrupt you
Proud of how you've done this morning?
You say
Proud yes to have been able to overcome the handicap
of four years of idleness

You are full face and you say
And proud to have shown that at fifty-three one is not
through

Delile   And the scene on the beach?

Béatrice   It's been cut

Delile   How come?

Béatrice   I did think a dive would make a good symbol
But the bike on the hill will do as well

Delile   Right that's what I'm good at

Béatrice   That's correct
Everything should be true
The tiniest detail should be ah well
You've come a long way since yesterday

Mme Delile   He's bitten the bullet haven't you Pierre

Béatrice   That's perfect
Of the two candidates left I'd incline towards you the
one with scars still visible that you don't try to hide and
even your injured hand
My colleague Adèle sees things a bit differently she and
I complement one another with our slightly different
points of view which is very important
She leans more towards Blache

Delile   You've seen him?

Béatrice   Vincent will decide
With Blache the broadcast would lose in truth what it
would gain in clarity the contrasts would stand out better
The current tendency on all channels is to move in that
direction

Mme Delile   So our chances aren't that good?

Béatrice   When it comes to the final selection all sorts
of considerations come in that only Vincent knows about
Does he even know himself?

Scene Fourteen

Magistrate's office. Early evening.

Phélypeaux   I put myself in Delile's place
I come in and I see the backs of my friend Blache and
my young wife Rose sitting in the kitchen side by side
Bang
Why?
A very ordinary scene really
Blache is a frequent caller at the house there's nothing
suspect about his presence
Nor about their posture

Mlle Belot   A back can be enormously expressive

Phélypeaux   Did Blache actually have it off with Rose?
Was the husband's shattering intuition right? Considering
how slowly he managed to rid himself of it
Perhaps it lurked deep within him in hibernation
The beast

Mlle Belot   In the jungle

Phélypeaux   Steady on
Reread me the passage of Rose's statement about the
cycle race being cancelled

Mlle Belot *(reading)*   That's how on returning from a
cycle race which didn't happen my husband came into the
kitchen where I was having a coffee with our neighbour
and friend Blache who came almost every evening to chat
with us and often spent Sundays in our company Pierre
had a sudden start he said a few things which weren't
very coherent for quite a long time he didn't want to
have Monsieur Blache around which upset me and
Monsieur Blache as well but with time all that calmed
down

Phélypeaux   Let's assume nothing happened

Mlle Belot   Let's hope something has

These people's lives were so hopelessly shallow

Phélypeaux   What may seem shallow to some allow me
Pierre and Rose love each other not a cloud in the sky
in addition they have a loyal friend Nicolas
None of the three is in want of anything they entertain
a fully gratifying relationship leaving nothing to be desired
What do you think of it?

Mlle Belot   I'm falling asleep

Phélypeaux   Harmony
And suddenly the accident
Talking with you is always stimulating your platitudes
are helpful
For you a triangle necessarily means a cuckold
The triangle Mademoiselle Belot dynamically speaking
is a geometrically bivalent figure it can have a tendency to
disintegrate but it can also maintain itself in a stable state
provided the respective pressure on the three sides is equal
and opposite
Stability rupture of equilibrium that's the alternation of
which the history of peoples is made up as is the life-
history of each individual
Let's assume that they did sleep together

Mlle Belot   Yes
You realise I am on overtime and you can't pay me for
it

Phélypeaux   That's correct
I have no funds to remunerate your extra time but you
are happy to stay on for me

Mlle Belot   That depends on the evenings Monsieur le
Juge
My triangle is you me and a friend with whom I have
a date this evening
He and I are keen not to miss the beginning of the film
at eight thirty-five on TF1 and beforehand I must have
the time to prepare an omelette

Phélypeaux   You can make it in two shakes of a lamb's
tail

Mlle Belot   Beat the eggs fry up the chopped bacon

Phélypeaux   Congratulate him
If it's him who chose it but don't come back with
This blouse you are
Lucky in love

Mlle Belot   As for that

A knock at the door.

One can't be unlucky in everything
You're abusing

Phélypeaux   Show that person in

She goes to open the door. Enter **Jacky**.

Phélypeaux   Hey it's you

Jacky   Good evening
Can I take a few minutes of your time?

Phélypeaux (*to* **Mlle Belot**)   Luck becomes you

Mlle Belot   On your nocturnal walks
D'you always go alone?
Wouldn't it become you to find yourself the right
person?

Jacky   Can I see you alone?

Mlle Belot   Can I go now?

Phélypeaux   And which film is it anyway?

Mlle Belot   *Choose your Weapon*

Exit.

Jacky   With Depardieu Montant Deneuve Galabru
Lanvin Anconina
Third-rate

Phélypeaux   Not at all
  I saw it when it came out at the Gaumont on the
Champs Elysées five years ago I was in the last year of
law school let me remember a retired gangster who
decides to go straight suddenly bumps into
  Like a flash out of his own past

Jacky   A former mate who's just escaped
  Along with a young lout
  Depardieu
  You're yawning your head off Hubert
  Looks as if you've been around all the bars and dance
halls

Phélypeaux   Two sleepness nights on the run

Jacky   You'll kill yourself

Phélypeaux   I'm on the Blache case
  How's life treating you Jacky?

Jacky   So so
  You've got nothing for me?
  A little something
  I need something
  For sure you've got something but you'll pass it on to
others
  You still serving the others before me?
  Well that's the way it is I suppose I haven't been
around long enough
  Or I don't know how to manage you I won't keep you
  I'll let you go and sleep
  But you know that I'm persistent you'll end up by
giving me something to get my teeth into

Phélypeaux   Can I offer you a drink? You know where
the bar is
  In the little cupboard
  Yes the packet of roasted almonds too

Jacky   Well that's something

She pours the drinks.

Here's good luck to you Hubert

Phélypeaux   And to you
My little Jacky you seem you
I don't know
On top of the world
Is that mohair? Angora?
Who gave you the jumper?
How's your love-life?

Jacky   I'm desperate
I must have something

Phélypeaux   Hungry little cat
Look
Ninety-two dossiers to manage at once

Jacky   Your problem is indigestion
Overfed Hubert? Worried by your obesity?

Phélypeaux   You can laugh
Run-of-the-mill stuff fraud shop-lifting exposure GBH

Jacky   You should complain
You have the Blache affair
Magistrates in the whole of France envy you for it

Phélypeaux   Great isn't it
I shake it in every direction and I feel it's ready to
squirt

He gets up, walks up and down.

You know about mirages in the desert
You see you go you believe and then nothing
Sand
Petty crimes and offences petty judge petty life

Jacky   Tell me should I cry now or later?
And what if I had something for you?

Phélypeaux   Do you mean it?

Show me the goods

Jacky   First we strike a deal
I don't work for nothing

Phélypeaux   If you know something that interests the
law

Jacky   What interests me ·
Is to get myself out of this hole you and me Hubert
Monsieur le Juge d'Instruction Phélypeaux
We're in the same boat and perhaps it is time to
change boats
So go and sleep on it
When you wake up tomorrow you can call me

She gets up.

Phélypeaux   Hold it

Jacky   No you're shattered you're reeling
(*On the point of leaving.*) Blache's murderer is Delile

Phélypeaux (*jumping up*)   Ah
Tomorrow morning I summons you as a witness

Jacky   Are you kidding?
I'm talking about a deal

Phélypeaux   You think you have

Jacky   Proof? By no means
Stuff you can build a consistent case on certainly

Phélypeaux   Go on then

Jacky   I'm telling you
Fair's fair

Phélypeaux   What are you asking?

Jacky   Twenty-four hours
Exclusive access for twenty-four hours to all information
on the case once you've decided
Or are forced

To hand over something to the press

Phélypeaux I'm bound by the secrecy of the
investigation

Jacky Okay
Since you take me for a fool
Let's each go and sleep on it Hubert good night
But you have my phone number

Phélypeaux I don't know if it's the alcohol or the
fatigue
You're beginning to amuse me

Jacky The obligation of secrecy okay so let's say this
Insofar as you decide for whatever reason
Take note these are the terms of our contract
To make public any information about the affair
You are committed to pay me back in my own kind
Hubert
Your word

Phélypeaux You have it

Jacky Can we drink?

Phélypeaux Let's drink

Jacky Delile's son

Phélypeaux Paul

Jacky Was born due to goings on between Nicolas
Blache and Madame Delile a liaison which two
neighbours Madame Colin and Madame Loineau if you
push them a little their tongues would loosen

Phélypeaux I've already considered that hypothesis

Jacky But I'm bringing you the means of backing it up
Second element Pierre Delile was cornered by a
television channel to be in a broadcast did you know that?

Phélypeaux Him too?
Well so what?

Jacky   You didn't know
Good
And then Pierre Delile learns that Nicolas Blache has
also been approached which makes him furious
There was only space in the broadcast for one long-
term unemployed person over fifty who had found a new
job
Next Delile learns that Blache has been preferred a
piece of news that knocks him out

Phélypeaux   Not conclusive

Jacky   Third element Delile who was staying out of
everyone's way especially Blache
Delile goes round to Blache

Phélypeaux   He does?
When?

Jacky   If I could give you the date there wouldn't be
much left for you to do

Phélypeaux   Your source?

Jacky   A little injured sparrow I picked up
The Delile son his son so to speak

Phélypeaux   Paul?
The source couldn't be more doubtful
He has a season ticket for this chair
He pilfers he takes drugs

Jacky   He lies like he breathes

Phélypeaux   He loathes his father

Jacky   Yes all that
But I have intimate reasons for thinking

Phélypeaux   The prettiest girl in the world

Jacky   I know the limits of what she can offer
In your mirages you will doubtless come across a source
which is more to your liking

I have your word?

Phélypeaux   You obviously have investigating methods that are beyond my own

Jacky   Your hand

Phélypeaux   Listen
I'm suspicious of a one track course it often leads to judicial errors

At last he takes the hand held out by **Jacky**.

Phélypeaux   Our pact holds whatever comes out but
Leave Delile aside I'll pursue this lead myself
You have the nose
Go sniff about on two or three other suspects I have in mind

Jacky (*pulls back her hand*)   You are kidding?

Scene Fifteen

Hotel room. Morning.

They are having breakfast sitting face to face. The telephone rings.
Béatrice *lifts the receiver. The call is brief.*

Béatrice   Understood

She hangs up.

Vincent
You are the winner
I'm not the loser
Vincent is

Adèle   Who's lost what?

Béatrice   Shame about the programme

Adèle   Could you perhaps tell me?

Béatrice   Blache try-out successful

Don't bother sending other candidates
Both to return to Paris pronto

Adèle   What a relief

Béatrice   For you maybe

Adèle   Be a good sport

Béatrice   This is not a game

Adèle   Uh oh take cover
Persecution complex
What time's the next train?

Béatrice   Should let Delile know

Adèle   I'll run you a bath

Béatrice   You've cheated lied betrayed my trust
The whole way through

Adèle   Neurotic
A nice soothing bath is what you want

Béatrice   Successful try-out sure and for good reason

Adèle   Why question it?
Unless you no longer trust his judgement

Béatrice   There was no judgement

Adèle   No judgement hell breaks loose
Beware of going off the rails

Béatrice   Our mission has
For him not even to bother to see Delile

Adèle   He read your report on Delile
He was in possession of all the information necessary

Béatrice   No doubt you took great trouble to distil it to
him down the phone
That's okay

Adèle   You forget one thing
There was no time left

If he'd chosen Delile fine
I wouldn't've made a fuss

Béatrice   Oh yeah?
Go on talking

Adèle   There's nothing more to say

Béatrice   Exactly what I think

She goes to run a bath.

You win
The programme loses
That's all
No that's not all

The phone rings.

There's the trust between us

Adèle   I did what I had to Béatrice
In the interests of the programme
Maybe Vincent has changed his mind who knows?
He's calling back
Perhaps you should answer it

Béatrice *lifts the receiver.*

Béatrice   Ah
Here she is

Adèle *takes the receiver.*

Adèle   Yes Madame Blache
Oh but

The receiver falls from her hands.

She found him

She picks up the receiver, hands the écouteur to **Béatrice**.

Adèle   I don't know what to say
I am so shocked sorry thank you for thinking of calling

They both hang up. A pause and **Adèle** *bursts into uncontrollable* *laughter which* **Béatrice** *gets too. They calm down.*

Adèle   Phone Vincent

Béatrice   I'd rather you did

Adèle   Think for a minute

Béatrice   Yes

Adèle   You're craftier than I thought

Béatrice   Eh

Adèle   Congratulations
You did well

Béatrice   In the meantime

Adèle   Just tell Vincent we're still in the race after a
short pit-stop

Béatrice   If you're sure you feel that way

Adèle   I never thought Delile
I simply thought it'd be a bit blurred a bit less clear-cut
But if the two of us join forces work him up
Dope him condition him

Béatrice   Good thing
I hadn't called him yet

Adèle   Just get him and say it's on

Béatrice   It would've flattened him

Adèle   Just think
Of that other disaster we're escaping from
Dissension between two angels

Béatrice   I'm so relieved

Adèle   Watch out trouble your bath's about to overflow

Béatrice *goes to turn off the water.*

Adèle   Are you going to call Delile?

Béatrice   Why don't you call Vincent first?

Scene Sixteen

Kitchen. **Delile** *villa. End of the afternoon.*

Mme Delile *is preparing dinner.* **Delile** *enters, in a white jacket, white trousers and white cap. He starts to get changed.*

Delile   I don't know how to take it
    They've hired someone else

Mme Delile   In your place?

Delile   Ah don't shout in my ears
    I get enough noise from morning to night
    They say the experiment has worked so conclusively
that the customer advisor team is being doubled we go
from one to two

Mme Delile   After only a fortnight?

Delile   Two is the right number they say taking account
of the area to be covered which is thirty alleys multiplied
by forty metres which equals one thousand two hundred
metres and taking account of the average number of
customers at any moment throughout the day within the
shop which is three hundred and fifty

Mme Delile   So it's good news

Delile   We're hedging our bets they say one young and
one old they've hired a boy who's not even twenty-five
    They're contradicting themselves because two weeks ago
they talked of nothing but the fund of know-how I had
behind me
    Now they're saying you're going to make a pair which
complement each other

Mme Delile   But they're pleased with you

Delile   They say the test is proving fruitful

Mme Delile   So you see

Delile   In one or two weeks they may say something
else again
  As for two being the right number there's no question
because one thousand two hundred metres to cover means
that one man alone can only pass the same point every
two and a half hours his presence isn't sufficiently felt
  But if they had followed their own logic they would
have hired another person over fifty
  All the more since they say that they're satisfied with
my performance

Mme Delile   Pierre the soup is ready
  And still no cloakroom?

Delile   Rose these people say what they feel like saying
  Tomorrow they may say that a single man is enough
and the lad is the one to keep
  Or equally two is the right number but young ones are
better and so Delile is replaced by a youngster

Mme Delile   Sit down
  There's no reason why

Delile   That's just it there is no reason for whatever
happens
  They fire me they replace me by a young lad or they
keep a single man the young one that they just hired
  Meanwhile their store will have been on telly after the
programme's been on no one is going to bother finding
out whether Delile is still trotting up and down the aisles
  Rose this broadcast we mustn't go
  Or else Blache should do it
  Not us

Mme Delile   Pierre
  They killed him Blache Blache was killed
  The radio was on

Delile   You're kidding

Mme Delile   They said so on the one o'clock news and something I didn't get about the weapon

Delile   Well go on the weapon

Mme Delile   I don't think they've found the weapon

Delile   So?

Mme Delile   That's all

Delile   Blache would've been the man
That's what I said right from the start

Mme Delile   So you did Pierre
Think of poor Caroline
What times we live in

Delile   Yes but hell
There've been murderers in every age
A handgun attack?
Caroline wasn't home?
Damn it are you going to speak up?

Mme Delile (*crying*)   After all it does mean something to me (*Stopping crying.*) it's over now
I just feel what a shame that we stopped seeing them that's all

Delile   It wasn't personal Rose

Mme Delile   I know

Delile   I had nothing against Nicolas

Mme Delile   You couldn't bear to see anyone

Delile   That isn't over mind you
And this shitty broadcast Rose we mustn't go

Mme Delile   You'd regret it Pierre particularly if they don't keep you on at Bricomarket
At least it will've got you known and there are things that you could say

Delile   Dead you say? On the spot?

Mme Delile   Put on the radio for the eight o'clock news

The telephone rings. **Mme Delile** *lifts the receiver.*

Hello yes it's me Béatrice I'll just get him

Delile *takes the receiver.*

Delile   Yes
Is that so? But I've changed my mind I don't want to
Perhaps but that's the way it is
No I've no reason to give you
Yes I'll hand you over

He returns the receiver to **Mme Delile**.

Mme Delile   Yes Béatrice it's me yes Béatrice

A very long pause.

I'll do my best Béatrice

She hangs up.

Those two girls are completely distraught
They beg to be allowed to come round they can't set
off for Paris without having tried to convince you one last
time

Scene Seventeen

Magistrate's office. Morning.

Phélypeaux   You can't leave me in suspense like that
It's not human

Mlle Belot   But I don't remember any more

Phélypeaux   What was there on it?

Mlle Belot   A landscape of rocks and trees in the
distance the mountain
On the left and right there were naked women who
were lifting their arms I couldn't see their faces

Phélypeaux   Bathers
That's a famous picture you're describing to me

Mlle Belot   And then I don't know
The painter was very angry

Phélypeaux   I can imagine it

Mlle Belot   So what use is it keeping on so furiously?
While he was negotiating with the motorists

Phélypeaux   The painter?

Mlle Belot   Yes there was this fireman who was
pointing the water jet at the canvas with his nozzle
It wasn't water coming out but red paint like blood
Is it you holding up the traffic? He was thrashing about
like a maniac I couldn't understand why they couldn't
leave him alone

A knock at the door.

Phélypeaux   Let him in

Mlle Belot *brings* **Delile** *in.*

Phélypeaux   Your surname first name age marital status
profession place of abode

Delile   Do we have to go through all that again?

Phélypeaux   It's necessary because this is a new
appearance

Delile   So
Delile Pierre fifty-three married one child customer
advisor at Bricomarket two Turret Way Orleans

Phélypeaux   Are you related to Nicolas Blache or have
you been in his service?

Delile   No

Phélypeaux   Swear that you'll tell the whole truth and
nothing but the truth

Delile   I swear

Phélypeaux   Your son Paul is a perfect little wretch he bears no resemblance to you does he? You are ashamed of him aren't you? A scoundrel of this sort can't have been begotten by you isn't that right? He isn't your son is he?

When did you have your first doubts concerning your paternity?

Delile   Me?

Phélypeaux   On that crucial day of the cycle race which didn't take place the suspicion didn't just cross your mind you knew

And now a television programme is in the making about which you deliberately avoided telling me even though it must be very much on your mind you were a candidate but Blache was too and they preferred Blache

Delile   What's that got to do with my son?

Phélypeaux   It's me asking the questions Monsieur Delile each of us must stick to his role

And so you went to see Blache

Delile   I went to see Blache?

Phélypeaux   I could charge you but for the moment I prefer to hear you as a witness

Unless you would prefer me to charge you which would give you the right to have a lawyer's assistance and to have access to your dossier

The choice is yours

Delile   I don't understand at all

You're mistaken

Phélypeaux   What role were you offered in this broadcast?

Delile   Perhaps it's your technique to knock me sideways

Phélypeaux   What day did you go and see Blache?

Delile   Me I went to see Blache?

Phélypeaux   Wednesday and you weren't ignorant of the fact that on the evening of the first Wednesday of the month Madame Blache
Wednesday a little before ten o'clock you had decided to have a discussion with him
One can understand it here you are being offered a chance to show yourself to ten million television viewers
After having lived like a worm for four years
You can show up on the big day and tell all about the insults that society made you endure
How could you fail to be excited at this prospect?
But between you and this dream stands Blache
For the second time in the last twenty-five years Blache stands in the way like a demon shattering your happiness
Blache who owed you everything
The first time he makes your wife pregnant you manage to extinguish the fire which had devoured you for so long
The second time it's too much
I'm here to take your confession it will give you relief and the circumstances are such that I anticipate a lenient verdict

Delile   Are you mad?

Scene Eighteen

Le New York Bar. Daytime.

They are seen standing side by side.

Jacky   Is she holding his hand

Paul   She's guiding him you have to know your way hell is made up of several circles see
The fresco goes round the four walls

Jacky   Like a cartoon

Paul   Here is the second to last circle she says
And remember that I am close to you

Jacky   What are those?
The turrets of a castle?

Paul   No those are giants in the well
Along the coping all planted there up to their navels

Jacky   I don't see a thing

Paul   It's pitch dark
It's going to disperse
The fog the vapour the smoke of cigarettes she says
Come closer so I can take you
And here I did the last circle

Jacky   These two here pressed against each other with
intermingled hair

Paul   Their eyes only are wet inside the ice hardens the
tears between them
Here the very tears prevent weeping

Jacky   And him coming out mid-chest from the ice

Paul   The emperor of the dominion of pain

Jacky   His head has three faces the front one is
vermilion the right one is whitish yellow the left one is
quite black

Paul   Beneath each one two huge wings come out

Jacky   They haven't got feathers they look like bats'
wings
In each mouth the teeth are at work grinding away

Paul   A damned soul
The bloody froth drips onto the three chins
It's day here when it's evening down there

Jacky   Have you done others?

Paul   I've messed about with hundreds which are piled

up in a cellar where no one ever goes

Jacky   I don't know when you're lying
Don't bring me here again Paul
I can't breathe here

Paul   Here I painted directly on the walls
The bar-owner Vatchek is from Lithuania he came via
Kolyma Siberia he told me go ahead put some colour
there that was two years ago it's already flaking off
Le New York is my adopted home he lets me come
here even when it's shut I have a key

Jacky   I'm not an expert
You should show it to someone

Paul   I'm going to do your portrait

Jacky   Like hell

Paul   You did mine

Jacky   I've got some corrections

Paul   I'll paint all of you even the bits of you that you
don't know

Jacky   Me with two other heads?
Paul I don't mind but not on the walls of Le New York

Paul   In the house that we'll have

Jacky   I'd be crazy
To get tied up with you

Scene Nineteen

Magistrate's office. Afternoon.

Phélypeaux   The moment's come
The lights are green
The missile is about to go off the finger is on the
button

The launch must succeed if it doesn't
But it will
The investigating magistrate stands alone to make his
decision
He'd better not miss
He's put together the clues unravelled the motives
It isn't as if a decision were taken
Suddenly the decision's there inside him like a flower
opening up
All is still
The minutest details have been checked a thousand
times
The button the finger off it goes
I press charges

Mlle Belot   Today?

Phélypeaux   The count down has begun
One of two things
He breaks down
Or conversely
I rather expect
The man's resilient

Mlle Belot   He was ready to jump at your throat

Phélypeaux   He kept kicking and struggling like a
trapped wolf

Mlle Belot   There came a moment I was scared

Phélypeaux   Some of us get gunned down you know

He looks for a piece of paper on his desk.

Three eight five one zero three one two get me that
number
If he persists
Denying it that's the beauty of it

Mlle Belot   At fifty-three years of age
Having found work again and then

Phélypeaux   Four years in the depths of the cesspit
And to fall back in

Mlle Belot   Yes hold the line
Magistrate Phélypeaux wants to speak to you

Phélypeaux (*on the phone*)   Yes
Only I can't give you twenty-four Jacky I'll give you six
hours
Impossible really
The devil himself
Let's split the difference you get twelve hours okay?
Get round here right away

He hangs up.

Mlle Belot   Let me know
Perhaps it would suit you better if I let you see her
privately?

Phélypeaux   I have nothing to hide

Mlle Belot   There's something about you today which I
don't like

Phélypeaux   Am I here for you to like me?

Mlle Belot   You're off the rails
I believe he's innocent

Phélypeaux   It seems to me you're overstepping your
role

Mlle Belot   Too bad
I can't help it

Phélypeaux   He has no alibi
I have no proof
That's the beauty of it
The two adversaries enter the arena with an equal
handicap each one confident he'll get the better of the
other
Everything points to a big rush on the part of the
media a throng of newspaper people will lay siege

I'm giving Mademoiselle Niel twelve hours head start

Mlle Belot   What sort of love-potion has she
administered to you?
  To what does she owe the favour?

Phélypeaux   She's helped me to disentangle the threads

Mlle Belot   You've fallen into her nets

Phélypeaux   Your remarks are out of place I know that
you're impressionable
  Last night's film is it? Mademoiselle Belot are you still
  Under the spell?

Mlle Belot   The film was just fine

Phélypeaux   And the omelette with chopped bacon

Mlle Belot   I didn't watch the film

Phélypeaux   And there was no omelette with chopped
bacon?

Mlle Belot   No

Phélypeaux   So you had a long evening

Mlle Belot   Yes
  I wouldn't want you to suffer any harm
  You have no proof

Phélypeaux   Nor a confession
  Proof there's no assurance there will ever be one
  I must have a confession even if a confession isn't proof
it carries weight

Mlle Belot   There are confessions of all sorts and some
don't even reach your ear

Phélypeaux   And I have my own inner conviction
  Under the shock of being charged this type of man
cracks

Mlle Belot   Assuming he's the murderer

Phélypeaux   I hear you Estelle
However my lot is to be
And I stand
Alone

A knock at the door.

Mlle Belot   Not for long
Here she comes swifter than the wind
You noticed they repaired the pane
So do you want me to go and have coffee?
Can I go and have coffee?

Phélypeaux   You can go and open the door
In fact that's what I'm asking you to do right now
Open it

Mlle Belot *stays as if paralysed then goes towards the door.*
Béatrice *and* **Adèle** *enter.*

Béatrice   Magistrate Phélypeaux?

Phélypeaux   Himself
Whom do I have the honour of addressing?

Scene Twenty

Delile *villa kitchen, and magistrate's office, simultaneously, in two distinct spaces which overlap. End of the afternoon.*

Delile *in his work clothes. He is finishing getting changed.*

Mme Delile   They suggested
I don't know if I was right Pierre I accepted
They want the table to be at right-angles with the cooker
So that you can sit there and me here
The camera will be there

Delile   It's never been like that
It's not bad like that

Mme Delile   It allows you to open the fridge door
without going out of shot
   When you go for the champagne

Delile   It's better like that
   We'll leave it like that
   Why've we never arranged it this way?

Mme Delile   And at the moment when you say
   And so the sadness is over now it's celebration time
   I'll get up and go behind you with my arms around
you to say
   There were some appalling moments

Phélypeaux   I understand but
   What you're asking me
   Do you realise

Béatrice   And do you
   Our position?

Delile   Hang on Rose it's such a change
   The table I can't get over it
   What should I say afterwards?

Phélypeaux   It's absolutely inconceivable
   If the law started to yield to such contingencies

Béatrice   The shooting is tomorrow

Adèle   The programme's on the air next Monday
   We need five days

Mme Delile   In my heart of hearts I thought

Delile   In my heart of hearts I thought
   It's because of your age Pierre you'll never find another
job

Mme Delile   Then you say
   Idleness is a terrible thing

Delile   A terrible thing your standing goes to pieces and
your self-respect

Adèle   A five days' reprieve that's all we ask of you it would be most kind

Phélypeaux   Basically your demand is quite straightforward
You're asking me to suspend the course of justice
You're asking me to park the justice jalopy on the verge
To give time for lady television's limo to overtake

Béatrice   Five days only
Don't be mean

Adèle   Television does a lot for justice justice could do something for television

Phélypeaux   Justice? You give it the full treatment
Bonnemalle likes to rip its clothes off
Show it up in embarrassing positions

Béatrice   We give all institutions a rough time that's our function but have you noticed? Always with respect
By virtue of which the institutions respect us
And invariably when it's needed they lend us assistance
Call it a tacit agreement you better play it by the rules

Delile   Between society and individual
The axe falls

Mme Delile   What axe?
Ad-lib but not too much

Béatrice   It's in our mutual interest

Delile   I'll cut that
No activity no dignity

Mme Delile   And there you stop

Phélypeaux (*loudly*)   And Phélypeaux what will be left of Phélypeaux?

Mme Delile   You mustn't draw it out

Phélypeaux   No more Phélypeaux
Phélypeaux a joke

Mme Delile   I've done the skirting tiles

Mlle Belot   No one has yet been apprised in the
department Monsieur le Juge
Of your decision to press charges

Delile   It's spick and span

Phélypeaux   You really believe that?
I tipped off Baron the deputy in a case like this one
does not present the public prosecutor's department with a
fait accompli by now Baron must have passed it on

Mme Delile   I did the windows as well

Phélypeaux   You mind your back

Mme Delile   I washed the walls the ceiling

Mlle Belot   You didn't give a date

Béatrice   We're in a fix

Delile   But activity dignity are abstract words
These words don't carry weight you have to say
something that no word can say

Béatrice   Only you can help us out

Mme Delile   The gas chamber
You missed out the gas chamber

Adèle   We're asking you this favour

Delile   They've installed it they open it tomorrow
A little room where we can get changed and shower

Phélypeaux   With the best will in the world

Béatrice   Vincent Bonnemalle is not used to being
refused a favour
He doesn't much like asking for one
When he asks it is given

Phélypeaux   I'm sorry

Delile   You know their young lad

Béatrice   In any case he's sitting in his office expecting you to phone him personally

Delile   The one they hired to do the job with me

Béatrice   Shall I dial his number?

Delile   He didn't last long

Phélypeaux   No point

Delile   They fired him

Mme Delile   Is that possible?

Phélypeaux   It's no

A silence.

Timing is of the essence

Mme Delile   That's good news Pierre it's him they decided to get rid of it's not you

Phélypeaux   In five days I've seen situations turn upside down
I handle live stuff

Delile   Yes Rose
Him and not me
It's got to be said
He was a layabout

Phélypeaux   Try telling the fisherman to wait in order to catch that fish that's swimming by at that moment

Delile   We'll see what happens once the programme has gone out but I'm starting to think because there are customers who know me by now they walk up to me for advice on their own accord
My presence is having an effect
It has made a difference to the atmosphere of the store

The supervisor told me it's something which has not passed unnoticed with the management

Mme Delile You've never talked like that Pierre
Words of hope

Delile I've got to the top of the hill

Béatrice You are obviously right Monsieur le Juge

Delile They would be fools
If now

Mme Delile Of course

Béatrice If it has to be today then it will be today we give in

Mme Delile That means you get on well with your boss

Delile The manager came past he shook my hand he's a young chap with loads of diplomas he's hardly older than Paul we talked for a moment
One mustn't draw too many conclusions it's all part of setting the stage for the programme
Yet the supervisor says that the new policy is to go a bundle on customer relations

Béatrice Say no more
Never mind the scandal we'll announce the cancellation of the broadcast which is unprecedented
Inconceivable we won't give the reasons but people will know we have the means to make them known
Have no doubt everyone will be talking of it and not just on the streets also in high places
A mere few days before the broadcast to get his name in the news a low-ranking magistrate throws into prison the one man that Vincent Bonnemalle had chosen to carry hope to those hundreds of thousands of miserable souls the unemployed whose only crime is to be over fifty
Did Bonnemalle go and pick out a murderer? Is that like him?

The little magistrate had better be very sure of himself
Doubtless he's in possession of material proof

A knock at the door.

If not wouldn't he have been cautious enough to hold it
for a few days? Five miserable days?

Phélypeaux   Mademoiselle Belot go and see say ah
I don't know what to say
Say that I'm in a meeting

Mlle Belot   So you are but

Phélypeaux   I'm not expecting anyone

Mlle Belot   You summonsed that young would-be
journalist that Mademoiselle Niel

Phélypeaux   Ah no absolutely not throw her out

*But **Jacky** is already there.*

Jacky   Hello oh but what a gathering
I know you
On the telly you're

Phélypeaux   Jacky I
Not now
I'll get in touch a bit later

*But **Jacky** stays and gazes at **Béatrice** and **Adèle**.*

Mme Delile   It's Veuve Cliquot

Jacky   Aren't you Béatrice Lefeuve?

Mme Delile   I'll put it in the fridge
They should arrive any minute now

Delile   The crew?

Mme Delile   The car

Delile   Ah can you believe it?
A CX

Mme Delile   Not a new one it must look as though it's been around
   Not an old one either last year's model
   And
   Then you can keep it

Delile   What is it you said?

Mme Delile   A present
   From Vincent Bonnemalle

Béatrice   Shall I dial

Delile   Béatrice said so?

Béatrice   He insists on talking to you right away

Phélypeaux   Wait

Béatrice   Vincent is not accustomed to waiting

Adèle   Not forgetting

She looks at the time.

   That he's on the point of leaving his office he must go home any minute now
   To get changed this evening he's dining

Béatrice   With the Minister of Justice

Adèle   They're friends
   Since way back

Béatrice   But considerations of the law must take precedence

Adèle   There's no question that this precipitous action will put you under the spotlight perhaps it's precisely what you're after

Delile   Really?
   The car's for me?
   White?

Mme Delile   That's what they said

Adèle   Nevertheless beware
Don't burn yourself

Mlle Belot   Monsieur le Juge remember that fireman
With his hose

Phélypeaux   Spouting blood

Béatrice   Watch the damage
When a journalist gets hold of a good story

Jacky   I'm a journalist myself you know when this
meeting is finished
I'll take you to Bussard's for a drink okay? A typical
joint on the banks of the Loire Parisians don't know about

Béatrice   A perfect story indeed
Watch how the press will package it in its own way the
programme scuttled the old unemployed man saved from
drowning and kicked back into the bitter waves the
eagerness of an up-and-coming judge who wants to make
his name

Jacky   You can get the best Pouilly in the region

Béatrice   And the case collapses the dossier matters little
Mediawise Delile's place in the story can only be that
of the victim

Phélypeaux   It's true that the Pouilly this year
She does
Mademoiselle Belot an aspirin

Adèle   Who does what?

Phélypeaux   Madame Bussard does a salmon with
whortleberries

Mme Delile   I'm not sure I should tell you
I passed her yesterday walking her dog she is quite
alone now

Delile   Who?

Mme Delile   That poor Caroline

Phélypeaux   I could
I could offer you a drink here
But at Bussard's

Mme Delile   She's only got that animal

Phélypeaux   We could all go together to Bussard's

Mme Delile   Azur is fourteen her sight is going it's her
diabetes

Phélypeaux   There's shade
A row of old weeping willows

Mlle Belot   Am I still required?

Phélypeaux   You are included in the party as well
Mademoiselle Belot

Mme Delile   Couldn't we invite her to dinner one
evening Pierre?

Jacky   And me?

Phélypeaux   I'll carry you off too

Jacky   Wow the more the merrier

Phélypeaux   She also does a whole salmon on the bone
Caught on the premises tossed into hot butter only just
out of the water

Béatrice   You're so kind
Nevertheless there's this meeting isn't there Adèle with
the cameraman and the lighting man at Delile's place
To do the final blocking install the spotlights

Adèle   Decide on their get-up and there's the usual
chasing up of props

Béatrice   We're shooting tomorrow

Jacky   Dare I? A resourceful girl can't get in the way
Do take me on as an assistant I've been dreaming for
so long
To see what goes into the making of television

Paul *rushes in, brandishing a revolver.*

Jacky   Programme

Paul   Hit the floor
On your bellies

Jacky   Paul

Agitation. Shouts. Everyone flattens themselves to the floor except **Jacky**.

Delile   Fifty sixty eighty kilometres I got high on it

Paul   No one move everyone stay put

Delile   It cleaned my mind

Mme Delile   If he hadn't had his bike I'm sure we would've done something really stupid

Delile   To say that you should be standing up

Paul   Watch out the mad marksman is going to empty his magazine

Mme Delile   You have to have something to aim at

Delile   Before that you should say
We wouldn't have stood the stress

Mme Delile   We wouldn't have stood the stress you have to have something to aim at

Paul *throws the revolver to* **Phélypeaux**'s *feet.*

Paul   The revolver that killed Blache

Pandemonium. **Phélypeaux** *snatches the gun. Everyone stands up.*

Mme Delile   We had the electricity cut off

Paul   It was me who killed Blache

Jacky   Paul
You bloody liar

Paul   If she's repeated what I told her don't believe it a

second
  There isn't one bloody word of truth in it Monsieur le Juge

Phélypeaux   A crucial point of course is what you confided to her
  About the visit your father paid him

Mme Delile   No light our morale hit an all-time low
  And we couldn't put the little telly on any more

Paul   What visit to whom?

Phélypeaux   The visit Blache paid to Delile

Jacky   You mean Delile's to Blache Monsieur le Juge
  Oh Paul you liar

Mme Delile   Can't be true Pierre it's a fairy tale

Phélypeaux   I beg your pardon
  The visit Delile made to Blache

Paul   What's that visit you're blabbering about?

Jacky   He didn't kill Blache

Paul   Who didn't?

Jacky   You didn't

Mme Delile   After those four dreadful years

Paul   Why shouldn't I've killed Blache
  Blache my father who wanted to take my father's place in this television programme that my father
  Was dying to do what else could I do but rid my father of my father?

Mme Delile   It's marvellous

Delile   We feel reborn

Jacky   Paul
  You shit
  You want to snarl everything up

Mme Delile   Yes a new life

Jacky   I love you

Phélypeaux   Are you ready to testify?

Paul   If you so wish but you know

Jacky   No Paul do not

Mme Delile   No more shame

Phélypeaux   Mademoiselle Belot take down this statement

Jacky   No Hubert
A perjury it'd get him into more trouble he doesn't know what he's doing
Oh Paul
Shut up

Paul   I love you Jacky
I'll testify to it
I am Delile Paul

Phélypeaux   Age marital status profession place of abode.

The phone rings. **Mlle Belot** *answers it.*

Mlle Belot   Vincent Bonnemalle for Magistrate Phélypeaux

Phélypeaux   Age marital status

Paul   Twenty-four single

Phélypeaux   Say that I'll phone back
Profession place of abode

Paul   Artist two Turret Way

Mme Delile   I never admitted it to you Pierre
I had tea with Caroline a few times

Phélypeaux   Artist?

Mlle Belot   He'll call you back sir

Paul   I tag fences

Mme Delile   It's a long time ago she realised her dog
That its sight is going

Phélypeaux   What fences?

Paul   Oh you know
Building site fences

Phélypeaux   Are you related to Nicolas Blache?

Paul   That's a question which is not completely resolved

Phélypeaux   Do you swear to tell the whole truth and
nothing but the truth?

Paul   That question is a somewhat difficult one

Delile   Today is a special day for me

Mme Delile   Wonderful

Delile   I've found my way back to a job

Mlle Belot   Of course

Delile   It's taken me four years
Let's drink to it

Lights out on the magistrate's office.

The occasion's well worth it

Doorbell.

Rose here they come

They stand still. A pause. Doorbell again.

Who d'you think?

A pause. Exit **Mme Delile** *to open the door. She returns.*

Mme Delile   The lighting man and the camera man
Good evening you're the first those ladies should arrive
soon

Delile   Take a seat
  Here
  They shouldn't be long

Mme Delile   Everything's ready

Delile   What can I offer you
  A little glass of Pouilly while we wait

Lightning Source UK Ltd.
Milton Keynes UK
11 December 2010

164192UK00001B/13/P